D0811785

Université d Ottawa
Social Sciences Sociales
University of Ottawa

The Responsiveness of Demand Policies to Balance of Payments: Postwar Patterns

NATIONAL BUREAU OF ECONOMIC RESEARCH
STUDIES IN INTERNATIONAL ECONOMIC RELATIONS

The Responsiveness of Demand Policies to Balance of Payments: Postwar Patterns

MICHAEL MICHAELY

1971

NATIONAL BUREAU OF ECONOMIC RESEARCH

NEW YORK

DISTRIBUTED BY

COLUMBIA UNIVERSITY PRESS

NEW YORK AND LONDON

HG
388 1
. M49
197 1

Copyright © 1970 by National Bureau of Economic Research
All Rights Reserved
L. C. Card No. 76-117954
Printed in the United States of America
ISBN-0-87014-221-6

NATIONAL BUREAU OF ECONOMIC RESEARCH

OFFICERS

Arthur F. Burns, *Honorary Chairman*
Theodore O. Yntema, *Chairman*
Walter W. Heller, *Vice Chairman*
John R. Meyer, *President*
Thomas D. Flynn, *Treasurer*
Douglas H. Eldridge, *Vice President-Executive Secretary*

Victor R. Fuchs, *Vice President-Research*
F. Thomas Juster, *Vice President-Research*
Hal B. Lary, *Vice President-Research*
Robert E. Lipsey, *Vice President-Research*
Edward K. Smith, *Vice President*

Joan R. Tron, *Director of Publications*

DIRECTORS AT LARGE

Atherton Bean, *International Multifoods Corporation*
Walter W. Heller, *University of Minnesota*
Joseph A. Beirne, *Communications Workers of America*
Vivian W. Henderson, *Clark College*
Arthur F. Burns, *Board of Governors of the Federal Reserve System*
Wallace J. Campbell, *Foundation for Cooperative Housing* John R. Meyer, *Yale University*
J. Irwin Miller, *Cummins Engine Company, Inc.*
Erwin D. Canham, *Christian Science Monitor*
Robert A. Charpie, *The Cabot Corporation* Geoffrey H. Moore, *Bureau of Labor Statistics*
Solomon Fabricant, *New York University* J. Wilson Newman, *Dun & Bradstreet, Inc.*
James J. O'Leary, *United States Trust Company of New York*
Frank W. Fetter, *Hanover, New Hampshire*
Eugene P. Foley, *Dreyfus Corporation* Robert V. Roosa, *Brown Brothers Harriman & Co.*
Eli Goldston, *Eastern Gas and Fuel Associates* Boris Shishkin, *AFL-CIO*
Lazare Teper, *International Ladies' Garment Workers' Union*
Crawford H. Greenewalt, *E. I. du Pont de Nemours & Company*
Donald B. Woodward, *Riverside, Connecticut*
David L. Grove, *International Business Machines Corporation*
Theodore O. Yntema, *Oakland University*

DIRECTORS BY UNIVERSITY APPOINTMENT

Moses Abramovitz, *Stanford*
Charles H. Berry, *Princeton*
Francis M. Boddy, *Minnesota*
Tom E. Davis, *Cornell*
Otto Eckstein, *Harvard*
Walter D. Fisher, *Northwestern*
R. A. Gordon, *California*
Robert J. Lampman, *Wisconsin*

Kelvin J. Lancaster, *Columbia*
Maurice W. Lee, *North Carolina*
Lloyd G. Reynolds, *Yale*
Robert M. Solow, *Massachusetts Institute of Technology*
Henri Theil, *Chicago*
Thomas A. Wilson, *Toronto*
Willis J. Winn, *Pennsylvania*

DIRECTORS BY APPOINTMENT OF OTHER ORGANIZATIONS

Emilio G. Collado, *Committee for Economic Development*
Douglass C. North, *Economic History Association*
Thomas D. Flynn, *American Institute of Certified Public Accountants*
Nathaniel Goldfinger, *AFL-CIO*
Charles B. Reeder, *National Association of Business Economists*
Harold G. Halcrow, *American Agricultural Economics Association*
Murray Shields, *American Management Association*
Douglas G. Hartle, *Canadian Economics Association*
Willard L. Thorp, *American Economic Association*
Walter E. Hoadley, *American Finance Association*
W. Allen Wallis, *American Statistical Association*

DIRECTORS EMERITI

Percival F. Brundage
George B. Roberts
Gottfried Haberler
Joseph H. Willits
Albert J. Hettinger, Jr.

SENIOR RESEARCH STAFF

Gary S. Becker
Charlotte Boschan
Phillip Cagan
James S. Earley
Solomon Fabricant
Milton Friedman
Victor R. Fuchs
* On leave.

Raymond W. Goldsmith
Jack M. Guttentag
Daniel M. Holland
F. Thomas Juster
C. Harry Kahn
John F. Kain
John W. Kendrick

Irving B. Kravis
Hal B. Lary
Robert E. Lipsey
John R. Meyer
Jacob Mincer
Ilse Mintz
Geoffrey H. Moore *

M. Ishaq Nadiri
Nancy Ruggles
Richard Ruggles
Anna J. Schwartz
Robert P. Shay
George J. Stigler
Victor Zarnowitz

RELATION OF THE DIRECTORS TO THE WORK AND PUBLICATIONS OF THE NATIONAL BUREAU OF ECONOMIC RESEARCH

1. The object of the National Bureau of Economic Research is to ascertain and to present to the public important economic facts and their interpretation in a scientific and impartial manner. The Board of Directors is charged with the responsibility of ensuring that the work of the National Bureau is carried on in strict conformity with this object.

2. The President of the National Bureau shall submit to the Board of Directors, or to its Executive Committee, for their formal adoption all specific proposals for research to be instituted.

3. No research report shall be published until the President shall have submitted to each member of the Board the manuscript proposed for publication, and such information as will, in his opinion and in the opinion of the author, serve to determine the suitability of the report for publication in accordance with the principles of the National Bureau. Each manuscript shall contain a summary drawing attention to the nature and treatment of the problem studied, the character of the data and their utilization in the report, and the main conclusions reached.

4. For each manuscript so submitted, a special committee of the Board shall be appointed by majority agreement of the President and Vice Presidents (or by the Executive Committee in case of inability to decide on the part of the President and Vice Presidents), consisting of three directors selected as nearly as may be one from each general division of the Board. The names of the special manuscript committee shall be stated to each Director when the manuscript is submitted to him. It shall be the duty of each member of the special manuscript committee to read the manuscript. If each member of the manuscript committee signifies his approval within thirty days of the transmittal of the manuscript, the report may be published. If at the end of that period any member of the manuscript committee withholds his approval, the President shall then notify each member of the Board, requesting approval or disapproval of publication, and thirty days additional shall be granted for this purpose. The manuscript shall then not be published unless at least a majority of the entire Board who shall have voted on the proposal within the time fixed for the receipt of votes shall have approved.

5. No manuscript may be published, though approved by each member of the special manuscript committee, until forty-five days have elapsed from the transmittal of the report in manuscript form. The interval is allowed for the receipt of any memorandum of dissent or reservation, together with a brief statement of his reasons, that any member may wish to express; and such memorandum of dissent or reservation shall be published with the manuscript if he so desires. Publication does not, however, imply that each member of the Board has read the manuscript, or that either members of the Board in general or the special committee have passed on its validity in every detail.

6. Publications of the National Bureau issued for informational purposes concerning the work of the Bureau and its staff, or issued to inform the public of activities of Bureau staff, and volumes issued as a result of various conferences involving the National Bureau shall contain a specific disclaimer noting that such publication has not passed through the normal review procedures required in this resolution. The Executive Committee of the Board is charged with review of all such publications from time to time to ensure that they do not take on the character of formal research reports of the National Bureau, requiring formal Board approval.

7. Unless otherwise determined by the Board or exempted by the terms of paragraph 6, a copy of this resolution shall be printed in each National Bureau publication.

(Resolution adopted October 25, 1926, and revised February 6, 1933, February 24, 1941, and April 20, 1968)

FOREWORD

The postwar era is essentially one of fixed foreign-exchange rates. Since the late 1950's, it is also an era of largely free international transactions. This combination has inevitably made the maintenance of the present international financial system dependent on the use of international reserves and on the adoption of appropriate adjustment policies when balance-of-payments equilibrium is disturbed. While the problem of international reserves has attracted much attention, particularly in recent years, empirical analyses of adjustment policies have been, it seems, underrated in comparison.[1] One is thus inclined to agree with Meade's statement that:

> I am saddened at the sight of so many people in such positions of great responsibility, and in such positions of intellectual and academic influence in these matters, spending such a high proportion of time discussing the differences—which I admit are very important, between the various ways of controlling and increasing international liquidity—relative to the proportion of time which they have given to what in my view is the much more important problem of how the countries in the free world—the developed, industrialized, liberal countries of the Atlantic community, if you like—adjust their payments to each other.[2]

It is this relatively neglected subject matter—the postwar pattern of response of policy measures to imbalances of payments—to which this study is devoted.[3] Determining the pattern of policies in actual use is an essential part of evaluating the policies, schemes, institutions and manuals of conduct needed to improve the international monetary mechanism and assure an optimal flow of international transactions. A system of fixed and stable exchange rates—like the one existing

---

[1] Probably the most inclusive effort to redress the balance is represented by the recent work of the OECD's "Working Party 3."

[2] J. E. Meade in *Monetary Reform and the Price of Gold*, Randall Hinshaw, ed., Baltimore, 1967, pp. 121–22. Quoted also in Samuel J. Katz's review of the volume, *American Economic Review*, September, 1968, p. 1022.

[3] An interim report of this study has been published as Occasional Paper 106, *Balance-of-Payments Adjustment Policies: Japan, Germany and the Netherlands*, New York, NBER, 1968. The present volume incorporates, with rather substantial changes, the contents of that report.

today, whether explicitly or tacitly—requires for its long-term maintenance a given manner of responses to imbalances of payments. The analysis of actual patterns of policies in view of this requirement would thus be indispensable in the examination of the degree of consistency, or stability, of the present international monetary regime.

This volume is divided into two parts. In the first (Chapters 1 and 2), the study's purpose and approach are outlined, and the findings pertaining to the system as a whole are presented. In the second part (Chapters 3 through 12), the experiences of nine countries are analyzed individually. The study was actually conducted, of course, in the reverse order. First, each country was analyzed separately to identify the policy reactions in the country. Following this, a synthesis of the individual studies was undertaken, in order to search for any general pattern, or patterns, in the international monetary system as a whole and to analyze the reasons for similarities or differences among countries. This part takes up such questions as whether the policies undertaken to adjust deficits and surpluses in the balance of payments are symmetrical to each other, or whether deficits and surpluses provoke different kinds of reactions; whether or not countries employ any strategy or strategies which assign certain policy instruments to balance-of-payments adjustment while reserving others for domestic targets; whether any general change in the policy pattern was discernible over the period under consideration; and if variables such as the size of trade or recent experiences with inflations and depressions explain differences in policy patterns among countries.

It must be emphasized that the study of individual countries is subordinated to the ultimate purpose of an over-all analysis of the international monetary system. The separate studies thus follow a uniform method, making it possible to incorporate them into a wider analysis. In the process, much specific information about each country is inevitably lost. In particular, each individual study does not purport to be a comprehensive description and analysis of all the policy actions taken by the country in question to adjust imbalances of payments. Such a comprehensive study of any single country would require much more attention than could be given to individual cases in an analysis of the present nature. In the present study, the individual patterns are, rather, presented with the aim of demarcating the most salient features of the system. This approach involved selecting certain policies for observation and excluding others: it led, specifically, to a concentration on aggregative monetary and fiscal measures, with only scant attention to other policies.

This study is, basically, a statistical undertaking. Conclusions about patterns of policy reactions are reached in an "objective" fashion: that is, they are inferred from policy actions, rather than from statements about policy motivations. This may, perhaps, create the impression that the statistical inferences presented here are the sole possible source of evaluating policy responses. In fact, of course, many policy makers are quite articulate, offering very often published explanations of the policies followed. Moreover, other analyses of policy conduct, particularly in individual countries, are rather common. Such statements and analyses have been paid attention to, in the present study, mainly as a means of suggesting possible hypotheses and of checking the study's findings. References to relevant literature, had they been made at every occasion, would have made the presentation very cumbersome. The text of this volume thus avoids, by and large, such references. Instead, a bibliographical list of pertinent publications for each of the countries studied is appended at the end of the country's chapter; and a list of references which are not restricted to single countries appears at the end of Part I.

The wide scope of this study inevitably imposes severe restrictions upon its execution. From a variety of potentially useful methods of investigation, some must be selected and others neglected. The coverage of a large number of countries and the need to force the country analyses into the same mold, so that their findings would be useful as raw material for the international synthesis, led to much compression—and possibly oversight—in these analyses. The present study should therefore be viewed as having largely an experimental nature. It does not purport to provide definitive answers but to suggest probable and tentative conclusions and, hopefully, to provoke other studies of the issue; these—following different routes, employing different techniques and, in particular, examining more thoroughly the experiences of individual countries—may conceivably yield different conclusions or suggest alternative interpretations.

A considerable amount of data had to be assembled for this study. All of it came from published material—partly from well-known international sources (such as the *International Financial Statistics*), and partly from publications of the individual countries. Much of the data was found in the source in the form required for this study, while certain compilations had to be performed for other parts of the data.

Due to the vastness of this material, it is not presented in this volume. But the data for each individual country, as well as descriptions of the sources and methods, can be obtained from the National Bureau.

I am greatly indebted to those individuals whose help and advice were given to me throughout the course of the study. My chief recognition and gratitude are owed to Hal B. Lary, whose constructive comments and congenial criticism contributed heavily to the substance, shape and form of the study, and without whose continuous involvement and concern the study could not have materialized. The early stages of the study benefited from the help of a distinguished Advisory Committee, consisting of Peter B. Kenen (Chairman), Arthur I. Bloomfield, J. Marcus Fleming, George Garvy, Gottfried Haberler, Charles P. Kindleberger, Irving B. Kravis, Fritz Machlup, and Robert Triffin. The draft has been substantially improved by the criticism and suggestions received from the National Bureau staff reading committee, composed of Irving B. Kravis, Robert E. Lipsey, Ilse Mintz, and Peter Temin. Among my other colleagues at the National Bureau, many of whom lent a supporting hand, Phillip Cagan merits a special mention. In its final stages, the manuscript has benefited from a review by John Meyer, and by Emilio G. Collado, Robert V. Roosa, and Willard L. Thorp, who served on the reading committee of the Board of Directors. I also wish to acknowledge the contributions made to the studies of individual countries by various staff members of the International Monetary Fund—in particular, Carl Blackwell and Hannan Ezekiel—who were kind enough to comment upon the drafts of these studies.

The main task of compiling and manipulating the mass of the data was undertaken by Maxine Nord. At a later stage, Richard DeFiore helped proficiently in further statistical elaborations. I am indebted to both, as well as to Shmuel Shraier for carrying out most of the compilation of the bibliographic sections, to George Santiccioli for his attentive editing of the manuscript and to H. Irving Forman for applying his masterly craftsmanship, and his patience, in drawing the charts.

Besides staff meetings at the National Bureau, I have had the opportunity to discuss the study in seminar presentations at the University of Chicago, Columbia University, the Hebrew University, M.I.T., Princeton University, Rutgers University, the I.M.F., and the World Bank.

Finally, I wish to acknowledge the financial aid of the National Science Foundation and of the Ford Foundation, which supported the study as part of the National Bureau's program of international economic studies.

TABLE OF CONTENTS

TABLES

CHARTS

PART

GENERAL APPROACH
AND FINDINGS

CHAPTER 1

APPROACHES, CONCEPTS AND METHODS

1. Subject Matter of the Study

The basic problem which this study seeks to explore is the responsiveness of demand policy in the postwar world to the balance-of-payments position. From this problem follow further questions which the study will investigate: Was the reaction to balance-of-payments fluctuations uniform among countries, or were marked differences apparent? Was it uniform over time, or did it change over the period? Could the manner of reaction of countries to imbalances of payments be explained, or predicted, by some general attributes of countries? Are there consistent differences between the manners of response to balance-of-payments surpluses and deficits? If demand policy is used for balance-of-payments adjustment, are the manner of its use and the instruments employed uniform among different countries? If demand policy is not responsive to the balance of payments, can this be attributed to the appropriation of the policy for the achievement of other economic targets which governments regard as having priority over balance-of-payments equilibrium? And, finally, do the policy patterns in the leading trading nations, as they appear in this study, tend to contribute to the maintenance of a stable international monetary system or to its deterioration?

Demand policy comprehends, in this study, the major instruments of monetary and fiscal policy deemed to affect the economy through changes in aggregate demand and to be fairly widely distributed over the economy rather than narrowly concentrated in special segments. Needless to say, instruments of demand policy are not the only tools available for balance-of-payments adjustment. The most obvious other tool is exchange-rate policy. This is not taken into account in the present study for the simple reason that it was very little used during the period and in the group of countries covered in this study. This study is thus confined to adjustment policies under a regime of fixed exchange rates.

But beyond exchange-rate and aggregate-demand policies, there is, of course, a whole array of policies which may be, and have often been, used for balance-of-payments adjustment: customs duties and export subsidies; quantitative restrictions of imports and of other international transactions; special measures of taxation; price controls and "incomes policy"—these are some of the most obvious. The exclusion of such policies is due to one overriding principle which guides the present exploration: the study seeks to reveal and compare patterns in the use of policies which are commonly found in the various countries, and which may be inferred from quantitative data rather than from some qualitative evidence. Instruments which are not part of aggregate-demand policy do not usually qualify by these criteria. They are, very often, used sporadically rather than regularly, and in only the minority of countries, so that no meaningful "pattern" of use may be looked for. Sometimes, even when such instruments are in regular use, their measurement faces overwhelming practical obstacles —this being true, for instance, of the level of customs duties. In other cases, such as price controls and incomes policies, no quantitative evidence may be expected at all.

It is believed—although this is certainly an impression rather than an inference from solid evidence—that insofar as any policies were followed for the purpose of balance-of-payments adjustment, instruments of demand policy were normally a major part of such set of policies; this probably holds true for most countries covered in this study and for most instances of imbalances of payments. Moreover, measures other than aggregate-demand policy or changes in the exchange rate may be of temporary help in containing balance-of-payments pressures. But they are unlikely to contribute to longer-term external equilibrium in the sense in which this term is usually understood, and are therefore of much less interest in a study of the present nature.[1] It should thus be emphasized that this study does not purport to provide a full description or analysis of balance-of-payments adjustment policies. Not only does it exclude all policy instruments which are not part of aggregate policy, it provides no description of actual developments, as they occurred, for the policies which are explored. In other words, this is neither a catalog nor a chronological description of policies undertaken in periods of imbalance of payments. It is a search for some general outlines, or patterns, of the use of policies —a search which inevitably abstracts from individual properties. The studies of individual countries in this volume should be understood in this way, since they claim no more; one should not—and this, again, cannot be overemphasized—seek in these country studies a proper description or analysis of the ways in which each of these countries tried to solve its imbalances of payments.

Moreover, even though the study seeks to base its inferences on quantitative data, the inferences themselves are qualitative rather than quantitative. In other words, the study will ask whether demand policy as a whole, or certain of its instruments, were or were not used for balance-of-payments adjustment. But, if a policy instrument is found to move in response to the balance-of-payments position, the *size* of this movement will not be investigated. Still less does the study attempt to measure the effect of policy on the balance of payments. When, for instance, a country is found to have generally conducted its demand policy in a way which indicates responsiveness to the needs of the balance of payments, this finding does not necessarily imply that the country did indeed handle well its imbalances and induced full and quick adjustments.

This is, then, a study which seeks to find the "rules of the game" of demand policy in relation to the balance of payments, but not to photograph the game, nor even to describe its major moves.

2. Coverage of the Study: Countries and Period

The criterion used in the selection of countries for observation is dictated by the purposes of the over-all study. They must be large coun-

---

[1] To use the terminology recommended by Machlup, the study covers, by and large, the instruments used for "real adjustment," to the exclusion of instruments used for "compensatory corrections." See Fritz Machlup, "Adjustment in

tries in terms of size of international transactions: if implications for the international monetary system as a whole are to be drawn, it is obviously more relevant to concentrate on countries whose impact on this system is large.

Since the study is defined beforehand as an investigation of policy patterns under fixed exchange rates, Canada is excluded. Canada had a fluctuating rate during most of the period covered; this deviation makes the case of Canada—interesting as it is in its own right— less useful as a subject of international comparisons and a study of international policy patterns. The study thus covers the other nine countries of the "Group of Ten": Belgium, France, Germany, Italy, Japan, the Netherlands, Sweden, the United Kingdom, and the United States. These countries conduct, in their aggregate, an overwhelming share of world trade and other international transactions, own an overwhelming share of the world's capital, hold most of the world's international liquidity, and produce most of the world's income. Conclusions which are valid for these countries as an aggregate are thus applicable, by and large, to the international monetary system as a whole.

The period selected is that following World War II. The experience of earlier periods is not entirely irrelevant, but is of less immediate application to current issues and to problems which are likely to be faced in the near future.[2] The early postwar years 1945–49 are excluded, too, on similar grounds. Circumstances in those years were definitely unique; although one cannot safely predict that they may not recur, it seems quite evident that such repetition is not likely in the near future, so that any conclusions derived from the experience of those years are bound to be less important to current economic problems. The study thus starts with 1950 and ends with the latest date for which information was available at the time of its collection, usually the end of 1966.

International Payments," in Baldwin *et al., Trade, Growth and the Balance of Payments* (Essays in Honor of Gottfried Haberler), Amsterdam, 1965, pp. 185–213.

[2] The experience of earlier periods has been investigated in two well-known studies whose methods are similar in essence to the one adopted here, although confined primarily to observations of a single policy variable. The interwar period was the topic of Ragnar Nurkse's classic study, *International Currency Experience,* Montreal, 1944, where this method of investigation was followed in Chapter IV. The prewar period was studied in Arthur I. Bloomfield, *Monetary Policy under the Gold Standard: 1880–1914,* New York, 1959, particularly Chapter V. These studies will be referred to later.

3. The General Approach

As indicated above, this study will seek to establish probable relationships between the position of the balance of payments and the policies undertaken: it will try to reveal the principles followed by studying actual behavior. The analysis will be of a statistical nature.

It should be emphasized that the analysis is confined to the search for causal associations in one direction: changes in the target variable are the cause, and changes in policy variables are the effect. When a consistent relation between imbalances of payments and the movement of a policy variable is established, this relationship will be tentatively interpreted as causal in nature. That is, if a policy instrument reacts consistently to imbalances of payments by moving in a certain direction, it will be assumed that this is not a coincidence but that the reaction is causally related to the imbalance and is, therefore, conscious behavior on the part of policy designers. An attempt will usually be made, in such a case, to give a plausible explanation for their conduct; that is, to see what model, or analytical structure, could be expected to yield this pattern of action. The models could, of course, be different for different countries and, in each country, for different periods or different governments. The study will thus not try to impose one model upon all situations; nor will it try to assess the theoretical credibility of any model which may be revealed. The purpose will be to establish what policy makers may have wished and anticipated, rather than to evaluate whether their actions were well-founded.

More generally, this study does not aim to pass judgment on the actions of the governments of the countries under investigation—either on the targets they have been pursuing or on the means selected to achieve them. True, in some final analysis such a judgment must be made. Studying past experience in order to improve future performance necessarily implies pointing out favorable and beneficial patterns of behavior and setting them apart from those which lead away from desired goals. The present study, however, is viewed only as a necessary preliminary step in such an assessment; it is concerned only with the attempt to find out what the policy patterns actually were, rather than with the subsequent question of which of these policies were "good," or "bad"—and why. This definition of the subject matter of the study probably cannot be overemphasized, particularly because the analytical method may lead the unwary reader in the opposite direction. The constant attempt to search for a positive relation between the balance-of-payments position and policy actions may easily create the impression that the existence of such a relation is regarded favorably, while the lack of it is scored. No such normative judgment is intended in the present study.

The study's emphasis throughout will be on the relation between policy instruments and the balance of payments. In addition, however, a few other major economic targets will be observed. This will serve two functions. One is to make certain that a consistent association between imbalances of payments and a certain policy variable could not be attributed to the impact of another target variable. To cite an obvious example: If the balance-of-payments surplus is positively correlated with the rate of unemployment, measures taken to relieve either unemployment or excess demand for labor, when investigated in isolation, would be erroneously interpreted as being intended for the sake of balance-of-payments equilibrium. The other purpose of observing competing target variables is to find out whether the absence of a consistent relation between imbalances of payments and a given policy instrument could be due to the employment of this policy instrument in the service of an alternative target.

It should be understood, however, that these are only auxiliary observations, not on a par—in the present study—with the direct investigation of the relation between policy instruments and the balance of payments. In other words, this study is not a general investigation of trade-offs among targets or of the over-all allocation of policy instruments. It is designed specifically to observe reactions to imbalances of payments; other policy targets are admitted only as a means of ascertaining, and possibly explaining, the existence of certain reactions or their absence.

4. The Analytical Method

The study's stated purpose is to reveal patterns of reactions to imbalances of payments. But care must be taken, it must be stressed again, lest reactions to movements of *other* policy targets mistakenly be considered as having been taken in response to the balance-of-payments position. This problem of separating out responses to one policy target from responses to others would seem to call for a multiple (or partial) regression analysis where a policy instrument is the dependent variable and policy targets—including the balance-of-payments position—the independent variables. For a number of reasons, this method has not been adopted in the present study; it has been experimented with, to some extent, and the results of these experimentations (which are presented in the appendix) are not very encouraging.

The basic information on which the analysis will rest consists of quarterly data (adjusted for seasonal variations, where these are found). But the study of interrelations among variables *within* each quarter could hardly be of great significance. The quarter is an arbitrary dissection of the continuum of time. Changes in policy variables could easily be due to movements of the policy targets in the previous quarter, or in still earlier periods. If these movements should change direction often from one quarter to another, observations of relationships would be very likely to yield misleading results. In recent years, a few attempts have been made to construct a "reaction function" for various policy instruments by regression analysis which uses forms of distributed lags to take account of this problem.[3] Such a procedure would, in this instance, have had a number of drawbacks. First, it would have required, for each separate country, an extremely large amount of experimentation.[4] Second, no logical rational model of distributed lags, uniform to all countries, seems to suggest itself. Thus, although it is conceivable that a large enough number of experiments

[3] See G. L. Reuber, "The Objectives of Canadian Monetary Policy, 1949–61: Empirical 'Trade-offs' and the Reaction Function of the Authorities," Journal of Political Economy, April 1964, pp. 109–32; and William G. Dewald and Harry G. Johnson, "An Objective Analysis of the Objectives of American Monetary Policy, 1952–61," in Deane Carson (ed.), *Banking and Monetary Studies,* Homewood, Ill., 1963, pp. 171–89. A study devoted specifically to the length of the time lags which are involved in policy reactions (as well as the lags between the taking of policy measures and their impact upon the economy) is Albert Ando, E. Cary Brown, Robert M. Solow, and John Kareken, "Lags in Fiscal and Monetary Policy," in Commission on Money and Credit, *Stabilization Policies,* Englewood Cliffs, N.J., 1963, pp. 1–163. Interesting information about the time lags in policy reactions is contained in another recent study, reflecting opinions about policy processes in approximately the same countries which are investigated in the present study. See E. S. Kirschen *et al., Economic Policy in Our Time,* Amsterdam, 1964, particularly Tables X.2 to X.5, pp. 274–76.

[4] It should be mentioned that, as is shown in the appendix, the introduction of a few simple assumptions of lags has not improved the outcome of the regression analysis.

with a variety of models in each country would finally reveal a model which yields high correlation coefficients, the meaning and validity of such findings would be subject to much doubt.

A regression analysis of this type would be subject, furthermore, to a large impact of extreme values of both the dependent and independent variables—an impact which could easily distort the implications substantially (and probably has done so in the regression analysis presented in the Appendix). Again, removal of extreme observations could probably improve the results, but this would be a rather arbitrary procedure.

A formal regression analysis would have made sense conceptually, if it could be assumed that governments indeed had some quantitative "reaction function" in mind. While this is not inconceivable, it does not seem to be usually probable; it is likely that large gaps in the achievement of various targets lead to strong reactions of governments, but that there is no precise, or even approximate, quantitative relationship. Be that as it may, it should be recalled that the purpose of the present study is to establish qualitative rather than quantitative associations—it looks for directions of movements rather than for their sizes.

Moreover, while the study seeks to avoid the attribution of spurious associations (of policy variables with the balance-of-payments position), it does not intend to separate completely the variable of the balance-of-payments position from all other target variables. A partial regression coefficient of, say, the discount rate and the balance-of-payments position, would show the extent to which the discount rate would move in response to a balance-of-payments movement on the assumption that other economic targets remain unchanged. But this response would be quite obvious; if other targets are separated out, the discount rate would move, assuming that the government behaves rationally, in the direction which balance-of-payments-adjustment calls for. The partial regression coefficients derived in this manner may be used to infer some "rates of transformation" among the various economic targets. But for a study like the present one, which seeks to establish patterns of reaction of policy instruments to balance-of-payments movements—in the world *as it is,* where all other economic targets are always taken into consideration—this is not the appropriate procedure.

Finally, aggregative regression and correlation coefficients would not suffice to answer some of the important questions posed in this study, which require a separation into classes of observations. They would not be appropriate, for instance, for the purpose of examining the possibility of changes in policy patterns over time; or of searching for differences between responses to balance-of-payments surpluses and to deficits.

For all these reasons, the procedure of regression analysis has been abandoned here. Instead, certain other analytical methods have been adopted.

First, as a device for suggesting hypotheses about policy reactions, subperiods of imbalances of payments are distinguished. The unit of observation for a study of policy responses to imbalances of payments is the time during which the balance of payments is continuously in deficit, or continuously in surplus. The term "continuously" should be interpreted in a liberal way: a divergence in the direction of movement which occurs for a rather short time should not be regarded as starting a new period, but as a random discrepancy which may be disregarded. Needless to say, any such dissection of time into subperiods involves some element of arbitrariness in determining precisely the points at which each subperiod starts and terminates, but this element will most often be rather slight. This issue will be discussed further in Section 6 of this chapter.

The statistical investigation starts, then, with the observation of relations among movements of policy and target indicators within each period. Had these periods been of very short duration, this procedure would hardly have been justified, for the same reasons that apply to observations of individual quarters: the movement of policy variables in any period is as likely to be a reaction to movements of target variables in earlier periods as to developments of the current one. Usually, however, the units of observation are considerably longer. Periods defined in the way suggested here normally last from two quarters to a number of years.

It may be assumed that, when periods are of that length, policies within each period are normally a reaction to developments within the period rather than earlier. If this asumption is valid, an observation of concurrent changes in target and instrument variables would, indeed, reveal causal effects of target changes on policies. It must be recognized, however, that this is an assumption which, while probably reasonable, is supported more by casual observations, statements of policy makers, and general beliefs than by any firm analysis. Moreover, the procedure adopted here would be justified only if it could be assumed that policy measures do not have an immediate impact on the target great enough to reverse the direction of change which originally gave rise to the policy action: if this is not so, associations of changes in target and policy variables are more likely to reveal the effects of policies on targets than those of targets on policies. In other words, this procedure requires that the "inside lag" (or "recognition lag") be materially shorter than the "outside lag." There can, of course, be no assurance that this assumption is generally valid; and it must be recognized that, whenever it does not hold true, the outcome of the present procedure may be doubtful. A few specific instances where the method used may be suspected, on this score, to yield unreliable inferences, will be noted. A somewhat similar related problem will be discussed later in this chapter.[5]

[5] The time-lag problem is touched upon in the aforementioned studies of Nurkse and Bloomfield. Both used annual data (and the year as a unit of observation) to analyze the relation between two variables. Nurkse stated: "Our observations relate to yearly intervals. It is possible that domestic assets may be adjusted in the same direction as changes in international assets, not immediately, but with a lag of more than a year, in which case the year-to-year figures might conceal a process of adjustment taking place on the traditional lines. A lag in the process of adjustment is, after all, natural. Suppose an expansion of domestic credit gets under way in some country; the central bank's domestic assets increase, while its international reserve is likely to fall, thus 'offsetting' part at least of the rise in domestic assets. It may be only after some time—say two or three years—that the central bank is 'pulled up short' by the fall in its international reserve and that it may feel obliged to start contracting its domestic assets; and this contraction, again, may go on for two or three years and is likely to be accompanied by a return flow of gold and exchange reserves. In both the expansion and the contraction phase, domestic and international assets may thus move in opposite directions from year to year, and yet the 'rules of the game' may operate, albeit with a lag." (Nurkse, op. cit., pp. 68–70.)

Similarly, Bloomfield said: "The period of a year that is the basis of our comparison is essentially an arbitrary one that may conceivably conceal the fact that domestic assets did move more frequently in the same direction with international assets than in the opposite direction, but with a lag of more than one year." (Bloomfield, op. cit., p. 50.)

Nurkse and Bloomfield were worried by the possibility that central banks reacted with a lag of a few years. From all available evidence, this does not seem to be a matter of grave concern. Normally, central banks would probably react within a fairly short time—certainly, it could be expected, less than a year. If they do not, this would be an indication not of a slow machinery of response but of an intentional policy, which should by no means be described as following some "rules" with a time lag. Nurkse himself appears to suggest as much in the sentence just following the passage quoted above: "It is not always easy to draw the line between such delayed adjustment and deliberate neutralization with a view to avoiding adjustment." (Nurkse, op. cit., p. 70.)

A much more important reason for the inadequacy of annual data would seem to me to be that a period as long as a whole year is likely to contain move-

Where balance-of-payments developments follow a pattern approximating cyclical movements, this method of establishing relationships among variables will be complemented by the reference-cycle analysis developed for the study of business cycles.[6] In this case, the turning points in the balance of payments will serve as the "reference dates." In principle, this method should yield essentially the same conclusions as that of observing subperiods of imbalances, since each such subperiod will be approximately—although not precisely—a phase of the reference cycle. This additional method of investigation may help in revealing the degree of consistency of each relationship. It may also uncover typical time lags between imbalances and reactions, when such typical lags exist.

Conclusions derived from these observations would, to repeat, be tentative. If an instrument (or policy) variable appears to move consistently in the direction required for balance-of-payments adjustment, it will be necessary to test whether this association may not be due to the consistent association of balance-of-payments fluctuations with the movements of another target variable, with which the changes of the instrument variable in question are genuinely associated. Also, when policy variables are seen not to move consistently with the balance of payments, or even to move consistently in a direction opposite to the requirements for balance-of-payments adjustment, this will require explanation. A few complementary methods of investigation will be used to deal with these problems. Thus, the possibility of an association of the movements of a policy variable with those of an alternative target variable will be examined by looking at the latter during periods

ments in opposite directions (in each variable) rather than a uniform movement, and the averaging of these movements must detract seriously from the validity of the investigation. Observations based on annual averages and on the year as a unit of investigation are thus likely to be of a limited significance. The only case in which this is less important is where the dominant movements took the form of rather long cycles, with a considerable number of years within each stretch of the cycle.

[6] Essentially, this is a method by which each "cycle" is first divided into two phases—the "trough to peak" and "peak to trough" (or the reverse order). In the graphic presentation, each phase is assigned the same horizontal distance (equal for the two phases, and for all cycles), and the various cycles are charted on the same graph, one below the other. Beside the upward and downward turning points, the position of the variable under investigation is shown also for three other points, equidistant in time, during each of the two phases. In this way, positions of the variable through the various stages of the cycle may easily be compared, and typical patterns of cyclical behavior of the variable be revealed. See Arthur F. Burns and Wesley C. Mitchell, *Measuring Business Cycles,* New York, NBER, 1947, particularly Chapter 2.

of a uniform movement of the former. This may also be done through the reference-cycle analysis in two ways: first, by taking as reference dates the turning points in the movements of the policy *instrument* and examining movements of alternative target variables during these cycles; second, by determining reference dates according to turning points in the movement of a target variable and observing the movements of instrument variables along these cycles.

Isolating periods in which balance-of-payments equilibrium and alternative targets called for opposite policies would, of course, make it easier to distinguish reactions to imbalances of payments from responses to changes in other targets. Unfortunately, for this purpose (but not for policy makers!) the number of such episodes of clear conflict has been rather small in the countries and periods covered in this study. Although the small number of such cases prevents a formal separate investigation of these episodes, special attention will usually be given to them.

The combined use of all these methods should yield answers to the following questions: Which instruments of aggregate demand policy were used for balance-of-payments adjustment? Which were not, or were even manipulated in a way opposite to balance-of-payments requirements? Why were the latter not used for balance-of-payments purposes; that is, what other policy targets might have prevented the use of these instruments for balance-of-payments requirements? The analysis should also be able to show consistent differences in policy reactions among chronological periods in each country, or consistent differences—if they exist—between policy responses to balance-of-payments deficits and to balance-of-payments surpluses.

By the nature of the study, the relationships revealed cannot usually be completely and definitely established. Given that the unit of observation is a period of more or less monotonic movements, the number of observations in each country is necessarily small. Typically, it may not be more than ten or twelve and sometimes considerably less. The conventional methods of verifying the significance of apparent relationships would thus be of very little help in the present instance.[7] Statements of conclusions must, then, involve an element of judgment, and findings have to be treated as plausible implications of the evidence rather than as unchallengeable truths. But that is, in varying degree, the nature of any empirical proposition.

[7] This refers also to the test of "indexes of conformity," which is used in cyclical analysis. See the warning, *ibid.*, pp. 183–85.

5. Policy Instruments and Adjustment Policies

The selection of policy instruments, or variables, for observation will depend on the circumstances of each country. Differences in structure, law, and tradition lead to the use of different instruments in different countries. Here, statements of other analysts and of policy makers may be helpful as guidelines for experimentation. If, for instance, the magnitude of "secondary liquidity" is claimed to be of concern to the central bank of a certain country, this magnitude may be investigated in the study of that country; in another country this variable may be ignored, but the yield of government debt instruments studied; and so on. The discussion of individual countries will be preceded in each case by a section indicating, on the basis of prior information, what the major instruments used in the country are and the specific attributes of each instrument in that country, where this seems necessary for an understanding of the policy mechanism.

A few instruments are common to most of the countries under investigation. These include the following: the discount rate, reserve-ratio requirements, central-bank lending to the commercial banks, central-bank lending to the government, central-bank total domestic claims, commercial-bank lending to the public, the money supply, government revenues, government expenditures, and the government's budgetary balance. Most of these variables require no comment, but some need a few words of explanation.

Central-Bank Lending to the Government.[8] This magnitude is calculated on a *net* basis—that is, it represents the size of the net indebtedness (either positive or negative) of the government to the central bank and is derived by subtracting government deposits at the central bank from its borrowing from the bank: central-bank credit to the government increases the amount of liquidity in the economy only when it is net lending.

Central-Bank Total Domestic Claims. Changes in this variable are usually primarily a combination of changes in three other variables which are recorded separately: central-bank lending to the commercial

---

[8] When used in a general way, the term "government" will refer, in this study, to all official policy-making agencies; specifically, it will include the central bank. But in discussions of the central bank vs. the "government," the latter should obviously be interpreted as excluding the monetary authorities.

banks, central-bank lending to the government, and open-market operations. Sometimes they may also reflect other components, such as central-bank lending to the public (other than commercial banks). For reasons indicated above, central-bank lending to the government appears in this total on a *net* basis. The "total" of domestic claims is thus a hybrid in which some components are gross while one is net.

The Government's Revenues, Expenditures, and Budgetary Balance. In the fiscal sphere, the major policy tool which one might expect to be employed for balance-of-payments adjustment is probably the over-all (surplus or deficit) balance of the budget. This may best be discussed in terms of the government's "excess demand" for goods and services.[9] An increase in the government's excess demand—whether an increase in a deficit, a reduction of a surplus, or a shift from a surplus to a deficit—is a contribution to the economy's aggregate demand, and thus an expansionary measure; and a reduction of excess demand is the opposite. The investigation will thus examine not the position of the government's balance (i.e., whether it is a surplus or a deficit) but the *direction of change* in the balance from one period to the other. It may also be interesting to look separately at changes in government revenues and in government expenditures. If the government does manipulate its excess demand in reaction to balance-of-payments fluctuations, this distinction may show whether it is mainly revenues which are changed or expenditures, or possibly the two in opposite directions or in different proportions.

In examining policy reactions to imbalances of payments, a judgment must be made as to whether a given change in a policy variable is "adjusting" or "disadjusting"—that is, whether it tends to relieve or to aggravate the imbalance. This judgment has to be made on two different levels.

First, it may be asked whether the change in the policy variable, *in and by itself,* has an impact in an adjusting direction: if it does, it will be termed "adjusting." Thus, when there is a downward imbalance any change which tends to reduce aggregate demand or to lower prices is an "adjusting" change. This would include an increase of the dis-

---

[9] The "excess demand" is the excess of the government's expenditures on goods and services over those of its revenues which reduce the public's disposable income. In effect, the expenditures include very often loans to other organizations (whether private or nationalized), the case for whose inclusion as an element in the government's "excess demand" is not clear. Also, the data actually used refer to cash budgets, while the use of accrual budgets—had they been available—might be held to be more appropriate.

count rate, an increase of minimum-reserve ratios, a decline of central-
or commercial-bank credit, and so on. To call such a change "adjusting" does not necessarily imply that the entire process of which this
change is a part will have an adjusting effect. For instance, the discount
rate may be raised, but demand for commercial-bank credit may increase, too, swelling credit volume and thus augmenting the balance-
of-payments deficits. Without the change in the discount rate, however,
the deterioration would have been even stronger, and this is therefore
an "adjusting" change in the discount rate.

Second, the pattern of behavior of the whole array of instruments
combined must be evaluated. Within this framework, what was termed
an "adjusting" change before may not be so, and vice versa. In other
words, when the over-all pattern is examined, attention is focused on
the magnitude of some crucial variable. If this variable changes in an
adjusting direction, the policy pattern as a whole is adjusting. A change
in another variable which was found to be "disadjusting" when examined in isolation may still be consistent with the adjusting change
in the crucial variable. To cite a simple example: Suppose the crucial
variable is deemed to be money supply; this variable could change in
an adjusting direction, even though credit supply—which is only one
of the factors which create money—changes in a disadjusting direction.
The disadjusting movement of credit supply, *when judged by itself,* may
then still be consistent with an adjusting shift in over-all monetary
policy. Judging the pattern as a whole would thus require focusing
attention on the crucial variable or variables. This, indeed, whether
explicitly or implicitly, has always been the way adjustment policies
have been analyzed.

The investigation of each individual country will thus consist of a
discussion on two levels. First, each policy variable will be examined
separately to see if, by itself, it reveals any consistent behavior, either
adjusting or the opposite. Then, by way of summary and interpretation,
the observations of individual instruments will be combined to see
whether they imply a typical pattern of reactions, and whether this
pattern may be expected, in accordance with any reasonable model,
to be of an adjusting nature.

It is important to note that judgments about the behavior of policy
variables—that is, whether they do or do not respond in an adjusting
manner to balance-of-payments fluctuations—are based on observations of actual sizes of these variables. This attribute of the study has
a few pertinent implications—or, to some extent, drawbacks.

First, no distinction is made, in the analysis of each policy variable, between discretionary policy actions and automatic responses. A simple (and important) example may be mentioned. If money supply rises with balance-of-payments surpluses, and falls with deficits, money supply wil be designated as a variable which moves in an adjusting manner—although it is quite possible that these movements in money supply are due solely to the automatic impact of changes of the country's external balances. The absence of a distinction between the two types of responses is due to two considerations. One is pragmatic: it would usually be very difficult—and sometimes downright impossible —to separate automatic from discretionary policy reactions. Secondly, apart from this consideration, it may be assumed that governments could usually counteract automatic impacts; if they do not, these impacts may be judged to have been deemed desirable, even though they were not initiated by the government. Also, if the automatic impact is offset—partly or fully—by the government, and only the offsetting policy measures (which are, of course, discretionary) are taken into account, inferences about policy patterns would certainly be misleading. In the evaluation and interpretation of the whole pattern, as distinguished from the observations of individual policy variables, an attempt will usually be made in this study to point out relations between policy actions that appear to be automatic and those that appear to be discretionary.

Another drawback which must be acknowledged is that, *ex post,* realized movements of each policy variable may often differ from the *ex ante* changes—the realized movement is not necessarily identical with that intended by the policy maker. This difficulty certainly increases in importance with the complexity of the process by which the policy variable in question is brought into play.

Monetary variables differ as to the directness with which they can be manipulated by the monetary authority. On the one hand, such variables include instruments that are controlled directly and precisely by the authority, like the discount rate, minimum-reserve requirements, or open-market operations. On the other hand, they include a variable such as money supply, which is affected by the monetary authority only through a complex and long drawn-out chain of changes, not all of which are immediately taken into account. In between are variables such as components of the central bank's assets, or the supply of credit, which are at various stages of remove from the direct action of the monetary authority. It may be debated at what stage a variable is too little affected to be an "instrument" in monetary policy.[10] The advantage of examining variables at different levels, as in the present study, is that it makes possible an analysis, as has been explained earlier in this chapter, which is not tied in advance to the investigation of one specific model.

This problem may be even more relevant for budgetary policies: the identification of realized, *ex post* magnitudes with *ex ante* policies might well be questioned. Thus, a realized reduction in the government's excess demand is treated in this investigation as a contractive policy, and a realized increase as an expansionary policy. It may be argued that this is a particularly dubious procedure in the fiscal sphere; that when, for instance, the government undertakes an expansionary policy—say, by reducing tax rates without changing expenditures—the ensuing expansion may lead to a budgetary surplus through its effect on

[10] Challenged by a similar problem of determining what could be instruments of monetary policy, Karaken and Solow stopped somewhat earlier on this road. They argue: "It is not true, except in some irrelevant long-run sense, to say that the Federal Reserve controls either M [money supply] or its rate of change. What the Federal Reserve can do is buy and sell in the open market, set reserve requirements, and set the discount rate. A little less directly . . . we may say that the authorities control the effective primary reserves of the commercial banks . . . and at one further remove we may say that the measure of monetary policy is the power of the banking system to carry earning assets. This is what the monetary authorities do. They do not move a pointer on a dial marked M or even ΔM." (John Karaken and Robert M. Solow, "Lags in Monetary Policy," Part I of "Lags in Fiscal and Monetary Policy," Stabilization Policies, pp. 17–18).

Later, however, the authors state: "Why stop, though, with the assumptions (or attributions of knowledge) so far suggested? Why stop, that is, with Max F [maximum earning assets of commercial banks] as the instrument variable? Why not continue making assumptions until the ultimate policy variables, the price level, the rate of unemployment, etc., emerge as the instrument variables of the Federal Reserve? Above it was suggested that the System can be regarded as knowing how the direct determinants of total member bank reserves are themselves determined, and as being able to predict future values of the arguments of these functions which it does not set. But then why not assume in addition that the System knows member banks' demand for excess reserves, in which case it can be regarded as setting actual as well as maximum earning assets. And with a few more assumptions, the System can be regarded as setting the price level.

"Evidently, there is no basis in logic for stopping at one point rather than another—for making certain assumptions rather than others. . . ." (*Ibid.*, p. 81.)

Indeed, with no basis in logic, the definition of instruments or the "assumptions" we make may change from time to time and from one country to another. As stated in the text, an advantage of always considering instruments on various "levels" is that it imposes fewer restrictions, by an investigator, on the assumed mode of behavior of the policy maker.

the amount of tax revenues. Identifying a budgetary surplus with a contractive policy would be entirely misleading in this instance.

Such a contradiction between intended and realized budgetary balance—due merely to induced changes rather than to autonomous changes in exogenous variables—would not be possible under the "textbook" assumptions of multiplier analysis. Specifically, it would not be possible when *ex ante* investment is held constant, or even assumed to be a function of income. Under different assumptions, however, this contradiction is conceivable. It could be produced, for instance, by an "acceleration principle," or by assuming investment to be a function of *tax rates,* either in general or for certain corporate tax rates.

Ideally, the anticipated budgetary balance should have been used rather than the realized balance. However, this cannot be achieved in practice. At best, estimates of this magnitude are available for a fiscal year as a whole; even then, they do not necessarily reflect fully the anticipations of policy makers. Estimates of planned budgets would be of only little use for the purpose of this study. It is hoped that the adoption of budgetary performance as a substitute for expected budgetary magnitudes will not bias the results seriously. This hope may be justified when the periods of observation are not unduly long—say, not more than a year or a year and a half. Within short periods, changes induced by measures taken during the period may be expected to be slight in comparison with the primary changes. Thus, the danger that realized magnitudes will give indications contrary to the intent of policies is probably small when the period is short. When partial, circumstantial evidence on the government's intentions is available, this information will be introduced.

Unlike the monetary area, the study of fiscal policy is confined here to the "ultimate" variables. It considers the government's over-all balance in its budget; at the level immediately below this, it observes the two components of the budget—revenues and expenditures. But there it stops. It does not analyze the means by which each of these components is, in turn, affected—means which could well be considered policy variables in their own right. This treatment of the fiscal area results from the practical limitations of the investigation. It is easy to tell how the discount rate or the minimum-reserve ratio was changed during a given period. It would be immensely more difficult to say how the "tax rate" changed. This "tax rate" is some weighted average of a myriad of individual tax rates, many of which may move in opposite directions in a given period and certainly in different proportions. Even the study of entire categories of these rates, e.g., excise duties or income taxes, would be extremely complicated. A component such as the personal income tax would in itself raise serious problems: it is a whole structure not all parts of which always move in the same direction. In a study of the present scope, any attempt to observe such "partial" variables in a systematic manner must be abandoned.

Another, somewhat related, aspect of the method of investigation followed here is that it disregards the extent of change in policy variables which might have been anticipated in the absence of policy actions. This may again be illustrated by an example. Suppose the government's excess demand rises at a time of balance-of-payments deficits. This will be considered a movement in a disadjusting direction. Actually, it might well have been that the government's excess demand would have risen even more during the period under consideration, due to exogenous factors, and that, because of the balance-of-payments position, the government took steps to reduce its excess demand—a response in an adjusting direction. But this would not be revealed by the observed values of the variables and would therefore be disregarded. This is certainly a drawback of the method. But it could not be feasibly overcome, except in a small number of instances.

A difficulty of a different nature involved in the present study's method of evaluation is concerned with the distinction—and possible contradiction—between *levels* and *changes*. Once more, an example may be helpful. Suppose that during a period of balance-of-payments deficits, the discount rate is not raised but remains at a high level (in comparison with some "normal" level). It is not always possible to decide clearly whether this is or is not an adjusting response of the policy variable to the balance-of-payments position. Most often, the study will compare *movements* of the policy variable and the balance of payments; but sometimes the *level* of the policy variable will be taken into consideration—in a manner which must be, admittedly, of an arbitrary nature.

In concluding this section, it should be noted that most of the drawbacks involved in the method of observing movements of policy variables are probably more important in relation to budgetary than in relation to monetary variables. Hence, the inferences of the study about patterns of response of budgetary policies should be regarded as particularly tentative.

6. Determination of Imbalances of Payments

Since the purpose of the study is to identify and examine the policy reactions of governments to imbalances of payments, the variables which would be required, ideally, to indicate imbalances are those which serve this purpose in the decision-making process of the government concerned. The lack, however, of direct information about these "ideal" variables makes it necessary to substitute the researcher's judgment for that of the government concerned and to experiment with alternative variables. Since circumstances vary from one country to another, there should be no attempt to determine a single exclusive principle for identifying imbalances in all the countries studied. Where no particular special circumstances are apparent, however, it would be a good rule to stick as closely as possible to commonly accepted principles of identifying imbalances, since these are likely to be adhered to by the government concerned. It should be obvious from these remarks that it may be necessary to experiment with more than one definition or principle, even in the case of a single country.

The variable which appears to be the simplest, most easily observed, and most frequently available, is the country's external reserves. An increase of these reserves would indicate an "upward imbalance," or surplus; while a decrease would be a "downward imbalance," or deficit. The category selected to represent this variable is that of gross official reserves. The definition of this series usually includes holdings of gold and foreign exchange by the central bank or government plus the country's net position in the International Monetary Fund.

Holdings of foreign exchange by commercial banks, on the other hand, are probably not usually counted by governments as part of reserves for the purpose at hand. Before the era of convertibility, banks in most countries were ordinarily allowed to hold abroad only necessary working balances. In later years, commercial banks have presumably been guided by their own initiative and considerations in determining the amount of their foreign-exchange holdings. They do not act as agents of the central authorities, and their foreign assets and liabilities, and changes in them, are presumably disregarded in the government's identification of imbalances of payments.[11] Yet when commercial bank

[11] This approach is similar to that taken for the United States by the Bernstein Committee. See Report of the Review Committee, *Balance of Payments Statistics*

holdings are substantial, it may be worthwhile to experiment with including them in the country's reserves for the purpose of determining episodes of imbalances of payments. In the countries covered by the present report, this inclusion seemed, usually, to affect the analysis very little.

Another series experimented with is balance-of-payments surpluses and deficits, as defined by the Balance-of-Payments Division of the International Monetary Fund.[12] It covers the period from 1958 onward and uses the "official settlements" concept: "A surplus or deficit is defined as the balance of all transactions other than 'official settlements' (i.e., excluding changes in official gold and foreign-exchange assets, in net IMF positions, and in liabilities to foreign monetary authorities, and adjusted for advance repayments of foreign debt by governments). The over-all surplus or deficit so defined is equal to the basic balance, unrecorded transactions, and all movements of short-term capital, excluding only those that constitute official settlements." [13] This definition thus includes not only changes in a country's reserves but also changes in its liabilities to foreign monetary authorities and advance repayments of foreign debt by governments. The two series usually demonstrate a very high degree of agreement in direction of imbalances, and most often also in their intensity, during the period covered by the two (that is, from 1958 onward).

In some cases, it may be advisable to experiment with still other variables. For instance, a government may be concerned only with an imbalance on current account, disregarding movements on capital account. If this is thought to be the target, representation of imbalances by deficits or surpluses on current account may be rewarding.

Still another variable which may have to be taken into account is the *level* of reserves. A situation may occur where the government wishes to see a change in reserves—an accumulation or, probably much less often, a reduction. The government would then be concerned not with any change in reserves but with any discrepancy between the desired level of reserves and their actual level (or, in other words, a change not commensurate with the change desired by the government). The determination of a "desired level" is, of course, not an easy task. When the level of reserves has been constant over an extended period,

of the United States: A Review and Appraisal, Washington, D.C., 1965, Chapter 9.

[12] This information was kindly provided by the Division.

[13] International Monetary Fund, 1965 Annual Report, p. 66.

it may be legitimate to assume that a shortfall of reserves below this level could be considered a downward imbalance even when reserves are rising (from a particularly low level), and vice versa. When reserves demonstrate a long-term movement, some form of determining their trend would be required, and the assumption that the "trend level" is the desired one may be attempted.

Most of the experiments that could be made are not usually required. Two guidelines help to indicate the need for experimentation: first, an explicit statement of policy makers, or of economic analysts, that a certain variable is used to measure balance-of-payments disturbances— in which case the variable in question would merit an investigation; second, a lack of definite conclusions when the simple variable of external reserve holdings is analyzed.

The problem arising from the substitution of *ex post* for *ex ante* magnitudes, which has been pointed out in the discussion of policy variables, is just as relevant to the definition of targets in general and to the specific target of balance-of-payments equilibrium. The study investigates relations among *realized* movements of variables. *Anticipations,* on the other hand, are entirely absent from this examination. In the government's "reaction function," manipulations of policy variables will in effect be related to the present stock and the anticipated future flow of each magnitude that represents a target variable. Past flows enter into the function only as a factor which affects these two. The statistical investigations can, in principle, take account of present stocks; this will indeed be done, as has been mentioned: the level of external reserves will be introduced whenever it seems to be a promising addition to the analysis. Anticipations, on the other hand, are replaced by the statistically observable flows which, in relation to each point of time in which a policy measure is undertaken, have either taken place in the past or will have been realized in effect in the future. This is certainly not a perfect substitute, but it is probably the best available. A conceivable alternative would be to construct each government's "anticipation function," and derive from it anticipated values for the target variables. This procedure might possibly be attempted, but it is certainly not feasible in this study.

Some qualification is now needed with response to the statement made at the beginning of this section that imbalances would ideally be measured in the same way as the respective government measures it. A government may be indifferent to the so-called imbalance, or may even welcome it. The double meaning of the term "imbalance" should therefore be clarified. As used in this study, "imbalance" does not necessarily indicate that the government so regarded the development in question. The attempt to achieve a certain level of reserves, which has just been mentioned, is an important illustration of this point. If a level of reserves higher than the existing one is considered a target, then not an accumulation of reserves but its absence would be regarded, by the government, as an "imbalance." It should therefore be emphasized that the use of this term does not necessarily imply an expression of the government's view; on the contrary, one of the outcomes of the study could be to identify what the government actually considered an imbalance by examining the government's policies. Yet it is important to keep in mind that the study is intended to draw inferences for the international monetary system as a whole. For the latter, the accumulation of reserves by one country may be an "imbalance" even if it is not so regarded by that country. And it is therefore imperative to learn how that country reacted to such imbalances. It should also be noted that into an appraisal of the performance of the international system may enter considerations which could change materially conclusions drawn from the observation of individual countries. Thus, for instance, when a country which holds an unduly large proportion of the world's reserves fails to deflate in response to a loss of reserves, this absence of "adjustment" may in effect contribute to stability of the international system as a whole.

As stated earlier in this chapter, the analytical method employed here starts by determining subperiods of imbalance of payments, and a distinction is made among subperiods of "upward imbalance," "downward imbalance," and "stability." Since, however, more than one indication is used to identify imbalances, the question which naturally arises, and which merits at least a brief discussion, is how such subperiods are determined.

Conceivably, subperiods for each country could be defined in several alternative ways, depending on the variable used to indicate the balance-of-payments position. For the countries and period covered by this study, however, it is almost universally found that all indicators point in the same direction (needless to say, this applies to conventional indicators such as the level of reserves or the balance-of-payments deficit or surplus by one definition or another, but not to variables such as the rate of change of external reserves). Significant exceptions to this rule, which are quite rare, are pointed out in the country studies. It has been decided, therefore, to use for each country just one set of subperiods of imbalances, rather than a few alternative sets which would have been very similar to each other.

The determination of starting and end points for each subperiod of upward imbalance, downward imbalance or stability is not always self-evident. Take, for instance, a period of a long upward movement interrupted, at some point, by a short downward movement. Should this be regarded as three subperiods (upward, downward, and again upward movements)? Or should the brief interruption be disregarded, and the whole period be classified as a single subperiod of upward imbalance? Particularly difficult is the determination of subperiods of "stability." Obviously, no single quarter exists, in any country in which a state of precise equilibrium of the country's external position could be found. Yet, it is also evident that quite often the imbalance, whether upward or downward, is so minor that it should be disregarded, and the external position be considered as one of "stability."

In determining subperiods, several factors enter into consideration, chiefly the following: (1) the length of the period of movements in a given direction; (2) the intensity of these movements; (3) the degree of agreement among the various indications of balance-of-payments position (external reserves, over-all balance of payments, and, sometimes, other series); and (4) the extent of deviation from past developments and trends. Subperiods could conceivably be determined by some statistical function, which would include all these factors, as well as perhaps a few others. Even casual observations would suggest that a predetermined function of this nature would often lead to absurd results. Instead, an element of arbitrariness and judgment has been introduced into the determination of turning points. A general rule (which has been disobeyed very rarely—mainly in the case of the United Kingdom), is that no subperiod may be shorter than half a year; movements of only a single quarter falling between opposite movements in the preceding and following quarters are disregarded. In general, little disagreement could probably arise in the determination of subperiods, and classifications found elsewhere (in other analyses or in statements of policy makers), roughly agree with those used in the present study. In a few instances, however, the demarcation is not self-evident or clear-cut, and judgment plays a more important role. In instances which look particularly difficult, the chronological determination of subperiods is discussed in some detail.

7. Other Policy Targets

Policy targets may be of various kinds and shades, and most of them could not be identified without intensive study. It would obviously not be feasible to try to secure information about all of these targets; and for the present purpose such an attempt would probably be unrewarding, even if it were feasible. As explained earlier, other target variables are introduced in this study partly to determine whether a policy pattern which appears to be a reaction to imbalances of payments can be explained instead by the movements of these other variables, and partly to examine the possibility that an absence of reaction to the balance-of-payments position might be explained by the appropriation of policy instruments for alternative targets. While the number of such explanations could be very large, it seems that the observation of a few major targets would go a considerable way toward satisfying the requirements of such an examination. These targets are maintenance of price stability, maintenance of full employment, and achievement of a high, steady rate of growth.

The observation of the first two targets is relatively simple. The indexes of consumer prices and of wholesale prices appear to be the most frequently used indicators of movements of the general price level. Usually, though not always, these two indexes will yield similar results, particularly when price movements are substantial. This is also true about measurements of unemployment. Although series such as registered unemployment and the number of unemployed projected from labor force surveys may differ significantly in absolute size, indicated directions and intensities of change are generally similar.

Statistical representation of the growth target is more complicated. This is, by its nature, a longer-term target. A measurement of developments during a given period will inevitably reveal the effect of (1) changes in the economy's productive resources and the productivity of these resources—which is, presumably, what the target of "growth" refers to—and (2) the rate of utilization of existing capacity, in which the rate of employment, considered as a separate target, is of crucial importance. The separation of actual performance into these components would clearly be beyond the scope of a study of this kind. The rate of growth will therefore have to be measured by some summary indication of the current performance of the economy, despite the limitations just noted.

Conceptually, the best available yardstick for measuring the economy's over-all performance is probably the rate of increase of gross national product or net national product (the difference between the two rates will usually be slight). For a number of reasons, however, a measure conforming better to the purpose of this study is the rate of increase of industrial production. In the first place, it is usually available within a fairly short time, whereas gross national product estimates are available in most countries only with a considerable lag. It may thus be assumed that, for the purpose of determining their short-term policies, governments which have this measurement available at the relevant time regard it as indicating the growth rate. The government may justly feel that this use is not likely to be very misleading, since industrial production is itself a major component of the national product in the countries concerned. Even aside from the advantage of being readily accessible, industrial-production data often attract particular attention. Industrial production is more susceptible to the effects of short-term governmental policies—and reflects them better—than do other economic activities, and in particular those of the agricultural sector. Likewise, the industrial sector is often assigned a particularly heavy weight—e.g., in comparison with the services sector —by government observers. For these reasons, the index of industrial production will usually represent the growth target in the present study.

Beyond the problem of what statistical series best represent the various target variables, the question of how these series should be interpreted must be raised. It must be assumed that a given change (or position) of a series indicates a desirable movement (or level) for a particular target; while another position is undesirable and calls for correction. The number of possible assumptions, i.e., of possible modes of governmental views, may again be very large. In general, the position of a given target, as indicated by a given time series, could be judged by its level, by its direction of change, or by its rate of change. Thus, where the price stability target is concerned, any increase in the price level (measured, for example, by the consumer price index) may be regarded as a disturbance which should be corrected. But if a general upward trend of prices exists, it is possible that a price increase no greater than the average is not a source of concern, or that faster increases are not considered a disturbance as long as the price level is below its "trend line." A similar variety of models is conceivable when unemployment is examined. When the rate of unemployment is high in comparison with its average level, and rising, this would certainly be considered a disturbance. It is not clear, however, how a situation in which unemployment is high but falling would be regarded; or, to take the opposite combination, how a situation of low but rising unemployment should be treated. The same ambiguity holds when the growth target is examined. A situation where industrial production is both below its "trend line" and falling would, almost certainly, be regarded as a disturbance. The answer is not clear, however, when the rate of increase is above average, but production is still below its trend level, or when the rate of increase is falling, but production is above its trend level; and so on.

It would not be feasible to examine all such possibilities. In any case, it should be recalled that the study does not purport to investigate *all* the possible targets, and cannot therefore be exhaustive. For this reason, only a very few models of reaction will be examined. In general, it will be assumed that price stability is contravened when prices rise more rapidly than in recent experience; that the target of high employment is contravened by an increase of unemployment; and that a decline in the rate of increase of industrial production (and, needless to say, a negative rate) indicates a deterioration of the target of rapid growth. In the countries which have been investigated, it appears from casual observation that other reasonable models would most often have given similar indications about the timing of disturbances. In some cases where these indications are clearly contradictory, this will be taken into account informally. It should again be emphasized, however, that this procedure does not purport to be an exhaustive and definitive study of all reasonable possibilities. It is restricted, as has been stated earlier, to the examination of a very limited number of the simplest, and probably most obvious, among the possible models. The expansion of the scope of assumptions concerning potential indicators of achievement of targets, and the adoption of alternative approaches to those which are followed here, may be a promising avenue for further investigations along the lines of the present study. This probably applies with particular force to the target of rapid growth.

CHAPTER 2

AN OVER-ALL VIEW OF POLICY
PATTERNS

1. The Use of Budgetary Policy

In summarizing and evaluating the findings on the policy responses of individual countries to their balance-of-payments disturbances, which are presented in detail in the next part, it may be convenient to start by the examination of budgetary policy, which offers quite clear—though negative—conclusions.

In country after country, it has been repeatedly found that budgetary policy throughout the period under investigation was not responsive to the requirements of the balance of payments. There is no single country out of the nine covered in this study in which a positive, consistent pattern of response is revealed. Even individual episodes in which budgetary policy might be interpreted as having been taken in reaction to the needs of the balance of payments are not very frequent. This may be seen from Table 2-1, which repeats in a summary form the observations brought out in the respective country analyses.

As Table 2-1 indicates, the only instance over any considerable length of time in which budgetary policy behaved in a manner which may be interpreted as a response to the balance-of-payments position is that of the United Kingdom from late 1952 to late 1956. All other episodes seem to be sporadic. The evidence is, it should be mentioned, based very often on deficient data or on data which pertain to only a part of the period under consideration. Likewise, the qualifications which must be attached to the interpretation of *ex post* budgetary data,

TABLE 2-1

BUDGETARY POLICY DURING PERIODS OF IMBALANCES OF PAYMENTS

Country	Consistent with Balance-of-Payments Requirements (1)	Inconsistent with Balance-of-Payments Requirements (2)	Indifferent to Balance-of-Payments Requirements (3)
Belgium	III 1957 – IV 1958	III 1960 – IV 1961	IV 1962 – III 1965
France	I 1952 – IV 1952 IV 1952 – III 1953	I 1951 – I 1952 III 1953 – IV 1955 IV 1955 – IV 1958 IV 1958 – IV 1965	I 1950 – I 1951
Germany	I 1963 – II 1964	IV 1958 – III 1959 II 1961 – I 1962	II 1964 – II 1966
Italy		III 1953 – II 1956 I 1963 – II 1966	I 1952 – III 1953 I 1957 – IV 1959 I 1961 – I 1962
Japan	II 1951 – III 1952 IV 1961 – II 1963	III 1952 – II 1953 II 1954 – IV 1955 IV 1956 – III 1957 III 1957 – II 1961	IV 1950 – II 1951 IV 1953 – II 1954 II 1961 – IV 1961 IV 1963 – II 1964
Netherlands	II 1953 – II 1954 IV 1959 – IV 1961	I 1950 – IV 1950 IV 1950 – III 1951 III 1951 – II 1953 I 1956 – III 1957 I 1963 – IV 1963 IV 1963 – II 1964	III 1957 – I 1959 IV 1964 – II 1965
Sweden		II 1951 – I 1952 III 1959 – I 1960 I 1960 – III 1962	II 1964 – I 1965
U.K.	III 1952 – III 1954 III 1954 – IV 1955 IV 1955 – III 1956 IV 1958 – III 1959 III 1959 – IV 1959 II 1960 – IV 1960	II 1951 – III 1952 III 1956 – IV 1956 IV 1956 – II 1957 II 1957 – III 1957 III 1957 – III 1958 IV 1960 – III 1961 III 1961 – III 1962 III 1963 – III 1965	III 1958 – IV 1958 III 1965 – IV 1965
U.S.	III 1951 – I 1952	I 1953 – IV 1954 IV 1956 – III 1957 I 1958 –	

should always be borne in mind.[1] Yet the weight of the evidence is substantial: it indicates strongly that budgetary policy was not used in the service of the target of balance-of-payments equilibrium.

While Table 2-1 is based on the indications about budgetary policy provided only by the variable of the budgetary balance, similar inferences would be reached if the government's revenues and expenditures were examined separately. It must be concluded that budgetary policy as an instrument of aggregate demand policy was not generally part of the set of tools used to correct imbalances of payments. This would not exclude the use of *specific* budgetary revenues or expenditures for this purpose; while such use was not, as a rule, examined in this study, there could be little doubt that a few such instruments were often used in response to the needs of the balance of payments.

It was most frequently found that, in the countries under investigation, the failure to use budgetary policy for balance-of-payments purposes *cannot* be explained by the assignment of this policy instrument to the service of other competing targets. Most often, budgetary policy seems to be excluded from the list of instruments available for the correction of domestic as well as of balance-of-payments disequilibria. One country for which this statement would definitely not be true is Sweden, in which budgetary policy is geared, by and large, to the needs of maintaining high employment and high production. To a large extent, this is also true for the United States. But in other countries, no such overriding rule for the use of budgetary policy seems to emerge.

Even more rare is the use of the "policy mix," which came to be heavily advocated in recent years, by which monetary policy is assigned to the service of the balance of payments, while fiscal policy is reserved for the achievement of the domestic targets of employment and production.[2] This policy combination would require a tight monetary policy and an expansionary fiscal policy in periods of a balance-of-payments deficit combined with high unemployment; and the reverse order of policies with payments surpluses and domestic booms.

Table 2-2 presents the instances which qualify for such policy combination (that is, in which opposite policy directions are called for by

[1] See Chapter 1, pp. 19–20.

[2] For theoretical discussions of this "policy mix" see, for instance: Robert A. Mundell, "The Appropriate Use of Monetary and Fiscal Policy for Internal and External Stability," *I.M.F. Staff Papers,* IX (March 1962), pp. 70–79; J. Marcus Fleming, "Domestic Financial Policies under Fixed and under Floating Exchange Rates," *I.M.F. Staff Papers,* IX (November 1962), pp. 369–80; and Anne O. Krueger, "The Impact of Alternative Government Policies under Varying Exchange Systems," *Quarterly Journal of Economics,* LXXIX (May 1965), pp. 195–208.

TABLE 2-2

POLICIES DURING PERIODS OF CONFLICTING
REQUIREMENTS OF EXTERNAL AND
DOMESTIC POSITIONS

Country and Period	Monetary Policy	Budgetary Policy
EXTERNAL DEFICITS AND DOMESTIC SLACK		
France, IV 1952 – III 1953	* mixed evidence	– restrictive
Germany, III 1951 – I 1952	* neutral	* neutral
Netherlands, I 1956 – III 1957	+ restrictive	+ expansionary
U.K., II 1951 – III 1952	+ restrictive	+ expansionary
EXTERNAL SURPLUS AND DOMESTIC BOOM		
Belgium, IV 1962 – III 1965	– restrictive	– expansionary
France, I 1950 – I 1951	+ expansionary	* neutral
Germany, I 1963 – II 1964	* neutral	– expansionary
Italy, III 1953 – II 1956	– restrictive	– expansionary
Italy, I 1961 – I 1962	+ expansionary	* neutral
Sweden, I 1960 – III 1962	* mixed evidence	+ restrictive
U.K., I 1950 – II 1951	+ expansionary	* mixed evidence

+ indicates a policy in the direction required by the policy "mix."
– indicates an opposite policy.
* indicates neutrality or conflicting evidence.

the country's domestic and external position). The presentation is rather rough: only subperiods of imbalance of payments are observed, without attempts of some other subdivisions; the indication of monetary or budgetary policy as "restrictive" or "expansionary" involves risks of oversimplification; and the total number of cases presented in the table is rather small. But so far as the evidence of Table 2-2 goes, it is rather clear. In only very few instances (one each in the U.K. and in the Netherlands) does the "mix" under consideration appear to have been undertaken.

2. Instruments of Monetary Policy

Monetary policy may be represented by numerous variables, each of which could conceivably measure the direction of the policy pursued by the government. The discussion will turn now to the examination of the variety of major monetary instruments which have been used in the countries under consideration.

Chart 2-1 describes the observations concerning the use of monetary instruments in individual countries. It covers, for each country, those instruments which on the basis of prior information and the findings of the present analysis are judged to have been used normally and regularly, during at least a substantial part of the period, as tools of over-all monetary policy. In each country, subperiods are shown according to the balance-of-payments position. Whenever the instrument under consideration is found to have behaved, during a given subperiod, in a manner which conforms with balance-of-payments requirements, this period is colored black in the part of the chart which describes this instrument. When the instrument behaves in the opposite way, the period is colored by diagonal lines; and when the instrument shows no movement during an imbalance of payments, the period is colored grey. Chart 2-2, which is added for reference, summarizes the balance-of-payments positions in the individual countries: periods of downward disturbances are colored by diagonal lines: periods of upward disturbances, in white; and equilibrium periods, in grey.

The pattern described by Chart 2-1 is illuminating. It is immediately apparent that two variables alone may claim recognition as instruments which have been often used in a manner consistent with balance-of-payments requirements: the discount rate and the (rate of expansion of) money supply. In Belgium, France, Japan, Italy, the Netherlands, and the United Kingdom,[3] at least one of these variables—usually both—is seen to have moved in conformity with the balance-of-payments position either through the whole period or during most of it. In the other three countries—and in the former six in other subperiods —these variables seem to be generally "neutral," but not usually to have moved in opposite direction to balance-of-payments requirements.

The variable of (the rate of expansion of) credit supply by commercial banks shows a different pattern. In general, it reveals neither widespread conformity with the balance-of-payments requirements, nor the opposite, and may therefore be judged not to have been usually assigned to balance-of-payments adjustment. In just two countries— Belgium and the United Kingdom—does it seem probable that during

[3] See, however, the discussion in the following section suggesting that in the United Kingdom credit supply, and not money supply, as in other countries, indicates the direction of monetary policy.

CHART 2-1

MOVEMENTS OF MONETARY POLICY VARIABLES DURING
IMBALANCES OF PAYMENTS, 1950–66

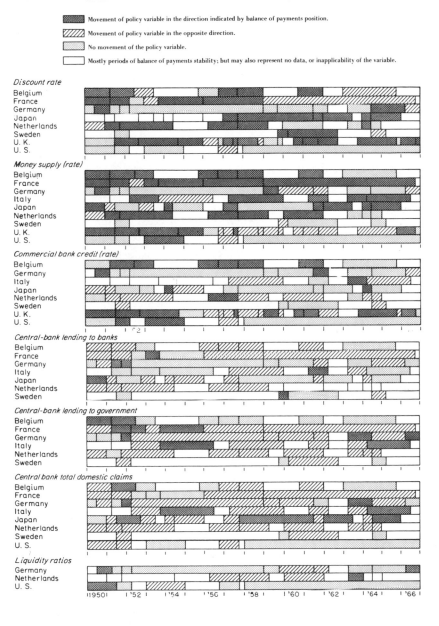

Movement of policy variable in the direction indicated by balance of payments position.

Movement of policy variable in the opposite direction.

No movement of the policy variable.

Mostly periods of balance of payments stability; but may also represent no data, or inapplicability of the variable.

Discount rate

Belgium
France
Germany
Japan
Netherlands
Sweden
U. K.
U. S.

Money supply (rate)

Belgium
France
Germany
Italy
Japan
Netherlands
Sweden
U. K.
U. S.

Commercial bank credit (rate)

Belgium
Germany
Italy
Japan
Netherlands
Sweden
U. K.
U. S.

Central-bank lending to banks

Belgium
France
Germany
Italy
Japan
Netherlands
Sweden

Central-bank lending to government

Belgium
France
Germany
Italy
Netherlands
Sweden

Central bank total domestic claims

Belgium
France
Germany
Italy
Japan
Netherlands
Sweden
U. S.

Liquidity ratios

Germany
Netherlands
U. S.

1950 '52 '54 '56 '58 '60 '62 '64 '66

CHART 2-2

THE BALANCE-OF-PAYMENTS POSITION, 1950–66

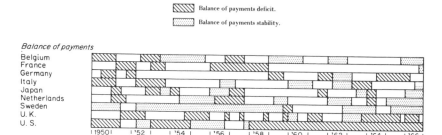

certain parts of the period under consideration the variable of credit supply was in fact manipulated to serve the needs of the balance of payments.

The next three variables, which represent central-bank lending, also show different patterns. One of these, central-bank lending to the government, seems to indicate "indifference," that is, a mix of episodes of movements which conform with balance-of-payments requirements, opposite movements, and "neutral" reactions, in about equal proportions. This is consistent with, and most probably related to, the findings concerning the budgetary policy. The most common—although not inevitable or universal—expression of a budgetary deficit would be government borrowing from the central bank. A surplus on the other hand would result in a repayment. Movements of the amount of government borrowing from the central bank may thus be expected to reflect, at least partly, movements of budgetary policy. Since the latter have been found to be generally nonresponsive to the balance of payments, it is not surprising to find no pattern of responsiveness of central-bank lending to the government.

The other component of central-bank lending—lending to commercial banks—reveals on the other hand a very obvious pattern of behavior, which is either neutral or (most often) runs *counter* to the direction indicated by the balance-of-payments position. Cases in which this lending declines with payments deficits and rises with payments surpluses are quite rare; whereas the opposite pattern, rising lending at times of deficit and declining lending with surpluses, is a very frequent phenomenon. This is true for countries in which other variables conform to balance-of-payments requirements, as well as for those in which no such positive response may be found.

The total domestic claims of a central bank consist overwhelmingly of lending to commercial banks and to the government.[4] Since lending to banks reveals a tendency to move in a direction opposite to balance-of-payments requirements, while lending to the government is by and large "neutral," the combination of the two may also be expected to reveal a disadjusting pattern. This, indeed, it does, with only slightly less consistency than does its component of lending to commercial banks. This is true for practically all countries in which the variable of the central bank's domestic claims is relevant and can be reliably estimated.[5]

The remaining monetary variable shown in Chart 2-1—liquidity, or reserve, ratios—is significant in only a small number of countries. In two out of the three countries in which this variable was of any importance, namely, Germany and the United States, a general indifference of its movements to the balance of payments is apparent, while the third—the Netherlands—even seems to show a pattern of behavior opposite to that which the balance of payments would require.

3. Compliance of Monetary Policy with Balance-of-Payments Requirements

It is thus seen that in a few countries none of the monetary instruments show a pattern of compliance with the needs of the balance of payments. In other countries, a few of the instruments do reveal such a pattern, and the most frequent policy combination is a change of the discount rate coupled with a change in money supply. With a down-

[4] In the United States, this total consists overwhelmingly of Federal Reserve credit created by open-market operations. In other countries open-market operations are either absent or insignificant or, even when substantial, are viewed as subsidary to the operation of one of the other monetary instruments.

[5] From Chart 2-1, Japan seems to be a case in which movements of the variable under consideration are as often in an adjusting direction as in the opposite. As has been pointed out in the chapter on Japan, however, data on Bank-of-Japan lending to the government are biased in the direction of conformity with balance-of-payments requirements (and are therefore not represented directly in Chart 2-1); this tends, naturally, to bias also the data on total Bank-of-Japan domestic claims in the same direction.

ward disturbance (that is, a balance-of-payments deficit) the discount rate is raised, and the rate of expansion of money supply falls. With balance-of-payments surpluses, the opposite movement takes place: the discount rate is lowered, and the rate of expansion of money supply rises.

If these two are considered the crucial variables of monetary policy in the countries in which this pattern is observed, then this pattern implies that the countries concerned manage their monetary policy so that it conforms with the needs of the balance of payments; [6] or, in other words, that these countries follow "the rules of the game" of a fixed-exchange-rate international monetary system. By most prevailing monetary theories, one or the other of these two monetary variables (the discount rate—representing the whole scale of interest rates —and the money supply), or both, would indeed be considered the crucial variable. In a simple Keynesian model, monetary policy could affect aggregate demand only to the extent that it affects the interest rate—which, in turn, has its impact on the demand for investment. The turn monetary policy is taking—that is, the question of whether its direction of movement is restrictive or expansive—would then be judged by the direction of movement of interest rates. The quantity theory of money would, on the other hand, assign crucial importance to the movement of money supply: aggregate demand is reduced by a reduction of the quantity of money, and raised by an increase of this quantity. But interest rates, too, would be expected to move in a manner consistent with movements of money supply: when the latter is lowered, interest rates must rise, hence the discount rate should be raised; and, similarly, the discount rate should be lowered with an increase of money supply.

In addition to its effect on the balance of payments through aggregate domestic demand, a change in the discount rate would be expected to affect the balance of payments through its impact on international short-term (and possibly also longer-term) capital movements. Regardless of what analytical model is employed, the "rules of the game" of balance-of-payments adjustment would thus require the discount rate to be raised in times of balance-of-payments deficits and lowered in times of surplus.

[6] The meaning given to "conformity" in this study, as stated in the preceding chapter, should be reemphasized here. It indicates "conformity" in *direction* alone, and not in size. Thus designating the monetary policy of a country as "conforming" with the need for adjustment does *not* convey the idea that the policy was necessarily sufficient, taken at the appropriate moment, or successful.

Neither of these two conventional monetary models would have required a definite movement in a specified direction of any of the monetary variables other than the money supply and the discount rate. Consider, for instance, the quantity theory (although the same conclusions would follow from the Keynesian model). A reserve-losing country is expected to lower its aggregate demand, and this would be done by a reduction of the money supply. But while the direction of the required movement of money supply is thus indicated, the *size* of this reduction is not. The more money supply changes, the faster the adjustment process will be. But certainly no one would expect this rule to require a rapid approach of the money supply to zero in the reserve-losing country, or to infinity in the reserve-gaining country. If a country were on the gold specie standard, the rate of change of money supply would be specified by the system itself: if money supply consists exclusively of gold, and so do the country's international reserves, the change in reserves and the change in money supply are one and the same thing. It can by no means be argued, however, that, if a country wants its monetary policy to serve the purpose of balance-of-payments adjustment, this indeed is the proper size of the required change in the quantity of money. The "proper" magnitude could be larger than, smaller than, or, by chance, equal to the magnitude of the automatic, direct fall in money supply which the loss of the country's international reserves involves.

Suppose the required change in the money supply is *smaller* than the automatic change. The monetary authority would then have to counteract—partly, not fully—this change by inducing an increase in commercial-bank credit to the public or by increasing central-bank lending to the government. An increase in either of these two magnitudes while the country's balance of payments is in deficit is thus not necessarily an indication of a lack of compliance with balance-of-payments requirements. Taking the opposite case, suppose that the required decline of money supply in the reserve-losing country *exceeds* the direct, automatic effect of the fall of reserves, and that commercial-bank credit would thus have to fall to reinforce the direct impact. The fall of international reserves involves a reduction of commercial banks' reserves and hence of their lending capacity when no excess reserves exist. This in itself would force the banks to reduce credit. If this automatic credit decline exceeds the amount which the monetary authority deems desirable, the lending capacity of banks will have to be *raised*, rather than lowered further. This may be done by relaxing minimum-reserve requirements, or by increasing the banks' reserves through the central bank's open-market purchases and its lending to commercial banks and the government. This, of course, is the case *a fortiori* when commercial-bank credit has to be raised rather than lowered. The lowering of minimum-reserve ratios and an increase in the central bank's domestic claims could thus well be consistent with a monetary policy which complies with balance-of-payments requirements in a reserve-losing country. It should therefore be emphasized that "compliance" in this sense does *not* necessarily indicate the use of monetary instruments directly controlled by the monetary authority in the "complying" direction: it may be entirely due to the automatic effect of the change in the country's external assets not offset—at least not fully offset—by policy actions.

In fact, as observed in the preceding section, the central bank's domestic assets do show, in most countries, a clear tendency to move in this way, that is, to rise with a fall in the country's external reserves, and vice versa. This has also been noted, by Nurkse and by Bloomfield, to be the case in earlier periods—although the tendencies revealed in these earlier studies do not seem to be as clear-cut as they appear here.[7] As has been pointed out, the direction of movement of the central bank's total domestic claims is governed, by and large, by that part consisting of its claims on commercial banks. As a rule, it appears that commercial banks are guided by a wish to prevent substantial fluctuations (particularly reductions) in their credit to their clients. A fall in the country's external reserves entails a similar loss of reserves by the commercial banking system. Rather than diminish their lending, the banks tend to replenish their reserves by availing themselves of the other source of bank reserves—that is, by borrowing from the central bank.[8] Nurkse has paid much attention to this pattern of behavior, which he termed "automatic neutralization." But the conclusions he drew from his observations were not warranted, due to an unjustifiably strict interpretation of the "rules of the game" of balance-

---

[7] Ragnar Nurkse, *International Currency Experience* (Montreal, 1944), Chapter IV; and Arthur I. Bloomfield, *Monetary Policy under the Gold Standard: 1880–1914* (Federal Reserve Bank of New York, 1959), Chapter V.

[8] In cases where commercial banks hold government securities which are not considered as reserves or otherwise required to be held, the banks would try to dispose of part of these securities. Normally, however, this would lead the central bank to acquire these assets; that is, the domestic assets of the central bank would rise to that exent that it would not be lending to the commercial banking system but by an increase of claims on the government.

of-payments adjustment. Nurkse's interpretation judges monetary policy to be complying with the "rules" if the central bank's domestic assets move parallel with its external assets, that is, with the country's external reserves. The central bank would thus be required not only to counteract the commercial banks' "automatic neutralization," but to take even stronger measures in that direction (that is, leading to parallel movements of the central bank's domestic and external reserves). As has just been argued, however, there is no need for such parallel movements; changes in the central bank's domestic assets in a direction opposite to the change in the bank's (and the country's) external assets could be perfectly consistent with an over-all pattern of monetary policy geared to the requirements of balance-of-payments adjustment.

In most instances, it may be recalled, a general pattern of responsiveness of monetary policy to the balance of payments is found to involve movements of the discount rate and of money supply in an adjusting direction—as a quantity theory of money would require from such a pattern. There are, however, a few exceptions. Most notable is the case of the United Kingdom. While the discount rate in the United Kingdom rarely failed to respond to the needs of balance-of-payments adjustment, no such consistency is shown by money supply. Until the mid-1950's, changes in money supply did indeed conform to changes in the balance of payments, but from 1956 onward this has been rare. A higher degree of conformity with the country's external situation is shown by commercial bank credit supply. This pattern is consistent with what appears to be the prevailing opinion among monetary analysts and policy makers in the United Kingdom, who would mostly disavow the quantity theory of money while attributing heavy weight to the availability, and perhaps the cost, of credit. In addition, changes of the discount rate have naturally been considered particularly important in the United Kingdom, as a reserve center, due to the direct impact of interest-rate levels on short-term capital movements and the (probably more important) indirect impact on movements of speculative funds of increases in the discount rate, in times of deficit, as a "declaration of faith" in the pound sterling's rate of exchange. For the United Kingdom, therefore, commercial-bank credit (rather than money supply) is taken here, along with the discount rate, as a guide to the intention of the monetary authorities. It should be emphasized that it is the intention, rather than the outcome, which is studied here. Thus, by this yardstick, the United Kingdom is judged to have, as a rule, responded to the balance-of-payments position, despite the mostly poor showing of the country's position—a performance which may well be partly due to the particular selection of policy variables in the United Kingdom.

Table 2-3, which is based on the findings of the studies of individual countries, shows the pattern of monetary policy in the nine countries covered in this study. Conformity of the pattern with the *direction*— though not necessarily the magnitude—of movement indicated by balance-of-payments requirements is represented by a plus sign, while a minus is assigned when no such conformity appears. The table specifies the monetary variables by which the pattern has been judged and, whenever there is a lack of agreement, gives the inferences for both variables. Since a possible change in the pattern of behavior may be found in a number of countries around the late 1950's or early 1960's, the table distinguishes between two periods, the 1950's and the 1960's.[9]

On the evidence of Table 2-3, countries may be divided into three groups. First come the United Kingdom and Japan, in which monetary policy may be said to have complied consistently with the direction of movement indicated by the balance-of-payments position of the country. This may also be true of Italy, though a judgment about that country has to be based on rather meager evidence. For one thing, Italy does not use changes in the discount rate as part of monetary policy, and the evaluation of its policy is based here on money supply alone. In addition, the small number of observations for Italy further reduces the reliability of this evaluation.

Second, there are several continental countries—France, Belgium, and the Netherlands—in which compliance with balance-of-payments requirements exists, but is less consistent than in the United Kingdom and Japan. Specifically, monetary policy in these countries seems to have become less responsive to the balance óf payments during the 1960's. In Belgium and the Netherlands this change is recent, occurring around 1962 or 1963. In France, it came as early as 1959, but is more ambiguous: a change in policy is suggested by the discount rate variable,[10] while the behavior of money supply remains consistent with changes in the balance-of-payments position in the more recent period as well. For the period under study as a whole, but subject to qualifi-

---

[9] The cut-off point between the two periods varies among the countries for which this distinction is relevant, from about 1959 to 1962.

[10] Even the implication of the movement of interest rates in France becomes less obvious when considered in conjunction with movements in other countries. See the subsequent discussion in Section 5.

TABLE 2-3

RESPONSIVENESS OF MONETARY POLICY
TO THE BALANCE OF PAYMENTS

Country	Indicator	1950's	1960's
Belgium	Discount rate Money supply Credit supply	} +	} −
France	Discount rate Money supply	} +	− +
Germany	Discount rate Money supply	} −	} −
Italy	Money supply	+	+
Japan	Discount rate Money supply	} +	} +
Netherlands	Discount rate Money supply	} +	} −
Sweden	Discount rate Money supply	} −	} −
U.K.	Discount rate Credit supply	} +	} +
U.S.	Discount rate Money supply	} −	+ −

+ indicates a policy in the direction required by the policy "mix."
− indicates an opposite policy.

cation for recent years, these three countries appear to conform, in their monetary policy, with the needs of the balance of payments. Lastly, in three other countries—the United States, Germany, and Sweden—monetary policy appears to be consistently nonresponsive to the needs of the balance-of-payments position. Isolated episodes of compliance may, of course, be found, but not for any length of time.

4. Policy Responsiveness to Surpluses and Deficits

In discussions of policy patterns in the postwar world, two conflicting claims have often been made. One argument leads to the conclusion that responses to balance-of-payments disequilibrium have a deflationary bias. The argument goes as follows: the ability of countries to sustain a balance-of-payments deficit for an appreciable period is limited by the availability of external reserves, whereas no such restriction exists when countries enjoy a balance-of-payments surplus and accumulate external reserves. It is more likely, therefore, that a country incurring balance-of-payments deficits would react by a restrictive policy than that a country experiencing balance-of-payments surpluses would respond by an expansionary policy. To put it differently, the reaction of the same country to surpluses and to deficits is not symmetrical but biased toward restriction.

The counter-argument claims a lack of symmetry in the opposite direction. In the postwar world, it is argued, developed countries are committed to a policy of full employment and, perhaps, of rapid growth. Due to rigidities in the economy, policies restricting demand must lead to unemployment and loss of production; hence, a strong resistance must exist to the adjustment of balance-of-payments deficits by such measures. No such resistance exists, on the other hand, to an expansionary policy when surpluses are realized—and some expansion in such circumstances is, of course, an automatic response. The overall tendency is hence expansionary or inflationary.

Table 2-4 is intended to provide a test of these claims. It describes the responsiveness of monetary policy to instances of surpluses and deficits in a shorthand manner, by singling out the exceptions to each country's general policy pattern. For a country which has been classified in the last section as complying with balance-of-payments requirements, only instances of noncompliance of policy are presented; for a noncomplying country, only instances of compliance are shown. Japan does not appear in Table 2-4, for the simple reason that no episodes of exception to the complying pattern of its monetary policy could be found.

The evidence of Table 2-4 lends strong support to the claim that countries tend to respond to deficits more than to surpluses. It is seen, first, that almost all instances of responsiveness to balance-of-payments requirements in countries in which such reaction was not the rule are found in times of deficit—four such instances against a single case of responsiveness at a time of surplus. Turning to the lower half of the table, it is seen that the large majority of instances in which generally complying countries have not responded in this manner occur in times of surplus: only rarely—once in Belgium, and three times, for the

TABLE 2-4

EXCEPTIONS TO POLICY PATTERNS IN
INDIVIDUAL COUNTRIES

Country	Period	
	Surplus	Deficit
COMPLIANCE WITH BALANCE-OF-PAYMENTS REQUIREMENTS IN NONCOMPLYING COUNTRIES		
Germany		II 1950 – I 1951
		II 1964 – I 1966
Sweden	II 1960 – III 1962	IV 1959 – I 1960
U.S.		I 1953 – IV 1954
NONCOMPLIANCE WITH BALANCE-OF-PAYMENTS REQUIREMENTS IN COMPLYING COUNTRIES		
Belgium	IV 1955 – III 1956	III 1952 – II 1953
	I 1963 – III 1965	
France	II 1952 – IV 1952	
	I 1959 – IV 1956	
Italy	IV 1953 – II 1956	
Netherlands	I 1950 – IV 1950	
	III 1953 – II 1954	
	I 1960 – IV 1961	
	II 1963 – IV 1963	
	III 1964 – IV 1964	
U.K.	I 1950 – II 1951	IV 1956
	I 1956 – III 1956	IV 1958
	I 1959 – III 1959	IV 1959
	IV 1965 –	

shortest duration, in the United Kingdom—did the policy pattern in these countries appear to be unresponsive to balance-of-payments deficits. The existence of a "deflationary," or "deficit-sensitive," bias of monetary policy thus stands out clearly. This bias may be due to either, or both, of two reasons. One, expounded earlier, is the asymmetrical attitude of governments toward losses versus accumulations of reserves. The other is the existence of the target of price stability, which would lead to a reluctance to undertake an expansionary policy during balance-of-payments surpluses, but would condone a restrictive policy at times of deficit. The wish to avoid losses of external reserves and, possibly, to avoid price increases, rather than to maintain full employment and fast growth, seems thus to be the stronger motivation of monetary policy in the group of countries investigated in this study.

It should be remarked that this is definitely not the case with budgetary policy. It has been demonstrated earlier that budgetary policy was in general unresponsive to the position of the balance of payments. But even in the minority of instances (represented in column 1 of Table 2-1) in which budgetary policy was consistent with balance-of-payments requirements, only very few are periods of deficits. A hypothesis that budgetary policy was used to adjust *deficits* may thus be refuted even more emphatically than the more general hypotheses of the application of budgetary policy for balance-of-payments adjustment.

5. Relative Trends of National Monetary Policies: Long-Term Movements

The analysis so far has relied mostly on inferences drawn from observations of policy responses to balance-of-payments fluctuations in each country. It is possible, however, that the monetary authority, while not reacting to the ups and downs of the country's external position, may conduct a more restrictive monetary policy throughout the period —if the general trend of the country shows a deficit—than it would have otherwise. The verification of such a possibility is by no means easy. In the few instances in which longer-term developments are analyzed in the individual country studies in Part II, this has usually not been very fruitful. It is possible, however, that cross-sectional, intercountry comparisons may shed added light. Specifically, it may be interesting to examine whether, in countries whose external reserves tended to fall, monetary policy tended to be more restrictive than in countries with generally favorable balance-of-payments positions.

Chart 2-3 traces discount-rate movements over the period of seventeen years covered by this study for each of the eight countries in which this instrument was used (in Italy, it should be recalled, the discount rate was practically unchanged throughout). In general, an upward trend in discount rates is apparent. The obvious exception is Japan, in which the rate tended to fall. In that country, which experienced during this period a very fast rate of growth, radical structural changes, and a rapid capital accumulation, a substantial decline of real interest rates was to be expected. It is thus impossible to tell whether the down-

CHART 2-3

DISCOUNT RATES, 1950–66

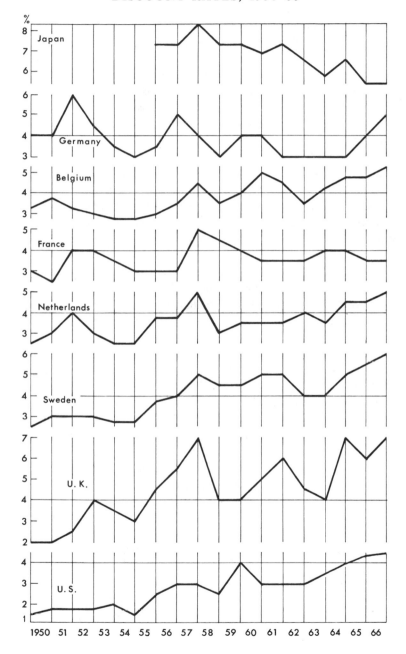

ward movement of the discount rate represents any trend of monetary policy. For his reason, and also owing to the lack of information on relevant discount rates in Japan prior to 1956, Japan will be excluded from the following comparisons.

Given the general upward trend of discount rates, the *relative* movement of each rate—relative, that is, to the movements of rates in other countries—is probably more significant than the individual movements taken separately. Table 2-5 shows changes in each rate, absolutely and in relation to movements in the seven countries together, during the period as a whole and during two equal subperiods: from the beginning of the period to the late 1950's, and from then to the end of the period.

The hypothesis under consideration would require a relative fall of discount rates in countries with generally favorable external balances, and vice versa. By and large, this seems to have happened. From the beginning of the period to the end, the relative discount rate went up considerably in the United Kingdom and in the United States, countries with unfavorable balance-of-payments developments. It went down in Germany and France, reserve-accumulating countries, and was about stable in Belgium and the Netherlands, whose balances were on the whole favorable but less so than those of Germany or France. Sweden, whose discount rate went up, had a favorable balance on the whole, but not a very large one.

Observations of the two subperiods confirm the general impression. But they also conform with the earlier inference of a generally more complying monetary policy in the 1950's than in the 1960's: most of the relative movements which were just described took place during the earlier years. The separate observations of the two subperiods also make the general impression more plausible. Thus, it is seen that the decline of the rate in Germany took place during the 1950's, the period of rapid accumulation of reserves in this country; in France, on the other hand, it took place in the later years—again the period of reserve accumulation. Likewise, the rise of the rate in Sweden appears to have taken place during the 1950's—a period with only little reserve accumulation in this country.

The impression conveyed by these comparisons is that monetary policy may have been guided by the balance-of-payments position in a few important instances in which the former analysis found it to be unresponsive: the United States, Germany, and France since the late 1950's. Such a conclusion would have, however, to be heavily hedged.

TABLE 2-5
DISCOUNT RATES
(END-OF-QUARTER AVERAGES)

Country	1950–52 (1)	1957–59 (2)	1964–66 (3)	1950–52 to 1964–66 Change (4)	1950–52 to 1964–66 Difference from Average Change (5)	1950–52 to 1957–59 Change (6)	1950–52 to 1957–59 Difference from Average Change (7)	1957–59 to 1964–66 Change (8)	1957–59 to 1964–66 Difference from Average Change (9)
Belgium	3.6	3.8	4.8	+1.2	−.2	+.2	−.5	+1.0	+.3
France	3.2	4.4	3.7	+.5	−.9	+1.2	+.5	−.7	−1.4
Germany	5.1	3.5	3.9	−1.2	−2.6	−1.6	−2.3	+.4	−.3
Netherlands	3.3	3.6	4.6	+1.3	−.1	+.3	−.4	+1.0	+.3
Sweden	2.9	4.5	5.3	+2.4	+1.0	+1.6	+.9	+.8	+.1
U.K.	2.7	5.0	6.1	+3.4	+2.0	+2.3	+1.6	+1.1	+.4
U.S.	1.7	2.9	4.1	+2.4	+1.0	+1.2	+.5	+1.2	+.5
Average of Seven Countries	3.2	3.9	4.6	+1.4	—	+.7	—	+.7	—

NOTE: All figures in per cent.

Long-term movements of the discount rate must reflect, at least in part, developments which have bearing upon the real rate of interest—as in Japan where it is obvious enough that such observations are to be discarded altogether. Likewise, other policy movements which reflect upon interest rates are excluded from consideration in such comparisons. It is very likely, for instance, that the upward trend of the discount rate (and of other interest rates) in the United States during the 1960's is a result of the general trend of budgetary deficits during these years—an effect which theory would lead one to expect; and these budgetary deficits were certainly not meant to respond to the balance-of-payments position. This may also be true (in the opposite direction) in Germany during the early 1950's, where the decline of interest rates accompanied a budgetary surplus. Germany is also another illustration of a case where, like Japan, the real rate of interest might have been expected to fall owing to a rapid accumulation of capital. These and similar considerations would thus make conclusions based on longer-term comparisons of discount rates at best very tentative.

These conclusions seem even more doubtful when contrasted with comparisons of longer-term movements of money supply. The latter are represented in Table 2-6 and in Chart 2-4. It has been noted earlier that, when responsiveness to balance-of-payments fluctuations is found, the variables of the discount rate and of money supply behave mostly as parts of a consistent pattern. It might be expected, therefore, that longer-term movements of these two variables may be similarly consistent. In fact, however, this is not generally the rule. Excluding the exceptional (Korean War) year of 1951, no trend seems to appear, over the period as a whole, in the level of the rate of expansion of money supply in the group of countries under study. In individual countries, on the other hand, trends are sometimes found—and in a way which usually contradicts the indications provided by trends of the discount rates. Most conspicuous is the case of the United Kingdom: the rate of expansion of money supply in that country shows an upward trend, particularly in the 1960's—in clear contrast with the restrictive indication given by the upward movement of the discount rate. This contrast is not surprising, in view of the dissimilarity of short-term responsiveness of these variables in the United Kingdom. But the contrast is also found in movements of the two variables in France, Belgium and the Netherlands, where consistency is mostly found in reactions to balance-of-payments fluctuations. Thus, an even larger measure of skepticism must be attached to inferences about the direc-

TABLE 2-6
RATES OF INCREASE OF MONEY SUPPLY
(FOUR-QUARTER AVERAGES)

Country	1951–52[a] (1)	1957–59 (2)	1964–66 (3)	1951–52 to 1964–66 Change (4)	Difference from Average Change (5)	1951–52 to 1957–59 Change (6)	Difference from Average Change (7)	1957–59 to 1964–66 Change (8)	Difference from Average Change (9)
Belgium	5.5	2.6	6.5	+1.0	+4.7	-2.9	+2.1	+3.9	+2.6
France	14.8	8.3	8.2	-6.6	-2.9	-6.5	-1.5	-.1	-1.4
Germany	14.0	12.3	6.0	-8.0	-4.3	-1.7	+3.3	-6.3	-7.6
Italy	15.7	9.6	11.4	-4.3	-.6	-6.1	-1.1	+1.8	+.5
Japan	30.0	11.4	13.8	-16.2	-12.5	-18.6	-13.6	+2.4	+1.1
Netherlands	6.7	4.5	9.3	+2.6	+6.3	-2.2	+2.8	+4.8	+3.5
Sweden	11.4	6.4	4.2	-7.2	-3.5	-5.0	—	-1.8	-3.1
U.K.	.9	1.5	7.0	+6.1	+9.8	+.6	+5.6	+5.5	+4.2
U.S.	4.6	1.8	3.6	-1.0	+2.7	-2.8	+2.2	+1.8	+.5
Average of Nine Countries	11.5	6.5	7.8	-3.7	—	-5.0	—	+1.3	—

NOTE: All figures in per cent.
[a] 1950 is omitted due to the absence of data for the year (or parts of it) in a few countries.

CHART 2-4
RATE OF CHANGE OF MONEY SUPPLY, 1951–66

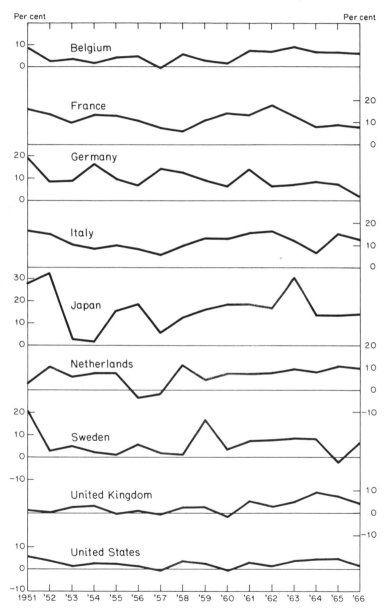

tion of monetary policy, and the conformity of this direction with the balance-of-payments position, which are drawn from longer-term international comparisons.

6. Interrelationship of National Monetary Policies: Short-Term Movements

While the longer-term international comparisons of monetary policies do not prove to be very fruitful, short-term international observations may add another dimension to the investigation. In the individual country studies, the assumed target variables are all indicators of performance of the national economy—its balance of payments, its employment, and the like. It may be worthwhile to study, in addition, the possibility that policies may also be undertaken in response not to these targets but to policies pursued by other countries. The examination of this possibility will be limited here to one policy variable—the discount rate—and to the group of countries covered in this study—more precisely, to just the seven countries of this group (Belgium, France, Germany, the Netherlands, Sweden, the United Kingdom, and the United States) in which discount-rate variations are relevant for the entire period.

If the discount rate in each country changed in response to fluctuations in its balance of payments, and if balance-of-payments fluctuations in the individual countries were positively correlated with each other, movements of the discount rate would also be correlated. A finding of comovements of discount rates could not be interpreted, in such a case, as responsiveness of policy in each country to other countries' policies. It is logically possible that changes in the balance of payments of the seven countries could be positively correlated, since the group constitutes only a part of the world. The share of this group in total world trade is so large, however, that such a correlation (that is, the group as a whole moving from a positive to a negative balance in trade with the rest of the world, and vice versa) is not very likely. A simple statistical test verifies, indeed, that the assumption of such positive correlation must be rejected.[11]

[11] The test is as follows: Assume, as a null hypothesis, complete randomness in the balance-of-payments position of individual countries. On the average, for the seven countries under consideration during the sixty-eight quarters from the be-

It is thus established that conformity of monetary policy with the direction indicated by the balance-of-payments position would *not* lead to a general similarity in the direction of these policies in the respective countries. Yet such similarity is definitely evident. This may be grasped from a casual observation of Chart 2-3. More convincing evidence is provided by Table 2-7, which compares discount-rate movements in individual countries with trends in the group as a whole. In each country, each movement of the discount rate is contrasted with the trend of discount rates in the other six countries during the quarter in which the rate was changed and the preceding quarter. When there

ginning of 1950 to the end of 1966, the balance-of-payments position was positive in 60 per cent of the quarters, and negative in the other 40 per cent (for the purpose of this test, a period of stability is considered, in an alternating order, as either a period of a positive or of a negative balance). The probability of any given quarter having a positive balance, in any given country, is thus .6. With this probability, and with the assumption of complete randomness (that is, complete lack of dependence of a country's balance-of-payments position on other countries' position), the observations of the sixty-eight quarters would be expected to be distributed as in column 2 in the table below:

Number of Positive Balances in the Quarter (1)	Number of Quarters	
	Expected (2)	Observed (3)
0	0	0
1	1	0
2	5	3
3	13	12
4	20	34
5	18	18
6	9	1
7	2	0
Total	68	68

The actual observations are recorded in column 3. A chi-square test shows (at the .999 level of confidence) that the nul hypothesis (of complete randomness) must be rejected. A look at the table reveals that the reason for this rejection is the high concentration of actual observations at the point of the four positive (against three negative) balances per quarter. That is, the observations concentrate at a position of an even division into positive and negative balances, *more* than a complete randomness (or lack of dependence) would lead to expect. Thus, with a random distribution the average proportion of countries with the same sign of balance-of-payments positions, as the majority of countries, in each given quarter, would be expected to be 67.5 per cent; whereas the average of this proportion among actual observations is only 62.0 percent. This conforms, of course, with the assumption that the country's positive balance is likely to be at the expense of another country of the group under consideration, which would then tend to have a negative balance.

TABLE 2-7

DISCOUNT–RATE CHANGES: RELATIONS
TO OTHER COUNTRIES

Country	Number of Changes Which Agree with General Trend (1)	Number of Changes Which Oppose General Trend (2)	Number of Changes Taken in Periods with No Clear Trend (3)	Proportion of Agreement with Trend[a] (per cent) (4)
Belgium	14	2	6	76
France	8	1	4	77
Germany	13	3	7	72
Netherlands	16	3	3	80
Sweden	10	2	2	79
U.K.	18	2	3	85
U.S.	14	7	3	65

NOTE: When the discount rate was changed more than once in a given quarter, this is considered a single change.

[a] For the calculation of this proportion, changes in periods with no trend are taken as changes both in agreement with trend and opposing it, with half weights assigned to each.

was a strong measure of agreement among the movements of rates during these quarters, a "trend" (positive or negative) was determined —with which the change in the country under consideration either agreed or disagreed; when no general agreement appears, or when there were only very few rate changes during this period, the period is judged to be without a trend.

It is immediately evident, from Table 2-7, that in all of the seven countries under consideration movements of the discount rate in each country were not independent of the movements of rates in the rest of the group but, on the contrary, strongly related to it. This is least true of the United States, where the link of rate movements with respective movements in the outside world seems to be weakest (but probably not entirely nonexistent). In all the rest of the countries the link appears to be strong and obvious.

It may be interesting also to examine in particular the relationship of exceptions to the normal patterns of monetary policy in each country to discount-rate changes in the outside world. Table 2-4, it will be recalled, records such exceptions: periods in which the monetary policy in a usually noncomplying country appears to be consistent with the needs of the balance of payments; or the policy in a country which usually conforms moves in the direction opposite to balance-of-payments requirements. Table 2-4 shows twenty-four such episodes. Of these, three are long enough to manifest more than a single trend of development of the discount rates and are therefore excluded from consideration. Of the remaining twenty-one episodes, in fifteen the direction of monetary policy was consistent with the trend of changes of discount rates in the group of countries in which discount rates were relevant. In three, the opposite was true; while in the remaining three no trend was evident. It may be concluded that, in general, movements of monetary policy which were exceptional to the normal pattern of policy in the respective country conformed to the trend of policies in the outside world, and could possibly be explained by the latter—although the speculative nature of such an inference would be obvious.

It thus appears that the direction of policies undertaken in each individual country is generally quite similar to the direction of policies followed in other countries in the group under consideration (and, one may presume, possibly also in other industrial countries which are not covered in the present study), and that this could not be attributed to chronological similarities in balance-of-payments developments. The comovements of policies might conceivably be explained by chronological coincidence of movements of other targets. Specifically, if business cycles happen to have similar chronological patterns in the countries under consideration, comovements of policies should have been expected. And if that were the case, changes in discount rates *relative* to rates in other countries would have been a most meaningful indication of a degree of responsiveness to the balance-of-payments position. The examination of such coincidence is very difficult, partly, at least, due to the lack of recognized business "cycles" in the analyses of the countries involved, and to the conceptual difficulties inherent in any attempt to determine such cycles. A rough comparison of developments as charted by the variables of unemployment and industrial production fails to uncover a chronological coincidence. It thus seems quite unlikely that this could be the explanation of policy similarities—although it must be emphasized that this statement is more in the nature of an impression than an inference drawn from a thorough investigation.

Two other explanations of the comovements of monetary policies may be offered. One is that policy makers are inclined by convention to follow policies in other countries, and are likely to feel restrained in undertaking opposite policies. The other explanation, which would make such behavior rational, is concerned again with the balance of payments. When discount rates (and interest rates in general) rise elsewhere, a country which keeps its rate stable, and *a fortiori* one which lowers its rate, is likely to experience outflows of short-term capital, and a loss of reserves. Likewise, a country which raises its rate while other rates fall is likely to experience an inflow of short-term capital, which, due to its expansionary impact, the country may find unwelcome.

Insofar as this is the explanation, monetary policy is directed not at the adjustment of actual imbalances of payments but at the prevention of balance-of-payments movements expected to result from other countries' policies. This, of course, is a pattern of policies which does not conform with the directives of balance-of-payments adjustment: the latter would require two countries which undergo opposite experiences in their balance of payments to undertake policies in opposite directions, rather than to coordinate their policies so that they will move parallel with each other.

7. Policy Responsiveness and External Positions

Before bringing this over-all view of policy patterns to a close, it may be worthwhile to inquire whether the existence or absence of policy responsiveness to balance-of-payments disturbances could be explained by structural differences among the external positions of the different countries. A few specific aspects of this possiblity come to mind.

First, it may be assumed that the larger the role of a country's international transactions in relation to its total economic activity, the greater the attention paid to its external position, and the more likely that demand policy will respond to balance-of-payments fluctuations.[12]

---

[12] It is not entirely certain that this assumption is valid. Compare two countries, one with large and the other with small imports relative to national income, and assume a balance-of-payments deficit of the same proportion of im-

The size of the country's trade may be considered an important factor in determining monetary developments also, insofar as these developments are an automatic response. Specifically, it may be expected that a country with a large trade in relation to its stock of money will realize automatically a large response of the variable of money supply, in an adjusting direction, to balance-of-payments disturbances of any given size (that is, of any given proportion of the country's external transactions).

One other possible determinant of policy patterns, the direction of whose influence seems quite obvious, is the size of a country's external reserves. A country with large reserves may be able to refrain from undertaking an adjusting demand policy in instances where such policy might have been unavoidable without these reserves. This may almost be said to be the *raison d'être* of holding reserves: to make it possible to maintain a fixed exchange rate *without* reacting in an adjusting manner to downward imbalances of payments. If this is so, countries with small reserves should be found to subject their monetary policy to the needs of the balance of payments more than do countries with large reserves.

Table 2-8 provides figures for the ratios under consideration in each of the nine countries. The size of trade in relation to the country's economic activity is represented by the ratio of merchandise imports to Gross National Product; while this is not the only possible (meaningful) indicator, it is probably the best single measurement for the purpose at hand.[13] The size of imports in relation to the stock of money is represented by the ratio of annual imports to the money supply (at year-ends). Had the ratio of money to GNP been similar

---

ports in the two countries. If income elasticity of demand for imports is the same in the two countries (abstracting, for simplicity, from consideration changes in exports), the same percentage amount of reduction of national income would correct the deficit in each country; on this basis, there seems to be no reason to expect one country to be more reluctant than the other to undertake demand policy in the adjusting direction. Moreover, automatic income effects would be expected, under certain assumptions (such as the existence of positive and equal propensities to save) to be more severe in the country with the larger imports; that country may, therefore, feel less obliged to undertake a restrictive monetary policy. Nevertheless, it is probably a general presumption that a country whose trade is small is likely to attach smaller weight to the target of balance-of-payments stability, and to try to achieve this stability, if it feels compelled to do so, by other means than demand policy.

[13] Taking exports rather than imports or an average of the two, would not have changed the indication significantly. This statement is restricted, of course, to the group of countries and to the period under study.

TABLE 2-8

MEASURES OF EXTERNAL POSITION

Period	Belgium	France	Germany	Italy	Japan	Netherlands	Sweden	U.K.	U.S.
			1. RATIO OF IMPORTS TO GNP						
1950–52	.29	.12	.12	.12	.12	.41	.23	.23	.03
1957–59	.32	.10	.14	.13	.11	.40	.22	.17	.03
1964–66	.39	.11	.15	.14	.10	.40	.22	.16	.03
		2. RATIO OF IMPORTS (ANNUAL) TO MONEY SUPPLY (END OF YEAR)							
1950–52	.70	.38	.78	.46	.56	1.17	1.09	.65	.08
1957–59	.81	.31	.85	.38	.45	1.48	1.26	.70	.10
1964–66	1.04	.31	.96	.35	.32	1.58	1.34	.47	.13
		3. RATIO OF EXTERNAL RESERVES (END OF YEAR) TO IMPORTS (ANNUAL)							
1950–52	.44	.20	.17	.50	.48	.29	.22	.25	2.42
1957–59	.40	.19	.67	.69	.31	.33	.20	.20	1.64
1964–66	.34	.56	.46	.52	.24	.31	.22	.08	.73

everywhere, this measure would have been merely a repetition of the ratio of imports to GNP; but the ratio of money to product is not necessarily similar either in general or among the countries under consideration. Finally, the size of reserve is represented by the ratio of (end-of-year) reserves to (annual) imports. This, again, is only one of the possible measures of size of reserves, and it may be expected to give only a very rough idea. Yet, since the complex matter of indicators of "adequacy" of reserves cannot be explored on this occasion, this is probably the best single measure that could be adopted, and presumably also the one most frequently observed by governments.

Table 2-9 summarizes in a descriptive way the indications provided by Table 2-8. The countries are classified into two groups—"conforming" and "nonconforming." Each respective measure is given a plus sign if, by the indication it provides, the country should be expected to adopt the policy pattern it has actually followed, a minus sign in the opposite case, and an asterisk if the indication is neutral.

It appears, from Table 2-9, that the three relationships under consideration could possibly explain some policy patterns, but not all or even most. No striking difference seems to exist between the two groups of countries in the relationships under study.

In observations of individual countries, the outcome appears again to be, at best, mixed. All the three ratios under consideration could explain the absence of responsiveness to the balance-of-payments position in the United States. Almost as consistently they could explain the high degree of compliance with balance-of-payments requirements in the Low Countries—Belgium and the Netherlands. But Sweden, with attributes similar to the two latter countries, is definitely a country in which monetary policy does not respond to the balance-of-payments position. Similarly, Japan would not be expected, by the evidence of these indicators, to follow the responsive monetary policy which it has devotedly followed; whereas the indication provided for France, the United Kingdom and Germany is unclear. Observations of these indicators, of what might be regarded as the structural position of a country's external transactions in its over-all economy, thus offer little explanation of the differences among countries.

Finally, it might be assumed that a "reserve-currency" country could be more inclined to subject its monetary policy to the needs of the balance of payments than one which does not fulfill this role. Since only two countries qualify for this category—the United States and the United Kingdom—no over-all conclusions about the significance of

TABLE 2-9

SUMMARY DESCRIPTION OF MEASURES OF EXTERNAL POSITION

	"Conforming" Countries					"Nonconforming" Countries			
	Belgium	France	Italy	Japan	Netherlands	U.K.	Germany	Sweden	U.S.
Ratio of imports to GNP	+ high	− low	− low	− low	+ high	− low	+ low	− high	+ low
Ratio of imports to money	+ high	+ high	− low	− low	+ high	− low	− high	− high	+ low
Ratio of reserves to imports	* medium	+ low[a]	− high	* medium	* medium	+ low	+ high	− low	+ high

[a] During the 1950's, when monetary policy in France tended to comply with balance-of-payments requirements.

this factor may be attempted. The two countries involved pursued, of course, almost diametrically opposite policy patterns.

8. Summary and Conclusions

The following summary of policy patterns in the postwar world will outline the main conclusions that have emerged from the present chapter; in addition, it will include a larger amount of speculation than there is in the main body of the analysis.

According to their patterns of responsiveness of monetary policy to the balance-of-payments position, the nine countries investigated in this study may be divided into three groups:

a. In two countries—the United Kingdom and Japan—monetary policy appears to have been played consistently according to the classical "rules of the game"; that is, to have been guided by the fluctuations in the country's external position.

b. In four other countries—France, Belgium, the Netherlands and, probably, Italy—monetary policy seems again to have been directed by balance-of-payments movements much of the time, but not with the same consistency as in the two former countries.

c. In the three remaining countries—the United States, Germany, and Sweden—monetary policy does not appear to have been generally, or even mostly, responsive to the balance of payments, and thus did not comply with the "rules of the game."

In countries of the first two groups in which compliance of monetary policy with the directives of the balance of payments tended to be the rule, the monetary tools which have been used for the purpose appear to be primarily the traditional instruments, namely the discount rate and the supply of money; the most important exception is the United Kingdom, where money supply is largely disregarded and credit supply takes its place as a major instrument of monetary policy.

Budgetary policy, on which attention has been so largely focused in theoretical discussions since the 1930's, appears to have responded to the balance-of-payments position only infrequently, definitely not as a rule, although this conclusion must be more heavily guarded than most others, due to the limitations of observations of this variable. It does not appear, moreover, that the failure to use budgetary policy for balance-of-payments adjustment stems from the use of this instrument in the service of domestic targets, whose requirements may contradict those of the target of balance-of-payments equilibrium. It seems more probable that, despite the heavy emphasis on it in analytical discussions or even in statements of policy makers, fiscal policy is largely unresponsive to the needs of major policy targets—either because it is too inflexible or because the principle of a balanced budget is still adhered to quite closely by policy makers.

It should be noted, in this connection, that the frequency of conflicts between the requirements of domestic targets—mainly the target of high employment—and the requirements of balance-of-payments equilibrium is not as high as the attention paid to these clashes in recent discussions would suggest. The impression that such a contradiction is of an overriding concern is probably due in large part to the recent experience of the United States, where from the late 1950's to the mid-1960's a high rate of unemployment accompanied a persistent balance-of-payments deficit. But this experience is by no means commonly shared: in most other major countries, the requirements of external and internal balance tended much more often to provide policy indications in the same direction, or at least not to contradict each other, rather than to point in opposite directions. As a result of this, and of the general lack of enthusiasm to employ budgetary policy, the use of the much discussed "policy mix," which would assign monetary policy to balance-of-payments adjustment and fiscal policy to the achievement of high employment (where the two targets call for policies in opposite directions), is a rarity rather than a common phenomenon.

Countries whose monetary policy generally responds to changes in the balance of payments tend to make exceptions to this pattern of behavior mainly when they are in surplus. Similarly, compliance of monetary policy with balance-of-payments requirements in generally noncomplying countries tends to be found at times of deficits. It thus appears that makers of monetary policy tend to gear their conduct to the country's external position more at times of deficits than at times of surpluses. It also appears that this tendency is not necessarily related to the level of external reserves: it is found when reserves are high as well as when they are low. It seems that countries tend to regard as their external target not so much the attainment of balance-of-payments equilibrium as the avoidance of deficits. The external target appears, that is, to be defined in a one-way manner. The loss of reserves is viewed with concern; but their accumulation—which might have been considered to be just as undesirable, due to its interference with the operation of the international system and to the real loss to the economy of holding reserves—is viewed, in fact, with satisfaction or indifference.

Aside from this disparity in reactions to external surpluses and deficits, differences among countries in their responses to the balance-of-payments position do not seem to be accounted for by any single factor in their structural positions or international experiences. The importance of external trade could explain the greater responsiveness in Belgium and the Netherlands than in the United States. Low external reserves may explain the tendency in the United Kingdom and, during part of the period, in France, to comply with balance-of-payments requirements; whereas high reserves could explain opposite patterns in the United States and in Germany; and a large automatic impact of balance-of-payments developments on money supply could explain, again, responsiveness in the Low Countries and in France, and its absence may account for the lack of responsiveness in the United States. But almost all these assertions must remain within the realm of possibilities, at best partly verified, rather than strongly supported inferences, since statements to the contrary could not, by and large, be entirely rejected on the basis of the evidence on hand.

There could be little doubt, moreover, that these factors do not nearly exhaust the list of possibly significant influences. Policy patterns are determined by general inclinations of policy makers, which eventually reflect the basic attitude of the public. The factors which have been investigated do, it may be presumed, play some role; but a much wider range of structural conditions and historical experiences takes place in shaping general attitudes: histories of depressions or of rapid inflations would, of course, be most obvious examples.

The fact that the majority of the nine countries under investigation appear to have conducted, during most of the time, their monetary policy in a manner which complies with the "rules of the game," should be interpreted with caution when implications for the international monetary system as a whole are drawn. It should be recalled, first, that the noncomplying group includes the United States and Germany—two of the most important countries in the system. Second, it should be noticed that the tendency of monetary policy to be guided by balance-of-payments requirements appears to have weakened during the 1960's: in France, Belgium, and the Netherlands, responsiveness of monetary policy to the balance of payments is absent or less frequent in this period in comparison with the 1950's, while no examples of an opposite shift are found among the other countries studied.

In view of the starting position in the world at that time, it would seem that policy patterns during the 1950's may have been consistent with the requirement of stability in the international monetary system. In the late 1940's and early 1950's, the distribution of international liquidity among the major countries was grossly uneven. Considerations of the *level* of external reserves in different countries could have justified a failure to react to developments which tended to equalize the distribution. Specifically, in view of the very high level of reserves with which the United States started this period, and the rather low level of reserves in Germany, the lack of response in the former to the loss of reserves, and in the latter to their accumulation, must have contributed to the stability of the international system.

From the late 1950's onward, on the other hand, policy patterns appear in a different light. While in earlier years the distribution of reserves had been moving toward greater equality, the tendency during the later period has been toward lesser equality. The failure to respond by adjustment policies to losses of reserves in the United States, and to their accumulation in Germany and, during most of the period, in France, now definitely ran counter to the requirement for a stable international system. Furthermore, the *general* level of reserves (when measured, by the conventional yardstick, as a proportion of the flow of external transactions) was lower in the later period—a fact which would have called for a stronger policy response to balance-of-payments fluctuations. Moreover, the 1960's have been characterized by practically full external convertibility, and considerable freedom of capital movements among the major countries. That is, instruments of control of external transactions, which could be (and most probably were) used in place of adjustments in demand policy in the earlier years, have been mostly foregone in the later period. It thus appears that, in contrast with the 1950's, patterns of demand policy in the 1960's cannot be judged to have been consistent with the target of stability of the international monetary system.

References

American Enterprise Institute for Public Policy Research, *International Payments Problems: Symposium Proceedings,* Washington, D.C., 1966.

Baldwin, Robert E., *et al.*, *Trade, Growth and the Balance of Payments* (Essays in Honor of Gottfried Haberler). Amsterdam, 1965.

Bank for International Settlements, *Annual Report*, Basle, 1930–66.

Bank of England, *Bulletin*, quarterly, London, December 1960–66.

Bank for International Settlements, *Eight European Central Banks*, New York, 1963.

Bloomfield, Arthur I., *Monetary Policy under the Gold Standard: 1880–1914*, New York, 1959.

Brown, Weir Messick, *The External Liquidity of an Advanced Country*, Princeton, 1964.

Corden, W. M., *Recent Developments in the Theory of International Trade*, Princeton, 1965.

Deshmukh, C. D., and Roosa, Robert V., *The Balance Between Monetary Policy and Other Instruments of Economic Policy in a Modern Society*, Washington, D.C., 1965.

European Economic Community, Commission, *The Economic Situation in the Community*, quarterly, Brussels, Publishing Services of the European Communities, 1961–66.

European Economic Community, Monetary Committee, *The Instruments of Monetary Policy in the Countries of the European Economic Community*, Brussels, 1962.

European Economic Community, *Report on the Activities of the Monetary Committee*, annual, Brussels, 1959–66.

European Monetary Agreement, *Report of the Board of Management*, annual, Paris, 1960–66.

Fellner, William, *et al.*, *Maintaining and Restoring Balance in International Payments*, Princeton, 1966.

Fleming, J. Marcus, *Toward Assessing the Need for International Reserves*, Princeton, 1967.

Fousek, Peter G., *Foreign Central Banking: The Instruments of Monetary Policy*, New York, 1957.

Franks, Sir Oliver, *Some Reflections on Monetary Policy in the Light of the Radcliffe Report*, New York, 1960.

Georgiadis, Hourmouzis George, *Balance of Payments Equilibrium: A Theoretical and Empirical Study*, Pittsburgh, 1964.

Haberler, Gottfried, *A Survey of International Trade Theory*, Princeton, 1961.

———, *Money in the International Economy; A Study in Balance of Payments Adjustments, International Liquidity and Exchange Rates*, London, 1965.

Hinshaw, Randall (ed.), *Monetary Reform and the Price of Gold*, Baltimore, 1967.

Institute of Bankers, Oxford University, *International Banking and Foreign Trade*, London, 1955.

International Monetary Fund, *Annual Report*, Washington, D.C., 1946–66.

——, *Balance of Payments Manual*, 3rd ed., Washington, D.C., 1961.

——, *Balance of Payments Yearbook*, Washington, D.C., 1949–66.

——, *International Financial News Survey*, weekly, Washington, D.C., July 1948–66.

——, *International Financial Statistics*, monthly, Washington, D.C., Jan. 1948–66.

——, *International Monetary Problems 1957–1963: Selected Speeches of Per Jacobsson*, Washington, D.C., 1964.

——, *The Revival of Monetary Policy*, Washington, D.C., 1953.

Kindleberger, Charles P., *Balance of Payments Deficits and the International Market for Liquidity*, Princeton, 1965.

Kirschen, E. S., *et al., Economic Policy in Our Time*, Vol. I: General Theory; Vol. II: United States, United Kingdom, Norway; Vol. III: Belgium, Germany, the Netherlands, France, Italy; Amsterdam, 1964.

Lary, Hal B., *Problems of the United States as World Trader and Banker*, New York, NBER, 1963.

Lederer, Walther, *The Balance of Foreign Transactions*, Princeton, 1963.

Liesner, L. L., *The Import Dependence of Britain and West Germany: A Comparative Study*, Princeton, 1957.

Machlup, Fritz, *The Need for Monetary Reserves*, Princeton, 1966.

McKinnon, Ronald I., and Oates, Wallace E., *The Implications of International Economic Integration for Monetary, Fiscal, and Exchange-Rate Policy*, Princeton, 1966.

Meade, James Edward, *Theory of International Economic Policy, Vol. I: The Balance of Payments*, London, 1955.

Nurkse, Ragnar, *International Currency Experience*, League of Nations, Montreal, 1944.

Organization for Economic Co-operation and Development, Economic Policy Committee, *The Balance of Payments Adjustment Process;* A Report by Working Party No. 3 of the Economic Policy Committee of the O.E.C.D., Paris, 1966.

Organization for Economic Co-operation and Development, *Economic Outlook*, semi-annual, Paris, 1967–68.

——, *General Statistics*, bimonthly, Paris, 1950–64. Issued 1950–Sept. 1961, by the Organization for European Economic Cooperation.

——, *Main Economic Indicators*, monthly, Paris, Jan. 1965–66.

——, *Statistics of Balance of Payments, 1950–1961*, Paris, 1964.

Rees, Graham L., *Britain and the Postwar European Payments Systems*, Cardiff, 1963.

Sayers, R. S. (ed.), *Banking in Central Europe,* London, 1962.

Scitovsky, Tibor, *Economic Theory and Western European Integration,* Stanford, 1958.

Seldon, Arthur (ed.), *Not Unanimous: A Rival Verdict to Radcliffe's on Money,* London, 1960.

Snider, Delbert A., *Optimum Adjustment Processes and Currency Areas,* Princeton, 1967.

Statistical Office of the European Communities, *General Statistics Bulletin,* monthly, Brussels, 1963–66.

U.S. Congress Joint Economic Committee, *Economic Policies and Practices; Comparative Features of Central Banks in Selected Foreign Countries,* 88th Congress, 1st Session, Washington, D.C., 1963.

———, *Economic Policy in Western Europe,* Report, 85th Congress, 2nd Session, Washington, D.C., 1959.

United Nations, Research and Planning Division, Economic Commission for Europe, *Economic Survey of Europe,* annual, Geneva, 1947–66.

United Nations, Secretariat, Department of Economic Affairs, *Governmental Policies Concerning Unemployment, Inflation and Balance of Payments 1950–51: Analysis of Replies by Governments to a United Nations Questionnaire,* New York, 1951.

———, Secretariat, Department of Economic Affairs, *Governmental Policies Concerning Unemployment, Inflation and Balance of Payments 1951–52: Analysis of Replies by Governments to a United Nations Questionnaire,* New York, 1952.

Van Campen, Ph. C. M., *On the Coordination of Monetary Policy within the E.E.C.,* Document 17, European Parliamentary Reports, 1962–63.

PAPERS

Allen, R. G. D., "Statistics of the Balance of Payments," *Economic Journal,* Vol. 61 (March, 1951), pp. 179–96.

Arndt, H. W., "Balance of Payments Equilibrium and Monetary Policy: A Comment," *The Economic Record,* Vol. 31 (May, 1955), pp. 105–11.

Badger, D. G., "The Balance of Payments: A Tool of Economic Analysis," *International Monetary Fund Staff Papers,* Vol. 2 (September, 1951), pp. 86–197.

Bernstein, E. M., "Strategic Factors in Balance of Payments Adjustment," *International Monetary Fund Staff Papers,* Vol. 5 (August, 1956), pp. 151–69.

Bopp, K. A., "Central Banking Objectives, Guides, and Measures," *Journal of Finance,* Vol. 9 (March, 1954), pp. 12–22.

Cooper, R. N., "The Balance of Payments in Review," *Journal of Political Economy,* Vol. 74 (August, 1966), pp. 379–95.

Dorrance, G. S., and Aubanel, G. R., "Survey of Monetary Analyses," *International Monetary Fund Staff Papers,* Vol. 5 (February, 1957), pp. 358–433.

————, and White, W. H., "Alternative Forms of Monetary Ceilings for Stabilization Purposes," *International Monetary Fund Staff Papers,* Vol. 9 (November, 1962), pp. 317–40.

Duesenberry, J., "Domestic Policy Objectives and the Balance of Payments," *Journal of Finance,* Vol. 21 (June, 1966), pp. 345–54.

Familton, R. J., "Balance of Payments Equilibrium and Monetary Policy," *The Economic Record,* Vol. 30 (November, 1954), pp. 209–24.

Fleming, J. Marcus, "Domestic Financial Policies under Fixed and under Floating Exchange Rates," *International Monetary Fund Staff Papers,* Vol. IX (November, 1962), pp. 369–80.

Gilbert, Milton, "Reconciliation of Domestic and International Objectives of Financial Policy: European Countries," *Journal of Finance,* Vol. 18 (May, 1963), pp. 174–86.

————, and McClam, Warren, "Domestic and External Equilibrium: European Objectives and Policies," *American Economic Review,* Vol. LV (May, 1965), pp. 189–99.

Havrilesky, Thomas, "A Test of Monetary Policy Action," *Journal of Political Economy,* Vol. LXXV (June, 1967), pp. 299–304.

Heller, H. R., "Optimal International Reserves," *Economic Journal,* Vol. 76 (June, 1966), pp. 296–311.

Henderson, H., "Internal Financial Policy and the Problem of External Disequilibrium," *Economia Internazionale,* Vol. 3 (November, 1950), pp. 952–62.

Høst-Madsen, P., "Asymmetries Between Balance of Payments Surpluses and Deficits," *International Monetary Fund Staff Papers,* Vol. 9 (July, 1962), pp. 182–99.

————, "Measurements of Imbalance in World Payments, 1947–58," *International Monetary Fund Staff Papers,* Vol. 9 (November, 1962), pp. 343–65.

Jaramillo, R., "Central Bank Discount Rates," *International Monetary Fund Staff Papers,* Vol. 13 (March, 1966), pp. 103–18.

Kenen, P. B., and Yudin, E. B., "The Demand for International Reserves," *Review of Economics and Statistics,* Vol. 47 (August, 1965), pp. 242–50.

Krueger, Anne O., "The Impact of Alternative Government Policies under Varying Exchange Systems," *Quarterly Journal of Economics,* Vol. LXXIX (May, 1965), pp. 195–208.

Machlup, F., "Adjustment, Compensatory Correction, and Financing of Imbalances in International Payments," in Baldwin, R. E., *et al., Trade,*

Growth, and the Balance of Payments: Essays in Honor of Gottfried Haberler, Amsterdam, 1965, pp. 185–213.

————, "Three Concepts of Balance of Payments and the So-Called Dollar Shortage," *Economic Journal,* Vol. 60 (March, 1950), pp. 46–68.

Mundell, R. A., "The Appropriate Use of Monetary and Fiscal Policy for Internal and External Stability," *International Monetary Fund Staff Papers,* Vol. 9 (March, 1962), pp. 70–77.

Murphy, H., *et al.,* "The Adequacy of Monetary Reserves," *International Monetary Fund Staff Papers,* Vol. 3 (October, 1953), pp. 181–227.

Olakanpo, J. O. W., "Monetary Management in Dependent Economies," *Economica,* Vol. 28 (November, 1961), pp. 395–408.

Patel, I. G., "Monetary Policy in Postwar Years," *International Monetary Fund Staff Papers,* Vol. 3 (April, 1953), pp. 69–131.

Romanis, Anne, "Balance of Payments Adjustment Among Developed Countries," *International Monetary Fund Staff Papers,* Vol. 12 (March, 1965), pp. 17–34.

Ross, C. R., "Monetary Control and Economic Policy," Oxford University, Institute of Statistics, *Bulletin,* Vol. 19 (November, 1957), pp. 293–305.

Sargent, J. R., "Monetary Policy and the Balance of Payments," Oxford University, Institute of Statistics, *Bulletin,* Vol. 19 (November, 1957), pp. 347–51.

Schere, J., "On Measuring Fiscal Policy," *Journal of Finance,* Vol. 20 (December, 1965), pp. 683–90.

Smith, J. S., "Asymmetries and Errors in Reported Balance of Payments Statistics," *International Monetary Fund Staff Papers,* Vol. 14 (July, 1967), pp. 211–34.

Smith, Warren L., "Are There Enough Policy Tools?" *American Economic Review,* Vol. LV (May, 1965), pp. 208–26.

Stein, Herbert, "The Evolving International Monetary System and Domestic Economic Policy," *American Economic Review,* Vol. LV (May, 1965), pp. 200–207.

PART

II

COUNTRY PATTERNS

CHAPTER 3

EXPLANATORY NOTE

Each country chapter starts with a brief institutional description of the major variables used in the country's demand policy. This is followed by the statistical analysis, and a summary and interpretation of the main findings concludes the chapter.

The statistical analysis normally starts with a basic table, "Movements of Policy Variables during Subperiods of Imbalances." The table presents the division of the whole period under study into subperiods. These subperiods are also represented in a basic chart, which describes the movements of the balance-of-payments variables, of other potential target variables, and of the policy variables. In the chart, subperiods of downward imbalances are shaded by diagonal lines, subperiods of stability are shaded gray, and subperiods of upward imbalances are not shaded.

In the basic table, the policy variables are considered during each subperiod of imbalance. For convenience of observation and exposition, each such movement is given a sign. It is marked by a plus sign when the movement of the variable complies with the assumption that the variable is manipulated in the direction required for balance-of-payments adjustment (for brevity, this will be referred to as an "adjusting direction"), by a minus sign when the variable moves in a direction opposite to that which balance-of-payments adjustment would require, and by an asterisk when the variable does not move, although balance-of-payments adjustment would have justified an upward or a downward movement.[1] It should be clear, in line with the discussion in the former

---

[1] Similar use of plus and minus signs, in a context limited to the study of a single policy variable (the central bank's domestic assets), was made by Nurkse

part, that at this phase of the analysis each variable is examined by itself, and not yet as part of the general pattern; the method is simply to judge each one according to whether it moves in an "adjusting" direction or not.

The stage is then set for the observation of policy variables. If a variable moves consistently in the direction conforming to the need for balance-of-payments adjustment, it would be tentatively concluded that manipulation of this variable was indeed motivated by the purpose of adjustment. If no such consistent behavior is found—and, *a fortiori,* when a variable consistently behaves in the opposite fashion—it would be concluded that the variable under consideration did not serve as a tool of balance-of-payments adjustment.

Quite often, tables will be presented in which the positions of alternative target variables are described along with the movements of a given policy variable. If the direction of such a movement is consistent with the assumption that it was made in order to adjust a certain target variable, in view of the concurrent position of that variable, the latter is given a plus sign for the period of the movement under consideration; if the change in the discount rate is in the opposite direction, the variable is assigned a minus. It is thus possible to get an impression at a glance of whether an assumption that manipulation of the discount rate was intended to serve a certain target is justified or, rather, not contradicted by the data.

It may be in order to repeat here a qualifying note about the scope of the individual country studies, which has been more fully stated in Part I. Each country study is viewed primarily as raw material for the international comparisons and synthesis, which has been offered in Part I. This aim of the individual analyses imposed, necessarily, a given

and by Bloomfield in their aforementioned studies. See Nurkse, *International Currency Experience,* pp. 68–70, and Bloomfield, *Monetary Policy under the Gold Standard,* pp. 47–51.

It should be emphasized—indeed, this point could not be overstressed—that the use of such signs does *not* have any normative connotation. Giving, for instance, a plus mark to a certain movement does by no means indicate that this movement is considered desirable in general, or by some particular yardstick, or that a different policy would be somehow less desirable. If any convenient "neutral" symbols could be used for the purpose of identification, they would have been adopted. The plus and minus signs were selected because no other symbols are completely neutral, while these signs enjoy the advantages of having been used in distinguished and well-known precedents and of being visually convenient.

mold upon all of them. Each of these analyses would have been carried out in a different—and more intensive—fashion, had the purpose been simply to describe and investigate the experience of that country for its own sake. It is with this view in mind that the individual country chapters should be approached.

CHAPTER 4  BELGIUM

1. Policy Instruments

The management of monetary policy in Belgium is formally more decentralized than in most other countries. Three separate institutions are in charge of the three "classical" monetary instruments. The National Bank of Belgium, the central bank, is responsible for setting the discount rates and for discounting bills and granting advances to commercial banks, although the discounting is done partly through a separate, intermediary institution. Open market operations are conducted by an autonomous institution, the *Fonds des Rentes,* and minimum reserve ratios are under the jurisdiction of still another agency, the Banking Commission. The latter two organizations are, however, heavily influenced by the National Bank and, as will be seen shortly, the areas in their charge are of a subsidiary nature in the conduct of over-all monetary policy. However, because of various checks limiting its operations, the Bank in turn cannot deviate materially from the policy of the government, particularly the Ministry of Finance.

The Discount Rate. The discount rate is by far the most important instrument in the conduct of monetary policy in Belgium. The basic discount rate applies to the discounting of most domestic bills. Other rates—some lower (for bills originating in foreign trade) and some higher—apply to the discounting of other bills and to advances made by the National Bank. As a rule, the whole schedule of rates is changed at once, with constant spreads maintained between the various rates, so that the position of the basic discount rate is representative of the whole rate schedule.

The discount rate is significant in more than one way. First, it affects the cost of borrowing from the central bank: National Bank lending to commercial banks, by rediscounting or by advances, is substantial and is subject to large variations. Second, and even more important, the schedule of rates charged by commercial banks on their lending (or paid to their depositors) changes almost automatically with changes in the discount rate; this relationship was particularly rigid until 1961. Lastly, as in many other countries, changes in the discount rate are taken as a signal of restrictive or expansionary intentions of the monetary authorities.

Open-Market Operations. These operations are not, as a rule, intended to affect over-all monetary conditions. The function of the *Fonds des Rentes,* the agency in charge of the operations, is primarily to regulate the market for government securities. Its dealings in that market are intended to prevent undue fluctuations and to lead to the conformity of movements of long-term rates with those of the discount rate, rather than to have an independent effect on interest rates. Since 1957, the *Fonds* has also been heavily engaged in transactions in its own certificates. But, again, these operations are intended to smooth movements in the money market rather than to change basic monetary circumstances. Open-market operations are thus not a relevant variable for the purpose of this study.

Minimum Liquidity Ratios. The Banking Commission supervises a wide schedule of liquidity ratios, starting from a "cash ratio" of 4 per cent and ending with a "cover ratio" of, at the extreme, 65 per cent. But this schedule has remained unchanged throughout the period, except for the abolition of the cover ratio at the end of 1962. It is intended to secure bank solvency and banks' holdings of government securities rather than to affect their lending capacity. In recent years, a system of minimum reserve ratios was introduced. In principle, this system is flexible and is intended to affect banks' lending capacity; however, its actual operation began only in 1963, so it is practically immaterial for purposes of the present study.

Other potential instruments are of even less importance. Quantitative control of credit existed for a short time—from early 1964 to mid-1965 and during most of 1966. The National Bank sets maximum quotas for its lending to each bank, but these quotas are rarely reached, and are thus ineffective. Among the direct instruments available for monetary policy, the discount rate is thus by far the most important, and is in practice the only instrument generally relied upon to effect monetary changes.

BUDGETARY AND DEBT POLICY

The Belgian government's budget consists of two parts, one for ordinary, and one for extraordinary, items although the criteria of division between the two parts are not clear and are subject to frequent changes. The extraordinary budget includes primarily investment expenditures, either made directly by the government or through lending for the purpose of capital outlays. Extraordinary expenditures are financed overwhelmingly by borrowing, so that the size of the deficit in the extraordinary budget approaches the size of the budget itself. But the ordinary budget too shows deficits more often than surpluses. The net result has thus been a practically uninterrupted deficit of substantial proportions in the over-all budget. The deficit is financed by borrowing from all sources: the central bank, commercial banks, the capital market and foreign lenders.

As a source of long-term lending, the National Bank is of only minor significance. By an agreement dating from 1948, total outstanding lending from the Bank to the Treasury cannot exceed 44 billion francs, of which 34 billion is a consolidated loan originating in the war years, while the remainder is a revolving fund.[1] Over the period as a whole, the outstanding amount of Treasury indebtedness to the Bank has been quite stable, although for some short periods its fluctuations are substantial. The outstanding amount of Treasury deposits in the Bank, and fluctuations in this amount, are insignificant in relation to the size of the debt; movements of the government's net indebtedness to the Bank are thus practically identical with those of the gross indebtedness.

The size of commercial banks' lending to the government was partly dictated, until 1962, by the "cover" regulations, which require the banks to hold liquid assets primarily in the form of Treasury Certificates. This lending, together with the acquisition of government securities in the capital market, are the main source for financing the large budgetary deficit. As will be recalled, the *Fonds des Rentes* seeks to regulate the sale of government securities so as not to disrupt existing market conditions. An excess of supply of these securities, at current market rates, is directed primarily to the National Bank; while an excess of demand is met by sales from the Bank's portfolio. Net changes in the Bank's lending to the government are thus determined

---

[1] The revolving fund has recently been increased to 16 billion francs.

as the difference between the government's deficit and the amount of financing obtained from other sources at existing market rates.

2. Statistical Analysis

For purposes of this analysis, turning points in Belgium's balance-of-payments position have been determined by the movements of the country's external reserves (shown in Chart 4-1) and, since 1958, by the series of over-all surpluses or deficits (not shown); both series give mostly similar indications.[2] The subperiods of imbalances are identified in Table 4-1, where the movement of external reserves (column 1) indicates the direction of the imbalance.

In column 2 of the table, movements of the discount rate during subperiods of imbalances are described. It is immediately apparent that until the end of 1961, movements of the discount rate generally conformed to what would be expected had they been taken in response to the balance-of-payments position. The only exception is the movement of the discount rate during II 1952 – II 1953, when the rate was lowered at a period of a downward imbalance of payments; but, as a glance at Chart 4-1 will show, the fall of reserves and the reduction of the discount rate were very slight, so that the rule was not seriously violated. From 1962 on, however, movements of the discount rate do not seem to be generally related to the needs of the balance of payments.

The association of the discount rate with the balance of payments is tested by means of Table 4-2, in which all changes of the discount rate are recorded. In column 1, the trend of the country's external reserves just before each change in the discount rate is shown.[3] It is again immediately clear that, up to the beginning of 1962, practically all changes in the discount rate could be interpreted as responses in an adjusting direction to the balance-of-payments position. The only

[2] The subperiod IV 1958–III 1960 is an exception: the over-all balance fluctuates, showing only a slight cumulative deficit over the period, which is therefore designated as a subperiod of stability, whereas the loss of external reserves over this period is more substantial.

[3] This refers to the direction of change of reserves during the last quarter before the change in the discount rate, but almost the same results are indicated when the last two quarters are observed. This applies also to indications of movements of alternative target variables, discussed below.

CHART 4-1

BELGIUM: TIME SERIES OF SELECTED VARIABLES

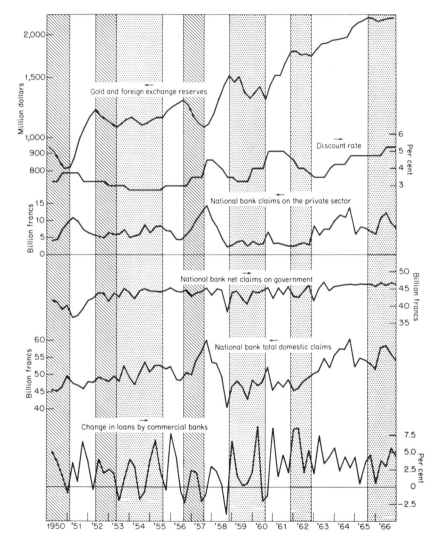

NOTE: Diagonal-line areas represent period of downward imbalances;

CHART 4-1 (*Concluded*)

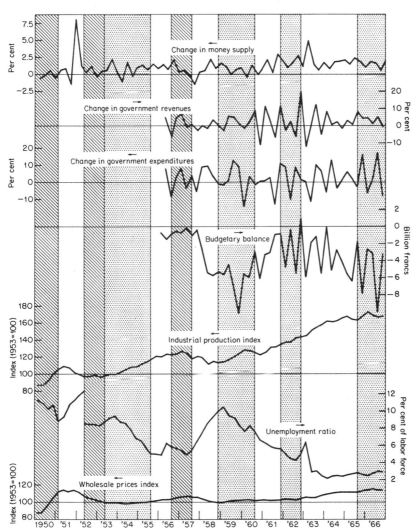

gray areas represent stability; white areas represent upward imbalances.

TABLE 4-1

BELGIUM: MOVEMENTS OF POLICY VARIABLES DURING SUBPERIODS OF IMBALANCES

Subperiod	External Reserves (1)	Discount Rate (2)	National Bank Claims on Commercial Banks (3)	National Bank Total Domestic Claims (4)	Commercial Bank Lending to Public (quarterly rate of change, per cent) (5)	Money Supply (quarterly rate of change, per cent) (6)
I 1950 – I 1951	fall	+ raised	– rise	– rise	+2.0	+.2
I 1951 – II 1952	rise	+ lowered	– fall	+ rise	(+) +3.0	(+) +1.9
II 1952 – II 1953	fall	– lowered	* stable	* fluctuate	(+) +1.1	(+) +.5
II 1953 – III 1955	stable	stable	rise	rise	+2.0	+.9
III 1955 – III 1956	rise	* stable	– fall	* fluctuate	(+) +2.5	(+) +1.3
III 1956 – III 1957	fall	+ raised	– rise	– rise	(+) +.6	(+) –.1
III 1957 – IV 1958	rise	+ lowered	– fall	– fall	(+) +1.7	(+) +1.2
IV 1958 – III 1960	stable	raised	rise	rise	+1.5	+.6
IV 1960 – IV 1961	rise	+ lowered	– fall	– fall	(+) +5.3	(+) +1.6
IV 1961 – IV 1962	stable	lowered	rise	rise	+4.6	+1.7
IV 1962 – III 1965	rise	– raised	* fluctuate	* fluctuate	(*) +4.1	(*) +1.9
III 1965 – IV 1966	stable	raised	fluctuate	fluctuate	+3.6	+1.4

NOTE: For explanation of symbols, see Chapter 3, explanatory note.

TABLE 4-2

BELGIUM: CHANGES IN THE DISCOUNT RATE
AND POSITION OF TARGET VARIABLES

Discount Rate	External Reserves	Level of Unemployment	Industrial Production (rate of change)	Change in Wholesale Prices (compared with trend)
	(1)	(2)	(3)	(4)
Raised:				
III 1950	+ fall	+ falls	+ rises	+ rises
III 1955	* stable	+ falls	+ rises	* stable
IV 1956	+ fall	+ low	− falls	+ rises
III 1957	+ fall	− rises	− falls	− falls
IV 1959	+ fall	− high	+ rises	* stable
III 1960	+ fall	− high	− falls	− falls
III 1963	− rise	+ falls	+ rises	− falls
IV 1963	− rise	+ falls	+ rises	+ rises
III 1964	* stable	+ low	* stable	+ rises
II 1966	* stable	+ low	− falls	+ rises
Lowered:				
III 1951	+ rise	* stable	− rises	* stable
IV 1952	− fall	+ rises	+ falls	+ falls
IV 1953	+ rise	+ rises	− rises	* stable
I 1958	+ rise	+ rises	+ falls	+ falls
II 1958	+ rise	+ rises	+ falls	+ falls
III 1958	+ rise	+ rises	+ falls	+ falls
I 1959	+ rise	+ rises	+ falls	* stable
III 1961	+ rise	− falls	− rises	* stable
IV 1961	+ rise	* stable	− rises	* stable
I 1962	+ rise	− falls	− rises	* stable
III 1962	* stable	− falls	+ falls	* stable
IV 1962	* stable	+ rises	− rises	* stable

NOTE: For explanation of symbols, see Chapter 3, explanatory note.

exceptions, out of a rather large number of observations, are a small reduction of the discount rate in December 1952 (which, as was noted before, was taken while reserves were slightly falling), and a slight increase of the rate in August 1955, which cannot be explained by the movement of reserves, then practically stable. Once more, no such association appears for the later years: starting with the lowering of the rate in August 1962, movement of the discount rate can no longer be explained by the need for balance-of-payments adjustment.

Columns 2, 3, and 4 are designed to test the possibility that changes in the discount rate before 1962, which we have tentatively regarded as intended for balance-of-payments adjustment, could not in fact be interpreted as having been taken in response to the needs of other targets. In column 2, the unemployment position is described. The evidence of this column does not contradict the assumption that changes in the discount rate were intended to achieve the target of high employment. This is true in particular with regard to discount rate reductions, almost all of which were taken at a time of high and rising unemployment. It is less true when discount-rate increases are examined: some of these were taken when unemployment was either rising or, though falling, was high. Taking together movements of the discount rate in both directions, the association between them and the employment situation would appear to be somewhat weaker than their association with the balance of payments, but it is still rather strong. To only a slightly smaller extent, this applies also to the target of high industrial production, which is represented in column 3. Once more, it is in the cases of reductions of the discount rate where the association of the instrument with the target is strong, while increases of the discount rate do not appear to be generally related to the state of industrial production.

On this evidence, changes in the discount rate are more weakly associated with the targets of high employment and high production than with the balance of payments. It is not, however, so weak an association that it can be dismissed without further consideration of the possibility that it was really these two targets, and not the balance of payments, to which the discount rate responded. One further test which may be attempted is to isolate those episodes of change in the discount rate in which either the target of high employment or that of high production, or both, would indicate a policy different from that which the balance of payments would call for. We find a number of episodes (July 1957, December 1959, and August 1960) in which the discount rate was raised when reserves were falling, despite high unemployment or slack production; and a number of other episodes (July 1951, and a succession of changes from August 1961 to March 1962) in which a lowering of the discount rate could be explained by the rise of foreign-exchange reserves but not by the requirements of employment and production. Only in the episode of December 1952, noted before, did the opposite occur: the rate was lowered while reserves were falling slightly, as would be required by rising unemployment and falling production at that time. These episodes cover only a minority of the movements of the discount rate; but, as far as they go, they indicate that preference was generally given to balance-of-payments requirements.

A similar test may be conducted by means of a reference cycle analysis, where the cycles are determined by movements of the discount rate: at the trough the discount rate is lowest; it rises towards the peak of the cycle, when it is highest; and falls again towards the next trough. The turning points of the discount rate cycles are as follows:

Cycle	Trough	Peak	Trough
1950–54	I 1950	I 1951	III 1954
1954–59	III 1954	IV 1957	II 1959
1959–63	II 1959	IV 1960	I 1963
1963–66	I 1963	IV 1966	—

Chart 4-2 describes this analysis. Parts A, B and C present, respectively, the movements of external reserves, the unemployment ratio and the rate of expansion of industrial production. The assumption that discount rate changes were made in response to these respective targets would require the patterns of movements of reserves and of the unemployment ratio to be V-shaped, while the industrial-production pattern should either have the reverse shape or show a relatively high average position during the trough-to-peak phases. In fact, no resemblance to the expected shape is found in the industrial-production pattern; some resemblance is apparent for the two other target variables during the three cycles up to 1963, though it is not perfect in either one. In view of these observations, the assumption that discount-rate changes were responses to the balance-of-payments position fares quite well, but again, alternative assumptions about the motivation of changes in the discount rate could not be entirely dismissed.

A final test of the possibility that the discount rate was manipulated in accordance with the needs of employment and production is made using a reference cycle analysis in which the cycles are determined by movements of these targets; this is done for the years 1950–60, in which two cycles can be clearly distinguished. The turning points in the cycles would be almost identical for both the unemployment ratio and the index of industrial production. It was therefore decided to select just one of those variables to represent both. Chart 4-3 thus presents

CHART 4-2

BELGIUM: PATTERNS OF TARGET VARIABLES DURING
DISCOUNT–RATE CYCLES

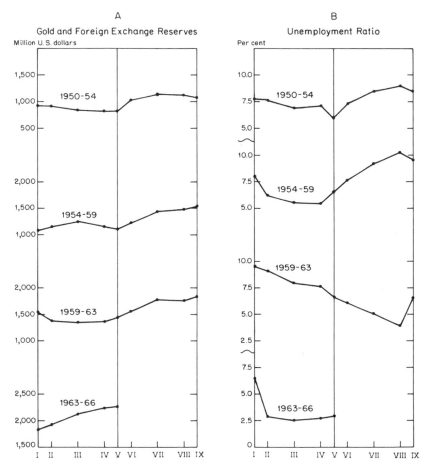

an analysis of cycles of industrial production, but it should also be understood to represent, in effect, patterns relating to cycles of unemployment. In the trough-to-peak phase of this cycle, the rate of expansion of production is high, and unemployment is low, whereas during the peak-to-trough phase the rate of expansion is low—sometimes even negative—and unemployment is high. The turning points are as follows:

CHART 4-2 (*Concluded*)

C

Change in Industrial Production

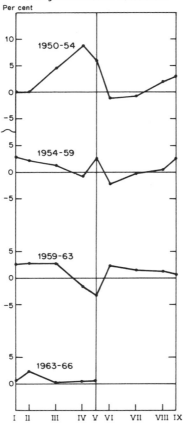

Cycle	Trough	Peak	Trough
1950–53	II 1950	II 1951	II 1953
1953–58	II 1953	I 1957	IV 1958

Part A of Chart 4-3 describes the pattern of movements of the discount rate along the two cycles. A conformity of these movements to the needs of production and of employment would result in inverted V-shaped patterns. Some resemblance to this pattern does appear for the cycle of 1950–53; in the cycle of 1953–58, on the other hand, no such pattern is revealed. Thus, the association of the discount rate with

CHART 4-3

BELGIUM: PATTERNS OF POLICY VARIABLES DURING
INDUSTRIAL–PRODUCTION CYCLE

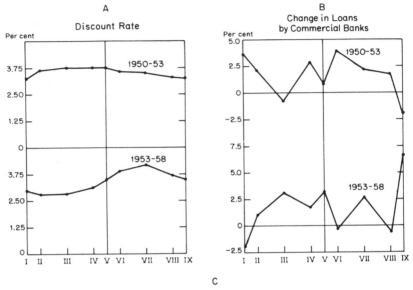

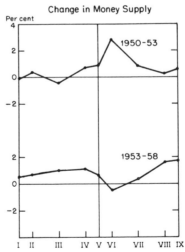

movements of the domestic targets of production and employment is rather weak.[4]

From the combined evidence of these tests we cannot categorically reject the possibility that discount rate policy was determined primarily in relation to the domestic targets of employment and production, but it seems more likely that, until 1962, the balance of payments was the main consideration and was given preference in the event of conflict with the requirements of employment and production. It must be emphasized, however, that such conflicts were rare and of minor significance. Most of the time, both the domestic targets and balance-of-payments developments required the same direction of policy action.

It remains to examine the possibility that, during the period up to 1962, discount rate changes were directed toward the target of price stability. As column 4 in Table 4-2 shows, such a possibility cannot be refuted altogether. Discount rate changes were often in the direction indicated by the need to maintain price stability and rarely in the opposite direction; but often also there seemed to be no association between rate changes and price movements, and the discount rate was raised or lowered while prices were stable. It should be noted that, although the price level did fluctuate during the period under consideration, the changes were not very large most of the time. Aside from a large rise from mid-1950 to mid-1951 (the Korean War period) and a considerable decline from then to mid-1953, the wholesale price level remained almost stable until late 1962. One may assume that price fluctuations could not have been a major reason for manipulations of the discount rate during these years.

It seems more likely, on the other hand, that from early 1963 to the end of 1966 it was, indeed, the movement of the price level to which the discount rate responded. As has been noted earlier, the discount rate during this period does not appear to be related to the balance-of-payments position. Over the period as a whole, it even moved in a disadjusting direction: it was continuously raised while external reserves were generally increasing, even though mildly. As can be seen from Table 4-2, this tendency of the discount rate does not appear to be associated with changes in the rate of expansion of production and probably not with changes in unemployment. Price movements, how-

---

[4] A direct comparison of the regularity of the pattern under consideration with the pattern followed by the discount rate during cycles in the balance of payments would have been helpful. It is unfortunate, for this purpose, that no meaningful "cycles" of the latter can be found.

ever, provide an easy explanation: after many years of stability, prices were rising continuously and substantially. It is plausible that during this period of rising prices and rising external reserves—two phenomena with conflicting requirements for policy direction—the target of price stability assumed preference over the target of balance-of-payments adjustment. The discount rate, the major direct instrument of monetary policy in Belgium, then began to be used more for the purpose of stabilizing prices than to achieve balance-of-payments equilibrium.

As for some other monetary variables, column 3 in Table 4-1 describes the behavior of the National Bank's lending to the commercial banking system. This variable generally moved in a disadjusting direction, i.e., in a direction opposite to the movements of the country's external reserves. Until about the middle of 1962, this inverse relationship was almost perfect, as may be seen from both column 3 and Chart 4-1. Since then, fluctuations in the amount of lending to the banks do not seem to correspond to any fluctuations in the amount of external reserves.

The amount of lending from the National Bank to the government does not seem to have any relationship to the balance-of-payments position. During nearly all of the subperiods of imbalance of payments, lending to the government was either quite stable or fluctuating with no general trend. While the outstanding amount of this lending was always substantially higher than the amount of National Bank lending to the banks, fluctuations in the latter were usually greater than fluctuations in the former. As a result, the direction of change in the National Bank's total domestic assets, which are made up primarily of these two categories, tended to be determined by the movements in its loans to the commercial banks. From column 4 in Table 4-1, it also appears that the total domestic assets of the National Bank generally moved in a disadjusting direction, although not quite with the same consistency as its lending to the banks.

The amount of commercial bank credit to the public, on the other hand, certainly seemed to move in an adjusting direction. This may be seen from column 5 in Table 4-1, where the rate of expansion of credit (positive throughout) is described. Without exception, this rate appears to have responded in an adjusting manner to the balance-of-payments position: it was higher in times of surplus, and lower when deficits appeared.

Practically identical conclusions may be derived for the rate of change of money supply (column 6 of Table 4-1). Once more, in almost all subperiods of imbalances of payments, movements of this variable appear to have been positively associated with movements of external reserves, that is, to move in an adjusting direction.

It seems very unlikely that these movements of credit and money supply were in fact intended to meet the needs of other major targets. This may be seen from Parts B and C of Chart 4-3, where the movements of the two variables during the cycles of industrial production (and unemployment) are described. If the two variables responded to the needs of these domestic targets, the resulting pattern would be V-shaped, or at least each line would be in a lower position during the trough-to-peak phase than during its opposite. In fact, however, no such patterns emerge.

Neither could it be assumed that the rates of expansion of credit and of money responded, as a rule, to the needs of price stability. It will be recalled that prices were practically stable until 1962, when a trend of price increases appeared. The high rates of expansion of money and credit since 1962, which may have been the source of the price rise, definitely cannot be interpreted as having been maintained in response to the need for price stability.

Unfortunately, it is difficult to evaluate the movements of the budgetary variables: quarterly data on revenues, expenditures, and the budgetary balance are available only from 1957. This limitation of the data not only shortens the period of observation, but also makes it impossible to examine reactions of these variables to balance-of-payments deficits. Evaluation of the available data, as far as they go, does not reveal any general relationship between the fiscal variables and the position of the balance of payments. The budgetary deficit appears to have been particularly large from about early 1958 to mid-1961. At the beginning of this period external reserves rose markedly, but during most of the period they were rather stable. The deficits increased once more from late 1964 to late 1966, the end of the period covered by the data—again mostly a time of stable reserves. Thus, there is no evidence to justify an assumption that movements of the budgetary deficit corresponded with movements of the balance of payments; nor do these data indicate a general responsiveness of the budgetary deficit to the requirements of high production, high employment, or price stability. It should, however, be emphasized again that any conclusions about the budgetary variables are very tentative at best, given the lack of data for the earlier years.

3. Summary and Interpretation

Throughout most of the period, until about 1962, monetary policy and developments in Belgium appear to have been quite closely and regularly linked with the country's balance-of-payments position. The following is a typical sequence of events.

Assume a downward imbalance of payments with a decline in the country's external reserves. Normally the National Bank would react to this position by raising the discount rate, by far the most important direct monetary instrument. By convention, a rise in interest rates charged by the commercial banks will follow the increase in the discount rate. This movement of the interest rates is consistent with the development of credit supply, which may be traced as follows. The loss of external reserves reduces the reserves of the commercial banks with the National Bank. The commercial banks compensate part of this reduction by increasing their borrowing from the National Bank, despite the increase of the discount rate. Yet, at the end of the process, the commercial banking system does restrict its credit outstanding—that is, more precisely, it does reduce the rate of credit expansion. The rate of expansion of the money supply is also reduced. Of the three major components which create money—namely, the accumulation of foreign assets, bank credit and National Bank lending to the government—the first falls, the second falls more often than not, while the last normally fluctuates without a regular trend, so that it usually does not offset the movement of the first two components. As a result, the money supply moves in the same direction as the external reserves. When a surplus appears in the balance of payments, and external reserves start rising, all these processes are normally reversed.

By the Nurkse definition, the "rules of the game" were not obeyed in Belgium: a loss of foreign assets by the National Bank was almost consistently accompanied, as has just been mentioned, by a rise in the Bank's lending to commercial banks, which usually was not offset by a change in the Bank's lending to the government. The National Bank's domestic assets thus tended to move in the direction opposite to the Bank's foreign assets. By the alternative definition suggested in this study, however, in which movements of the discount rate and of money supply serve as yardsticks, the "rules of the game" of monetary policy were indeed observed in Belgium more consistently than in most other countries. Judged by the behavior of these two variables, as well as credit supply, monetary policy was used regularly in Belgium for the purpose of balance-of-payments adjustment.

Most of the time the requirements of balance-of-payments adjustment were not in conflict, but rather in agreement, with the demands of the domestic targets of high employment and high production. A loss of reserves most often came at a time of fast expansion of production and low unemployment; that is, when the economy was characterized by high aggregate demand, although in Belgium during most of the period studied, this did not also mean rapid price increases. In the same way, balance-of-payments surpluses coincided as a rule with a slack in production and with high unemployment. This is a likely concurrence in a small country, where the effect of domestic policies on the balance-of-payments is presumably more important than developments in the world market. The cycle of developments might very well be as follows: with a balance-of-payments deficit, a restrictive monetary policy is followed, as indicated above. This leads, in time, to balance-of-payments surpluses accompanied by a domestic slack resulting from the contraction of domestic demand. And this, in turn, calls for an expansionary monetary policy, which would lead again to a deficit in the balance of payments.

During the last few years of the period covered—from about 1962 or 1963—a change in the policy pattern may be apparent. This is a period in which reserves accumulated most of the time, although at a mild pace, while the price level, which had been rather stable before, started to rise at a relatively fast rate. During these years, the discount rate appeared to be responsive to the target of price stability, rather than to the needs of the balance of payments. Yet movements of the money supply and bank credit still seemed to conform largely to the position of the balance of payments. It thus may be argued that monetary policy in Belgium in these years also acted partly to restore balance-of-payments equilibrium. By permitting a fast expansion of money and credit it allowed prices to increase as they did, which in turn prevented a still greater accumulation of external reserves. Yet, these adjusting movements were mitigated by the restrictive act of raising the discount rate.

Limitations of data—only the latter half of the period is well covered —restrict the possibility of deriving conclusions about the pattern of budgetary variables in Belgium. As far as the data go, they show no evidence that the budgetary balance was generally responsive to the balance of payments. Neither is there any indication of policy "mix" by which budgetary policy is assigned the task of serving the domestic targets of employment and production, while monetary policy is engaged in balance-of-payments adjustment.

References

Banque Nationale de Belgique, *Bulletin d'Information et de Documentation,* quarterly, Brussels, 1925–66.

Banque Nationale de Belgique, *Report Presented by the Governor,* annual, Brussels, 1949–66 (in French from 1870).

Ministère des Affaires Economiques, *L'Economie Belge,* annual, Brussels, 1947–66.

Organization for Economic Cooperation and Development, *Economic Surveys: Belgium-Luxemburg Economic Union,* annual, Paris. Reports for 1953–61 issued by the Organization for European Economic Cooperation.

CHAPTER 5  FRANCE

1. Policy Instruments

In France, monetary policy is conducted by the National Credit Council, which is nominally headed by the Minister of Finance, while the Governor of the Bank of France serves as Vice President. As a rule, however, the Minister is absent from the Council's meetings, and the operation of the Council is directed by the Bank's Governor. Although the Bank is theoretically only the executive agency of the Council, carrying out the latter's policy, in practice the Bank of France brings recommendations for policy actions before the Council, and the Council's staff is provided by the Bank. The Council may thus be viewed as the means by which the Bank of France submits its suggestions to representatives of the public and the banking community for approval, and by which it coordinates its policy with that of the government, particularly the Ministry of Finance. In this way, the Bank of France enjoys a smaller degree of formal independence than do most central banks, but this does not mean that the Bank is in a subordinate position: it probably wields greater influence on the operation of other government organs than do central banks in most other countries.

While there are many deposit banking facilities in France, banking is quite concentrated, both in number of banks and in location; the greater part of banking transactions is conducted by seven banks, only one of which has its headquarters outside Paris. More than half of the banking business, measured by the amount of deposits or by total assets, is concentrated in the four largest banks, all of them in Paris. These four banks have been nationalized since the end of World War II, yet they still operate as private enterprises. Despite the high degree of concentration and the nationalization of banking establishments, there are no indications that informal associations within the banking community, or "moral suasion" by the central bank, play an important part in the conduct of monetary policy in France.

The Bank of France uses all of the classical monetary instruments, but in forms and combinations that are uniquely its own.

Discount Policy. Rediscount policy—effected through changes in the discount rate and in rediscounting quotas—is the major instrument of monetary policy in France. Because of the massive amount of rediscounting at the Bank of France, changes in the discount rate are bound to be effective, for they operate on both the supply of credit and the demand for it. A semi-rigid relationship is maintained, by regulation, between the discount rate and the commercial banks' interest rates on customer loans. Formerly, the difference between the interest rates and the discount rate was fixed; a change in the discount rate thus led to a similar change in rates charged by commercial banks, leading in turn to a change in the amount of credit demanded by the public. Since November 1963, however, the regulations allow the commercial banks' lending rates to change only half as much as the discount rate changes.[1] A change in the discount rate thus affects the profitability of commercial banks' credit transactions (combined with rediscounting) and the supply of credit.

Since 1948, discount policy has also included the establishment of a ceiling for each bank, up to which it can discount at the Bank of France at the basic discount rate. Further rediscounting (or selling paper to the Bank of France with a repurchase stipulation) within a limit of 10 per cent of the discount quotas has been allowed since 1951, but a penalty rate, higher than the basic discount rate, is applied to such transactions. Since 1957, still further discounting has been permitted at a second, higher, penalty rate. Both changes in the ceilings and changes in the penalty rates are among the discount policy measures used. Unlike the situation in a country like Japan, where the basic discount rate was rather meaningless during most of the period in which penalty rates were in effect, it appears that in France the basic rate has been significant; that is, for most discounting transactions, this basic discount rate is relevant at the margin. Discounting at the penalty rates is usually taken only for brief periods, as a last resort; the very high level of the penalty rates forces the banks generally to stay within their basic rediscounting quotas.

---

[1] This change in the relationship between the rates was officially introduced in early 1960, but from then until late 1963 the change was applicable only to discount-rate movements outside the range of 3.5 to 4.5 per cent, and in fact the discount rate remained within this range during those years.

Reserve Requirements. The minimum-reserve requirements customary in most countries—requirements for the holding of deposits at the central bank, or cash, at a certain ratio to designated bank liabilities—did not exist in France during the period under review. Usually, commercial banks in France have maintained only small working balances at the Bank of France—not more than 2 to 3 per cent of their deposit liabilities. There have been, however, liquidity requirements of a somewhat different form considered secondary to, and intended mainly for the support of, rediscounting policy.

When the rediscount ceilings were introduced in September 1948, commercial banks held sizable amounts of Treasury bills. By selling these, the banks could have overcome the restrictive effect of the limitations imposed on rediscounting by the ceilings. In order to prevent such circumvention, the rediscount ceilings were accompanied by Treasury-bill "floors": banks were required to hold Treasury bills to the value of a given minimum amount. At first, each bank was required to maintain the amount of Treasury bills in its portfolio at the time the system was introduced; for all commercial banks at that time, the average was 28 per cent of designated liabilities. Each bank was also required to hold additional bills to the value of 20 per cent of the increase in its designated liabilities since the base date. In 1956 this mixture was replaced by a uniform ratio of 25 per cent of all liabilities, which was the average ratio for all commercial banks.

Early in 1961, a more inclusive reserve requirement was introduced. Under the new regulation, the banks were required to maintain portfolios of several types of assets, *including* the Treasury bills held under the floor regulation, at a given minimum ratio to the liabilities specified under the floor regulation. In addition to Treasury bills, these assets include certain commercial bills, all of which can be discounted at the Bank of France beyond the limitations of the ceilings under the existing regulations. Thus, this measure, too, was enacted as a supplement to discounting policy. Because of these new reserve requirements, the floor regulation ceased to be a necessary part of monetary policy, and changes in floor ratios were thereafter determined primarily by the needs of the Treasury. Consequently, the floor ratio has, gradually and substantially, declined from the level of 25 per cent at which it was maintained before 1961.[2]

[2] The system of floor ratios and reserve requirements described here was replaced in 1967 by a system of reserve ratios in which deposits at the Bank of France constitute reserves.

Open-Market Policy. Open-market operations have been a minor, subsidiary part of the management of French monetary policy. Banks were assigned open-market quotas which gave them limited recourse to open-market selling before starting to rediscount at the Bank of France at the penalty rates. In effect, then, open-market operations did not function as an independent instrument, but rather as part of the discounting mechanism.

Other Measures. The Bank of France has considerable power to intervene in the granting of credit by commercial banks; to grant various forms of credit, beyond some given size of transaction, the banks must obtain prior authorization from the Bank of France. This regulation has been used to control the allocation of credit, i.e., to discourage lending to certain industries, and encourage lending to others, but not, apparently, as an instrument of general monetary policy. Monetary circumstances influenced the regulation of instalment credit, but there is not enough of this instalment credit in France for direct intervention by the Bank of France in that area to make any substantial impact on the total amount of credit.

On occasion, however, direct control has been exercised over the credit volume. From February 1958 to February 1959, the total amount of credit which could be granted by each bank was frozen by directive of the monetary authorities at its level for the last quarter of 1957; expansion up to 3 per cent of that base was permitted only when credit for exports was concerned. Direct control was introduced again in early 1963, and was maintained throughout the rest of the period.

FISCAL POLICY AND THE TREASURY'S FINANCIAL TRANSACTIONS

Because of the Treasury's functions and the structure of its operations, its role in French economic life is rather complicated. The French government's budget is divided into two parts. One, by far the larger, includes "permanent items." On the expenditure side, this includes the government's real transactions and transfer payments; on the revenue side, it covers taxes and similar items. Generally speaking, this part of the budget is roughly balanced. The other part includes "temporary items," and essentially consists only of payments in the form of loans granted by the government (net of repayments), primarily for development purposes. These loans (the acquisition of financial assets) are financed mostly by sales of various government financial obligations; but the proceeds from these transactions are not recorded as revenue in the budget. The temporary-items part of the budget, hence the budget as a whole, thus necessarily shows a deficit, roughly the size of the expenditures on temporary items. This deficit does not therefore indicate the government's "excess demand," which would approximately correspond to a deficit in the budget of permanent items.

As is implied above, the government is heavily involved in the capital market, mainly in the sale of Treasury bills. These are of two kinds: "paper" bills are sold to savings institutions and other firms and to households in order to channel savings through the government; "current account" bills are the Treasury bills sold to commercial banks. Since the banks are compelled to buy the latter under the "floor" regulations, there is strong incentive for the Treasury to set low yields for the bills; consequently, the banks tend to invest as little as possible in Treasury bills. As a rule, then, the amount of acquisition (or disposition) of Treasury bills by commercial banks is determined by changes in their deposit liabilities and the floor ratio. During the last few years of the period surveyed, the strong financial position of the government led to a marked decline in the amount of outstanding Treasury bills which, in turn, made possible the abolition of the floor requirement in 1967.

The Treasury also influences the monetary situation in many other ways. It holds large sums on deposit for individuals, firms, special agencies, and governmental units, such as local authorities, and the governments of overseas members of the franc area. Some of these deposits, such as those widely held in the postal system, are even considered part of the French money supply. Changes in these accounts will, in turn, be reflected in the Treasury's accounts at the Bank of France, for the Treasury does not maintain deposits in commercial banks.

It is clear that while the government's deficit, and changes in it, must be related to the government's net indebtedness to the Bank of France, there is no necessary correspondence between the two. The latter reflects not only the size of the deficit but also the form in which it is financed (whether by sales of Treasury bills or by a change in the government's indebtedness to the Bank) and changes in the Treasury's monetary accounts, some of which move independently, while others are related directly to the budget.[3]

[3] An important instance of the latter case is given by budgetary allocations to governments of other countries of the franc area, which are accomplished by crediting the account of the government concerned at the Treasury, and do not

Université d'Ottawa
Social Sciences Sociales
University of Ottawa

It is also clear that neither the budgetary balance nor changes in the government's net indebtedness to the Bank of France accurately reflect the expansionary or contractionary impact of the government's transactions. For the reasons just explained, the cash deficit, as it is measured, does not represent the government's excess demand, while the change in the government's indebtedness to the Bank does not take into account the effect of changes in accounts held at the Treasury, and thus does not fully represent the effect of the government on the economy's liquidity.

2. Statistical Analysis

The study of monetary and fiscal reactions to balance-of-payments disturbances in France is restricted to a rather small number of observations. For about half of the total period—from the beginning of 1959 to the end of 1966—the balance of payments showed continuous surpluses, and external reserves increased monotonically. Episodes of balance-of-payments fluctuations are thus limited to the 1950's. Nevertheless, conclusions are suggested by the data.

First, as may be seen from Chart 5-1 and from column 2 of Table 5-1, movements of the discount rate appear consistently in the direction indicated by the need for balance-of-payments adjustment. This is certainly true for the years 1950–60; in later years, there were hardly any movements in the discount rate—only two minor changes in 1963 and 1965—and the changes were apparently unrelated to the movements of external reserves.

This impression is supported by Table 5-2, in which all changes in the discount rate are recorded. From column 1, it may be seen that almost all of these changes were in the direction required for balance-of-payments adjustment. The single apparent exception during the 1950's is the lowering of the discount rate in the third quarter of 1953, when external reserves were falling. The fall of reserves during that quarter was, however, minor; moreover, when the discount rate was

give rise to any immediate change in the Treasury's accounts at the Bank of France. In the longer run, however, these allocations will take the form of an excess of imports from France by the country concerned. This, in turn, must be reflected in a transfer of accounts at the Treasury from the foreign government to a French bank, which will lead to an increase in bank liquidity and corresponding increase in the Treasury's net indebtedness to the Bank of France.

CHART 5-1
FRANCE: TIME SERIES OF SELECTED VARIABLES

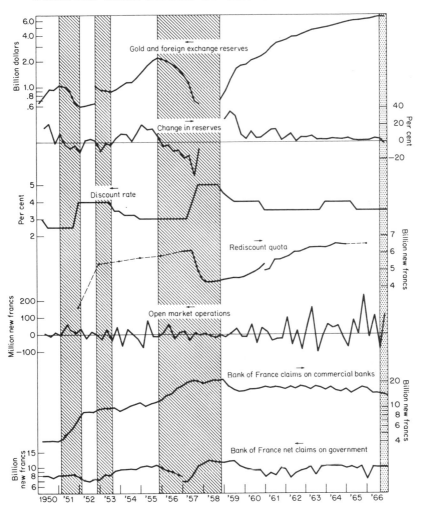

CHART 5-1 (*Continued*)

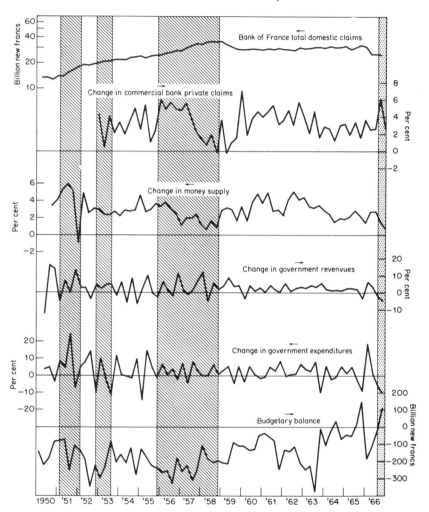

CHART 5-1 *(Concluded)*

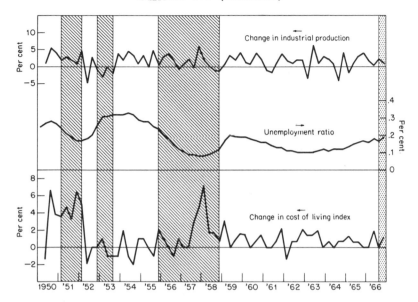

NOTE: Diagonal-line areas represent period of downward imbalances; gray areas represent stability; white areas represent upward imbalances.

actually changed, in September 1953, external reserves were already slightly rising. This episode thus cannot be considered an exception either.

Table 5-2 also provides an indication of the influence of targets other than the balance of payments on the movements of the discount rate. Unemployment, even at its peaks, was so low throughout the period that its fluctuations could not conceivably bring about monetary policy reactions. Table 5-2 is therefore confined to two other target variables. The rate of change of industrial production is represented in column 2; movements of the discount rate show no consistent association with this variable. But the rate of change of the cost-of-living index (column 3) seems to perform quite well. It appears that, on the whole, there was no contradiction between the requirements of balance-of-payments equilibrium and those of price stability. A fall of external reserves was more often than not accompanied by a greater than usual increase in prices, so that both targets required (or did not contradict the need for) an increase in the discount rate, whereas the opposite was usually true for periods of balance-of-payments surpluses.

TABLE 5-1

FRANCE: MOVEMENTS OF POLICY VARIABLES DURING SUBPERIODS OF IMBALANCES

Subperiod	External Reserves (1)	Discount Rate (2)	Bank-of-France Lending to Banks (compared with trend) (3)	Bank-of-France Lending to Government (4)	Bank-of-France Total Domestic Claims (compared with trend) (5)	Money Supply (quarterly rate of increase, per cent) (6)	Budgetary Balance (quarterly average, in billions of francs) (7)
I 1950 – I 1951	rise	+ lowered	– falls	* stable	– falls	(+) 4.4	(*) –.25
I 1951 – I 1952	fall	+ raised	– rises	+ falls	– rises	(+) 3.9	(–) –1.36
I 1952 – IV 1952	rise	* stable	* stable	+ rises	* stable	(–) 2.9	(+) –2.47
IV 1952 – III 1953	fall	– lowered	+ falls	– rises	* stable	(+) 2.5	(+) –2.02
III 1953 – IV 1955	rise	+ lowered	* stable	+ rises	* stable	(+) 3.2	(–) –1.65
IV 1955 – IV 1958	fall	+ raised	– rises	* fluctuates	– rises	(+) 2.0	(–) –2.29
IV 1958 – IV 1965	rise	* no trend	– falls	* fluctuates	– falls	(+) 3.1	(–) –1.32

NOTE: For explanation of symbols, see Chapter 3, explanatory note.

TABLE 5-2

FRANCE: CHANGES IN THE DISCOUNT RATE AND
POSITION OF TARGET VARIABLES

Discount Rate	External Reserves (1)	Industrial Production (rate of increase) (2)	Cost-of-Living Index (rate of increase) (3)
Raised:			
IV 1951	+ fall	* normal	+ high
II 1957	+ fall	− low	− low
III 1957	+ fall	− low	* normal
IV 1963	− rise	* normal	+ high
Lowered:			
II 1950	+ rise	+ low	+ low
III 1953	− fall	+ low	+ low
I 1954	+ rise	− high	+ low
IV 1954	+ rise	− high	+ low
IV 1958	* stable	+ low	* normal
I 1959	+ rise	+ low	* normal
II 1959	+ rise	* normal	* normal
IV 1960	+ rise	− high	+ low
II 1965	+ rise	+ low	* normal

NOTE: For explanation of symbols, see Chapter 3, explanatory note.

The long period of continuously rising external reserves deserves a special examination. During most of this period—throughout the 1960's—the discount rate was practically stable, while balance-of-payments adjustment would have called for a lowering of the rate. It is conceivable, however, that even though the discount rate was almost stable during these years, its *level* may have been determined by a consideration of the fact that the balance of payments was in a continuous surplus. If this is true, the level of the discount rate would be low, in comparison with other periods, but this is not what actually took place. The average, almost stable, level of the discount rate from 1960 or 1961 onward was about the same as the average, much more fluctuating, level of the rate during the 1950's. Therefore, by this yardstick, too, discount-rate policy cannot be said to have conformed to the requirements of balance-of-payments equilibrium during the 1960's. But, as the analysis of the over-all view in Chapter 2 has shown, a different conclusion is reached when the rising trend of discount rates in other countries is taken into consideration: in relation to rates elsewhere, the discount rate in France was indeed lowered during the 1960's.

It may be worthwhile to inquire whether the *level* of external reserves fulfilled a function in the determination of discount-rate policy. If it did, reversals of policy should follow, in general, reversals of movements of external reserves only after the latter have persisted over a long period of time, so that this cumulative effect on the level of reserves is significant. By and large, this does not seem to be the case. The only important episode in which the policy pattern would conform to this hypothesis is that of 1956–58. The decline of reserves in this period followed a very sharp increase which brought reserves to a high level. Indeed, discount-rate policy came to be restrictive only in the second quarter of 1957, after a sharp decline of reserves had already been in progress for a year and a half. But, contrary to the hypothesis under examination, discount-rate policy became expansive at the end of 1958, continued to be expansive in 1959, while reserves were rising but still below their 1955 peak. From the middle of 1959, the discount rate remained almost stable while reserves were rising rapidly and surpassing by far any previous level. In the latter part of 1951, the raising of the discount rate followed soon after a fall in reserves after a sharp rise. In late 1953 and in 1954, when reserves were only starting to rise from a low level, the discount rate was lowered a few times, whereas in 1955, when reserves were rising fast to much above previously maintained levels, the discount rate remained stable. On the whole, then, the proposition that the *level* of foreign-exchange reserves—as distinguished from the direction of change—fulfilled a significant role in determining the movements of the discount rate must be rejected.

The two "penalty rates" (not shown in Chart 5-1) may be seen to have played a supporting role to the basic discount rate: the movements of the former were always in the same direction as those of the latter. The penalty rates seem to be important mainly during 1957–59, when their movements and the basic discount rate conform to the requirements of balance-of-payments adjustment: the penalty rates were raised (the second, in effect, only introduced) during 1957 and the first half of 1958, when external reserves were falling; lowered slightly during the second half of 1958, when the balance of payments stabilized; and lowered considerably during 1959, when reserves were rising rapidly.

The movement of the basic rediscount quotas shows, as Chart 5-1 indicates, a slight upward trend most of the time. The increase in the quotas was very sharp during 1952. External reserves were, indeed, rising during that year, but this rise was only slight, and is not likely to have been the proper explanation for the increase in the quotas. The other deviation from the trend—a substantial decline in the quotas during the second half of 1957—is more significant; and it conforms to the movements of the basic discount rate and the penalty rates, and to the requirements of balance-of-payments adjustment during that period.

The floor regulations for the holding of Treasury paper (not shown in Chart 5-1) do not seem to fulfill any independent function. From the introduction of those regulations to the end of 1960 the floor ratio was stable, except for the previously noted change in structure, and consequently in its "marginal" level from 20 to 25 per cent, in 1956. On the other hand, as has been mentioned earlier, since the introduction of a more inclusive reserve ratio in 1961, the floor regulations have been of little relevance to over-all monetary policy. The reserve ratio, which was stable during 1961, increased in number of steps from early 1962 to the middle of 1963, then decreased from late 1964 to the end of 1965. All these changes took place during the period of a consistent, large rise of external reserves, and cannot thus be explained by the position of the balance of payments. In a rough way, they corresponded to changes in the same direction in the discount rate, and were, presumably, intended to reinforce discount-rate policy during these years.

Substantial changes in the amount of the Bank of France's lending to commercial banks clearly were opposite in direction to changes in external reserves, as may be seen from Chart 5-1 and from column 3 of Table 5-1. These movements in the Bank's lending to commercial banks appear to be related to three factors: the movement of external reserves, discount policy, and Bank of France lending to the government. Commercial-bank borrowing from the bank, generally rather stable, rose substantially during 1951 and from the end of 1955 to the middle of 1957, both of which were periods of substantial declines in external reserves. From mid-1957 to the end of 1958, the amount of such borrowing was stable, although foreign reserves were still falling sharply. This must have been due, first, to the discounting policy, which became restrictive during this period, and, second, to a substantial increase in the Bank of France lending to the government. It may be assumed that a fall of the latter during 1956 was a contributing factor to the rise of borrowing by commercial banks that year. In 1959, with the sharp increase in external reserves, commercial-bank borrowing from the Bank of France declined, despite the reduction of the discount rates. During 1952–55 and from 1960 onward, when external reserves were rising substantially, the commercial banks' borrowing was roughly stable. Given the fact that the commercial banks' lending to the public increased continuously during these periods, it is clear that the rise of external reserves relieved commercial banks from the need to resort to borrowing from the Bank of France as a means of financing this credit expansion. In sum, therefore, the relationship between external reserves and Bank of France lending was unmistakable: a fall of the former led to an increase in the latter, while a rise of the former brought a fall, or prevented a rise, in the latter. In France, as in other countries, the "automatic" disadjusting effect of commercial bank borrowing from the central bank clearly seems to be operative.

Fluctuations in Bank of France claims on the government, on the other hand, apparently have no consistent relation to the balance of payments, as may be gathered from Chart 5-1 and from column 4 of Table 5-1. The most important movement of disadjusting nature took place during 1957, when this lending increased while external reserves were falling, but a positive correspondence between the movements of the two variables is found on other occasions, until about the middle of 1961. From then on, claims on the government, while sometimes fluctuating, have been relatively stable, while external reserves have risen rapidly.

The movement in total domestic claims of the Bank of France—which is primarily the combination of the previous two components—seems to follow the same trend as the Bank's lending to commercial banks. The result, as Chart 5-1 and column 5 of Table 5-1 show, is that such changes are largely in a disadjusting direction. This holds true both for shorter-term movements and for longer-term trends: at the end of 1958, external reserves were on the same level as in 1950 (while fluctuating mildly between those years), whereas the Bank of France's total domestic assets increased appreciably over that period; from 1959 to 1966, on the other hand, the latter variable remained stable, or even declined slightly, while external reserves rose substantially. The inverse relationship frequently observed between a central bank's foreign assets and its domestic assets is clear in the case of France.

Data on lending by commercial banks to the public, presented in Chart 5-1 (i.e., commercial bank private claims), are available only from 1953 and thus do not cover earlier instances of imbalance. But in subsequent years—which comprise most of the total period—the amount of commercial-bank lending does not seem to be related in any consistent way to imbalances of payments. The rate of expansion of credit was rather stable throughout, and averages for subperiods are very similar to each other. The only important deviation from the average trend occurred from the middle of 1957 to the end of 1959, when credit expansion was particularly low. This covers a period when external reserves fell sharply during 1957; a period when they fell slightly during most of 1958, and a period when they increased sharply during 1959. The decline of the rate of expansion of credit during 1957–58 was probably due to the restrictive measures of those years (including the direct control of credit during 1958), which measures, in turn, were most probably taken as a response to the imbalance of payments. But this single episode—followed immediately by a reverse relationship in 1959—would not allow one to conclude that commercial-bank lending showed a regular response to imbalances of payments.

It is worth noting, however, that during the long period of uninterrupted accumulation of external reserves in the 1960's, the rate of expansion of commercial-bank lending does seem to be correlated, in a rough way, with the *rate* of expansion of reserves. Thus, if this period is divided into two—1960–62 and 1963 through the third quarter of 1966—changes in these two variables between the two subperiods appear to be similar. The quarterly rate of expansion of external reserves declined from 7.6 per cent in 1960–62 to 3.4 per cent in 1963–66, while the rate of expansion of commercial-bank lending fell from 4.8 per cent to 2.5 per cent. The particularly fast expansion of credit during the early 1960's might have come about without the rapid accumulation of external reserves, but this accumulation enabled the banks to maintain the rapid credit expansion without borrowing from the Bank of France. During 1963–66, on the other hand, credit expansion was restricted by direct control measures. It is sometimes argued that these restrictions were due to the declining balance-of-payments surpluses and the declining rate of accumulation of external reserves. If this is true, credit policy during this period would appear to be responsive to balance-of-payments fluctuations in a manner which assumes not balance-of-payments equilibrium, but a given, high rate of accumulation of external reserves to be the external target.

Money supply clearly seems to respond to changes in external reserves in an adjusting manner. This may be observed from Chart 5-1 and from column 6 of Table 5-1. The rate of expansion of money supply was, almost invariably, positively related to the movement of reserves. The only exception is the subperiod 1952, when the rate of increase of money supply fell and external reserves increased slightly.

Table 5-3 presents episodes in which the rate of expansion of money supply deviated markedly from its trend; that is, the expansion was particularly fast or particularly slow (it was practically never negative). It may be seen that, until 1960, such episodes could be explained by the need for balance-of-payments adjustment much better than by other targets. From 1960 onward, on the other hand, none of the targets appears to provide a good explanation of the developments in this instrument variable.

Like the amount of credit, money supply in the 1960's appears to be related to the rate of accumulation of external reserves: between 1960–62 and 1963–66 the quarterly rate of expansion of money supply fell from 3.8 per cent to 2.6 per cent. This association is almost inevitable: of the three major factors which contribute to the creation

TABLE 5-3

FRANCE: SIGNIFICANT CHANGES IN MONEY SUPPLY
AND POSITION OF TARGET VARIABLES

Period	Rate of Increase of Money Supply (1)	External Reserves (2)	Industrial Production (rate of increase) (3)	Cost-of-Living Index (rate of increase) (4)
II 1951 – II 1952	low	+ fall	+ high	+ high
I 1956 – III 1958	low	+ fall	* normal	* fluctuates
III 1958 – III 1960	high	+ rise	* normal	* normal
I 1961 – IV 1961	low	– rise	* normal	* normal
IV 1961 – IV 1962	high	+ rise	* normal	+ low
I 1964 – IV 1965	low	– rise	– low	– low

NOTE: For explanation of symbols, see Chapter 3, explanatory note.

of money, the stock of the central bank's net lending to the government was found to be rather stable during the 1960's, while the rate of expansion of commercial-bank credit and the rate of accumulation of external reserves—the other two major factors which determine money supply—moved, as has just been observed, in the same direction. The association of the rate of increase of money supply with the rate of accumulation of external reserves during the 1960's is similar to its aforementioned association with credit supply.

Movements of the budgetary deficit, which are represented in Chart 5-1 and in column 7 of Table 5-1, do not seem to have any consistent relationship to imbalances of payments. This would also be true if the deficit were calculated not in absolute terms but, say, as a ratio of the size of the budget, or of the national product. As has been explained before, the size of the budgetary cash deficit in France does not represent the government's excess demand for goods and services. Since data on this excess demand are not readily available, no presumption about its relationship to balance-of-payments adjustment can be offered. From Table 5-4, which lists episodes in which the budgetary deficit was clearly rising or falling, it appears that no alternative target could explain the movements of the budgetary deficit. A comparison of columns 4 and 7 in Table 5-1, or the corresponding series in Chart 5-1, will also show no consistency in the movements of the budgetary deficit

TABLE 5-4

FRANCE: THE BUDGETARY BALANCE AND POSITIONS
OF TARGET VARIABLES

Period	Budgetary Deficit	External Reserves	Industrial Production (rate of increase)	Cost-of-Living Index (rate of increase)
	(1)	(2)	(3)	(4)
II 1951 – II 1953	high	* no trend	+ low	* fluctuates
I 1955 – III 1956	high	* no trend	– high	+ low
III 1957 – III 1961	low	– rise	* normal	* fluctuates
III 1961 – III 1963	high	+ rise	* normal	* normal
III 1963 – IV 1965	low	– rise	– low	– low

NOTE: For explanation of symbols, see Chapter 3, explanatory note.

and of the government's borrowing from the Bank of France. This illustrates the point made earlier, that the government's cash position in France is affected significantly by components other than the budgetary deficits.

3. Summary and Interpretation

In examining policy patterns in France, a distinction should be made between the 1950's, a period of fluctuations in the balance of payments, and the 1960's, a period of consistent surpluses and continuous accumulation of external reserves.

During the 1950's, a consistent response to imbalances of payments is evident, and a regular pattern emerges. In the event of a deficit or a fall of reserves, the discount rate is raised. Such changes in the discount rate are the most important measure of over-all discount policy, which is, in turn, the major instrument of monetary policy. In addition to the basic discount rate, the penalty rates may also be raised in response to the deficit of payments. During the substantial downward movement of 1957, the discount quota was lowered significantly, as an added measure. The contractionary discount policy is not associated, however, with a contraction of commercial-bank borrowing from the Bank of France. In itself, the discount policy must obviously have this contractionary effect, as is clearly revealed by the movements of commercial-bank borrowing which follow the discount policy measures. But this would only partly offset the tendency of banks to increase their borrowing from the Bank of France during a period of falling external reserves, in order to overcome the reduction of their lending capacity which the fall of reserves must involve. In such a period, commercial banks' borrowing from the Bank of France increases, rather than diminishes: the rise of demand for this lending more than offsets the increase in its cost. In France, as in other countries, one encounters the paradox of increased bank borrowing from the central bank at times of a rise in the discount rate.

Bank-of-France lending to the government does not seem to respond in a consistent manner to a balance-of-payments deficit. Movements of total domestic assets thus tend, following the movement of the Bank's lending to commercial banks, to be in a disadjusting direction: when the Bank of France loses external assets its domestic assets tend to rise fast, whereas at other times they tend to be stable or to rise only slowly.

Commercial-bank lending to the public does not reveal any consistent pattern. This, as has just been mentioned, is true also for the Bank of France's net lending to the government. These two components participate, along with external reserves, in determining the size of money supply. Since the first two components do not as a rule contradict the movement of external reserves, the rate of expansion of money supply is correlated with the latter: in times of declines of reserves, this rate falls.

For this period, no asymmetry between upward and downward imbalances is evident: when external reserves rise, the opposite pattern appears. Therefore, it may be said that the discount rate—or discount policy in general—was manipulated, as a rule, in an adjusting direction. The rate of expansion of money supply also moved in an adjusting direction during this period whereas total domestic assets of the central bank behaved in a disadjusting manner. The latter phenomenon conforms to the findings by Nurkse and by Bloomfield on the assets of the central bank. By the Nurkse criterion, this monetary policy would then be classified as one which contradicts the "rules of the game." On the other hand, by the definition which employs the variables of the discount rate and the money supply, this pattern would be described as one which follows the "rules" rather consistently.

While consistency of the pattern during the 1950's seems evident, it cannot be ascertained whether the movements of the policy variables were indeed a response to the needs of the balance of payments. The movements, it was observed, could be interpreted almost as well as being directed by the "domestic" target of price stability. During the 1950's in France, these two targets usually appear to require the same policy response rather than to have contradicting requirements. This would suggest, in turn, that balance-of-payments fluctuations were normally due to changes in internal circumstances—and, presumably, to internal policy measures—rather than to external changes: balance-of-payments deficits went along with domestic inflation and price rises, whereas balance-of-payments surpluses were accompanied by domestic contraction and price stability.

Unlike monetary policy, fiscal policy does not reveal any consistent pattern of reaction, either by itself or in some "mix" with monetary policy. It does not appear that this was due to the employment of fiscal policy in the service of some other major target; this is not a surprising finding in view of the observation that other targets did not usually require measures opposite to those intended to bring about balance-of-payments equilibrium. Fiscal policy might, of course, have been aimed at some other target not examined in the study. It must also be remembered that data on the cash budgetary deficit, which were used to identify budgetary policy, may not have been on many occasions even a good approximation of the size of the government's excess demand. Thus, it is conceivable that more relevant data, if available, would have revealed some other pattern.

During the period extending from 1960 or, perhaps, 1959 to the third quarter of 1966, the pattern is significantly different. External reserves kept rising during these years at a very substantial rate. A monetary policy responsive to the need for balance-of-payments equilibrium should have been generally expansionary. Actual policy might be interpreted to have been such, but the evidence is not clear-cut. The discount rate was kept rather stable, instead of being lowered, and the two slight variations in it cannot be interpreted as having been motivated by balance-of-payments developments. Moreover, the level of the discount rate over this period as a whole was not lower than its average level in the preceding years, as an adjusting policy would have required. In relation to discount rates elsewhere, on the other hand, the discount rate does appear to have been lowered. The rate of increase of money supply seems to be roughly correlated with the rate of accumulation of external reserves—the two are considerably higher during 1960–62 than during 1963–66. But the average rate of expansion of money over this period of rising reserves as a whole is roughly equal to its rate of expansion during 1951–58, when no over-all trend of increase of external reserves existed. In these years, the only variable whose pattern of movement appeared to be similar to that observed for it in earlier years was the Bank of France's total domestic assets (and as part of it, the Bank's lending to commercial banks): it remained stable during the rapid increase of external reserves, while it increased substantially in the earlier period in which no over-all increase of reserves took place. This is yet another demonstration of the generally negative correlation between the two parts of the central bank's assets.

The conclusion that emerges is that monetary policy during this period was not meant to adjust the upward imbalance of payments. Nor does fiscal policy seem to have been used for this purpose: the budgetary deficit for these years was, on the average, smaller even in absolute terms than in the earlier period. Claims of alternative targets which have been examined do not seem to explain this lack of response of the policy variables. It is conceivable, of course, that other target variables, not observed here, could provide the explanation. But it seems more likely that the continuous and substantial accumulation of reserves during the 1960's was not considered a disturbance which should be corrected. It might even have been regarded as a desirable target. The fact that the rates of expansion of money and credit appear to be roughly correlated with the rate of accumulation of external reserves gives added credibility to the assumption that a high rate of accumulation of reserves was indeed a policy target during these years.

In this connection mention should be made of the French devaluations of 1957 and 1958. Both, unlike the changes in the rate of exchange in Germany and the Netherlands in 1961, were rather substantial: the first, taken in a few steps during the latter half of 1957, brought the rate of exchange from 350 to 420 (old) francs per dollar —an increase of 20 per cent; and the second, taken at the very end of 1958, raised the rate further to 490 francs per dollar—an increase of about 17 per cent. The first devaluation was taken at a time when external reserves were very low and still falling rapidly, and at about the same time as a contractionary monetary policy was undertaken. It may certainly be regarded as intended to adjust the balance of payments. The second devaluation, on the other hand, came at a period in which a balance had already been achieved. This devaluation might have been due to a fear that stability was only temporary and further deterioration likely. While this is a possible explanation, it is not supported by the fact that, by that time, discount policy had already become expansionary. It seems more likely that the devaluation was in fact caused by the low *level* of reserves, and was intended to raise that level. It may have been related also to the need to insure the success of external convertibility, undertaken in conjunction with devaluation.

The situation in France during the 1960's is thus very similar to that of Germany during the 1950's: the two countries may be said to have exchanged their roles around the late 1950's. In both situations, a devaluation (in Germany, that of 1949) is followed by a substantial, long, and uninterrupted accumulation of reserves; by the yardstick of maintenance of equilibrium in the balance of payments, the currency is undervalued. Yet no policy is undertaken to reverse this situation, apparently because it seems desirable. It may also be mentioned that a remarkable similarity exists between the situation in France during the 1960's and from 1926 to the early 1930's.[4] In 1926, too, the rate of exchange was determined (following a period of a fluctuating rate) at too high a level, and reserves started to accumulate rapidly.[5] Thus, as in the 1960's, this accumulation was apparently deemed desirable, and possibly even intended when the rate of exchange was determined.

References

Banque de France, *Compte Rendu des Operations,* annual, Paris, 1887–1966.

Berger, Pierre, "Interest Rates in France," *Banca Nazionale del Lavoro Quarterly Review,* Vol. 17 (September, 1964), pp. 263–95.

Organization for Economic Cooperation and Development, *Economic Surveys: France,* annual, Paris. Reports for 1953–61 issued by the Organization for European Economic Cooperation.

Wilson, J. S. G., "Post-War Monetary Policy in France," *Banca Nazionale del Lavoro Quarterly Review,* Vol. 8 (March, 1955), pp. 16–29.

[4] See Nurkse, *op. cit. passim.*

[5] Even the developments of the composition of reserves seem to be similar, in a very rough way, in the two episodes: first came a rise in both foreign exchange and gold; then the former stabilized, but not the latter; eventually, the amount of foreign-exchange was reduced, while the amount of gold kept rising at a rapid rate.

CHAPTER 6   GERMANY

1. Policy Instruments

Monetary policy in Germany is conducted by the Deutsche Bundesbank, which was established by the Bank Act of July 1957. The Bundesbank is headed by a Central Bank Council, which consists of its president, the vice president, and the presidents of the Central Banks in the states (*Länder*). All of these are appointed by the President of the Federal Republic. The *Länder* Central Banks are, in fact, branches of the Bundesbank. Before 1957, central banking in Germany was conducted by the *Bank Deutscher Länder* (BDL), which was established in November 1948. This bank differed somewhat in concept from its successor by having a more decentralized structure. It was conceived as the coordinating body of the *Länder* Central Banks, and its president was elected by their directors. However, the differences in mode of operation between the Bundesbank and its predecessor, the BDL, were of minor significance.

The Bundesbank is autonomous, and is not subject to any direction by the federal government. The 1957 Bank Act provides for participation of government representatives, without voting rights, in meetings of the Bundesbank Council, and of the Bundesbank president in the government's deliberations on monetary policy. But the Bundesbank is not bound in any way by the government, nor is it committed to fulfill any government request or requirement. The Bundesbank does, of course, act as the government's banking agent. The federal government and the *Länder* are committed to hold their deposits at the Bundesbank, and may hold deposits at other banks only with the Bundesbank's consent. Under this provision the Bundesbank has granted the *Länder* governments rights to hold deposits, within specified quotas, at certain financial institutions. The Bundesbank is entitled to grant the federal government, the *Länder,* and certain public special funds short-term credits within quotas specified in the Bank Act, but is not committed to extend these credits. Decisions on credits within the quotas are made at the Bundesbank's discretion.

The Bundesbank has at its disposal all of the major conventional tools of monetary policy and has used them extensively. These instruments will be surveyed here briefly.

Discount Rate. The bank buys and sells short-term bills (up to three months), which fulfill certain requirements, at the fixed discount rate. These include, among others, Treasury bills and bills issued by the *Länder* or other public authorities. The discount rate has in fact been uniform, at any given point of time, for all the bills; but the Bank, in principle, has the right to discriminate among various categories of bills.

The Bank also makes loans to commercial banks against the collateral of government bills and bonds or other debentures listed by the Bank at an interest rate usually 1 per cent above the discount rate. Lending in this form is not automatic; it is presumably intended to meet short-term liquidity gaps at the commercial banks. The interest rate charged by banks on loans to their customers is tied by law to the discount rate, which it cannot exceed by more than a specified percentage. As long as the difference between the two rates is this maximum, any reduction of the discount rate leads directly to an equivalent reduction in the interest rate charged by banks on their lending (although this would not necessarily hold true for an increase). Often, however, the gap between the two rates is less than the specified maximum, so that the effect of discount rate changes on rates charged by the banks is not automatic and is less direct.

The Bank is entitled, and has consistently used its rights, to specify a maximum rediscount quota for each individual bank. This quota is usually determined on the basis of the bank's capital: it is a certain coefficient of the size of the capital, but the coefficient may vary among classes of banks. The Bank has used changes in this coefficient, and thus in the individual quotas, as an instrument of monetary policy on a number of occasions.

Open-Market Operations. The Bundesbank is entitled to buy and sell all the bills eligible for rediscounting at the Bank, as well as other bills or bonds issued by the federal government, the *Länder,* and other public authorities, and also private bonds quoted on the stock exchange.

In fact, open-market operations were of minor significance in the earlier years, since the central bank (at that time, the BDL) had had almost no portfolio of marketable securities. By mid-1955, however, the central bank reached an agreement with the government, which in 1957 was incorporated in the Bank Act, putting a substantial amount of such securities at the Bank's disposal. This was done by transforming the character of the "equalization claims," i.e., the Bank's claims on the government resulting from the Bank's assumption of the government's obligations toward the commercial banks—obligations which originated in the currency reform of 1948. Originally, these claims carried an interest rate of 3 per cent, and could be sold only at their nominal value; in fact, this provision meant that the claims were not marketable. The agreement under consideration freed the Bank to sell (and buy) these claims at other prices. The claims, which subsequently became known also as the "mobilization paper," originally amounted to some eight billion marks. Open-market operations, which since 1956 have assumed large proportions, have been conducted primarily in this paper.

An agreement between the Bank and the commercial banks leads, in fact, to excluding the nonbank private sector from participation in the market for the paper in which the Bank's open-market transactions are conducted; that is, open-market operations are made only between the Bank and commercial banks, without any immediate effect on the nonbank sector.

An important attribute of open-market operations in Germany is that the Bundesbank directly determines not quantity but *price* in these transactions. The Bank specifies an interest rate—that is, by implication, prices of securities—at which the Bank is willing to buy or sell eligible securities offered to it or demanded from it. The interest rate varies, as a rule, with the length of maturity of the security (mobilization paper has been issued with various maturities). This, of course, is a procedure quite similar to determining the Bank's discount rate. Indeed, the open-market rate has, as a rule, been quite close to the discount rate; but variations in the open-market posted rate have been much more frequent than in the discount rate.

Reserve Requirements. Minimum reserve requirements have been in effect since 1948, and are incorporated in the Bank Act of 1957. The Bundesbank is entitled to require that the commercial banks hold reserves in the form of current balances at the Bundesbank. The requirements may vary among classes of banks and according to the type of liability against which reserves are held. The maximum ratios provided for in the act were 30 per cent for sight deposits, 20 per cent for time deposits, and 10 per cent for savings deposits. In addition to the distinction as to the type of liabilities, the Bundesbank requirements distinguish between banks in "bank places"—that is, places in which branches of the Bundesbank are located—and other banks; the former are subject to higher reserve requirements. Likewise, banks are divided into six categories according to the size of their liabilities; the larger the bank, the higher the reserve requirements. The number of different reserve-ratio requirements existing at any moment of time is, thus, quite substantial (approximately fifteen to twenty). As a rule, this structure moves in a coordinated way, and the proportional differences among the various ratios remain about constant.

Most of the time, reserve requirements were put on an average (or total) basis for each class of bank and liability. During a short period, however, marginal reserve ratios were added. In July 1960, all increases in liabilities above their average level of March–May 1960 were subject to the maximum-reserve requirements, while liabilities of the average size of March–May 1960 were subject to lower requirements. This situation lasted until December 1960, when the marginal reserve requirements were withdrawn.

Shortages of reserves are subject to penalty rates of 3 per cent above the rate in force for the Bank's advances against collateral. This means, as a rule, an interest rate 4 per cent over the discount rate.

Changes in reserve requirements were made about as often as they were in the discount rate; they were, thus, much less frequent than variations in the Bank's open-market rates. It seems that the Bundesbank regarded open-market operations as the main instrument for effecting gradual changes in bank liquidity and in interest rates; while changes in the discount rate and in reserve-ratio requirements were made at longer intervals as a means of consolidating and reinforcing the effect of open-market operations.

Reserve requirements were used by the Bundesbank on a few occasions to influence directly commercial banks' policy toward holding assets or borrowing abroad. This was done by subjecting foreign deposits in German banks, and the latter's borrowings from abroad, to special reserve requirements and by varying these requirements. Likewise, German banks' holdings abroad were regarded as a reserve asset held against liabilities to foreigners on a number of occasions when the Bundesbank considered short-term investments of German banks abroad to be desirable.

FISCAL POLICY

For most purposes of analyzing fiscal policy in Germany, the category "government" should include the *Länder* as well as the federal government. The reason is that the budgets of these two bodies are quite closely integrated, particularly on the revenue side. The German constitution specifies the allocation of the various tax revenues. In some cases (such as the business tax), all tax proceeds belong to the *Länder*. In others, they belong to the federal government. The proceeds of the income tax are divided between the two—about two-thirds to the *Länder* and one-third to the federal government. In addition, revenues are reallocated among the *Länder*—those with higher tax proceeds transfer part of their revenues to the others. Likewise, most of the tax laws of each *Land* have to be approved by the appropriate federal bodies. All of this would indicate the need to add the *Länder* to the federal government in discussions of budgets and budgetary policy.

In the federal government, budgetary policy is left in the hands of the executive branch to a probably greater extent than in most other Western countries. The Cabinet (and within it the Chancellor and the Minister of Finance) has a veto power over budgetary decisions. The executive branch's leeway is particularly large in "negative" acts; that is, the Cabinet is quite free not to make certain expenditures, or not to raise revenue from certain taxes, even though it is entitled to do so by the budgetary law of that year.

The federal budget is divided into "ordinary" (above the line) and "extraordinary" (below the line) components. In principle, "ordinary" budget expenditures should be covered by tax revenues, while expenditures of the "extraordinary" budget could be covered by loans as long as they result in the acquisition of "self-liquidating" assets. In fact, this requirement is interpreted in a way which puts very few restrictions on the type of expenditures in the latter budget. Yet, the declared policy of the German government has been to maintain a (cash) balance of the overall budget; and this indeed has been the policy over long stretches of time.

2. Statistical Analysis

Table 6-1 divides the period into subperiods according to the balance-of-payments fluctuations. The subperiods are determined by both the

TABLE

GERMANY: MOVEMENTS OF POLICY VARIABLES

Subperiod	External Reserves	Discount Rate	Open-Market Rate	Reserve Ratio Requirements
	(1)	(2)	(3)	(4)
III 1950 – I 1951	fall	+ raised	a	+ raised
I 1951 – III 1951	rise	* stable	a	* stable
III 1951 – I 1952	fall	* stable	a	* stable
I 1952 – IV 1958	rise	* fluctuates	* fluctuates	* fluctuates
IV 1958 – III 1959	fall	* fluctuates	* fluctuates	* stable
III 1959 – II 1961	rise	* fluctuates	* fluctuates	– raised
II 1961 – I 1962	fall	* stable	– lowered	– lowered
I 1962 – I 1963	stable	stable	raised	stable
I 1963 – II 1964	rise	* stable	* stable	* stable
II 1964 – I 1966	fall	+ raised	+ raised	* fluctuates
I 1966 – IV 1966	rise	– raised	– raised	+ lowered

NOTE: For explanation of symbols, see Chapter 3, explanatory note.

series of foreign exchange reserves and, since 1958, by balance-of-payments surpluses or deficits. By and large, the two series give the same indications for the years covered by both. Sometimes, the two may differ by one quarter in their indication of the turning point. In the very few cases of clear conflict between the two series, the turning point was selected by reference to the series of balance-of-payments surpluses and deficits.

It will be immediately observed that one subperiod covers about half of the whole period: from the beginning of 1952 to the end of 1958, balance-of-payments surpluses persisted. The discussion will turn later to a separate examination of these years.

A look, first, at the discount rate (column 2) shows clearly that this instrument has not been used generally for balance-of-payments adjustment. In only two downward imbalances, the one following the outbreak of the Korean War and the one which started in mid-1964,

6-1

DURING SUBPERIODS OF IMBALANCES

Central Bank Claims on Commercial Banks	Central Bank Net Claims on Government	Central-Bank Total Domestic Claims	Commercial Bank Lending to Public (quarterly rate of increase, per cent)	Money Supply (quarterly rate of increase, per cent)	Budgetary Balance (quarterly average, in billions of marks)
(5)	(6)	(7)	(8)	(9)	(10)
− rise	* stable	− rise	(+) 9.6	(+) 2.0	n.a.
+ rise	* stable	* stable	(−) 6.7	(+) 5.0	−.33
+ fall	+ fall	+ fall	(−) 8.0	(*) 4.2	(+) +.13
* fluctuate	− fall	− fall	(−) 4.4	(−) 2.8	(−) +.12
* stable	− rise	− rise	(*) 3.5	(*) 2.6	(−) −1.73
* fluctuate	− fall	− fall	(*) 4.1	(−) 2.0	(−) −.05
− rise	− rise	− rise	(+) 2.4	(−) 2.8	(−) −.28
rise	fluctuate	fluctuate	4.2	1.7	−.49
* fluctuate	+ rise	+ rise	(−) 3.0	(*) 2.0	(*) −.57
− rise	− rise	− rise	(*) 3.1	(*) 1.9	(+) −.35
* fluctuate	+ rise	* fluctuate	(−) 2.1	(−) .1	(+) −.55

n.a. = not available.   a = not applicable.

was the discount rate manipulated in the direction that balance-of-payments adjustment would require. During the other imbalances, the discount rate was either kept stable or moved in both directions within each subperiod of imbalance.

The posted rate for open-market operations (column 3) shows much the same behavior. Again, in one recent imbalance only—the downward movement of mid-1964 to early 1966—this rate changed in the direction required for balance-of-payments adjustment. Thus, open-market operations do not appear to have been intended to serve generally the target of balance-of-payments equilibrium.

The same impression is conveyed by the fluctuations of reserve-ratio requirements, which are shown in column 4. Once more, only during 1950–51 and during one recent period (1966) did reserve-ratio requirements move in the direction necessary for adjustment.

It thus appears that all the three major direct instruments at the disposal of the German Central Bank—changes of the discount rate, open-market operations, and changes of minimum reserve-ratio requirements—have not been used, as a rule, for balance-of-payments adjustment. There are only two instances which may be exceptions, i.e., the downward disturbances of late 1950 and early 1951 and of mid-1964 to early 1966.

Looking at the policy variables which involve the Central Bank's assets, similar indications appear, perhaps even more strongly. Central Bank lending to the commercial banking system (represented in column 5 of Table 6-1) appears to be unrelated to balance-of-payments fluctuations. Central Bank net lending to the government (in column 6) seems to move less often in the direction required for balance-of-payments adjustment than in the opposite direction. Changes in this category are mainly due, in the case of Germany, not to changes in the Central Bank's gross lending to the government but to changes in the amount of government deposits at the Central Bank. As may be seen by comparing column 6 with column 10 (or the appropriate lines in Chart 6-1) fluctuations in the Central Bank's net lending to the government are to some extent related to the government's budgetary surpluses and deficits. But the correlation is not perfect due to the reflection of two other factors aside from the budgetary balance in the size of the government's net indebtedness to the Bank; namely, open-market operations and the distribution of government deposits between the Bank and other banks.

Since the Bank's lending to commercial banks does not move in conformity with the requirements of balance-of-payments adjustment, while net lending to the government moves most often in the direction opposite to these requirements, the Bank's total domestic assets—the combination of these two—most of the time moves counter to the requirements of balance-of-payments adjustment. This is shown in column 7 of Table 6-1. According to the Nurkse yardstick, Germany is thus seen to follow a pattern of monetary policy, during the sub-periods under observation, opposite to what the classical "rules of the game" would require.

Commercial bank lending (shown in column 8) does not seem to vary in any consistent way with imbalances of payments. In only two instances—the downward imbalances of III 1950–I 1951 and II 1961–I 1962—did the rate of credit expansion change in conformity with the requirements for balance-of-payments adjustment: it was considerably below the rate in the preceding period and, in the latter episode, also

CHART 6-1

GERMANY: TIME SERIES OF SELECTED VARIABLES

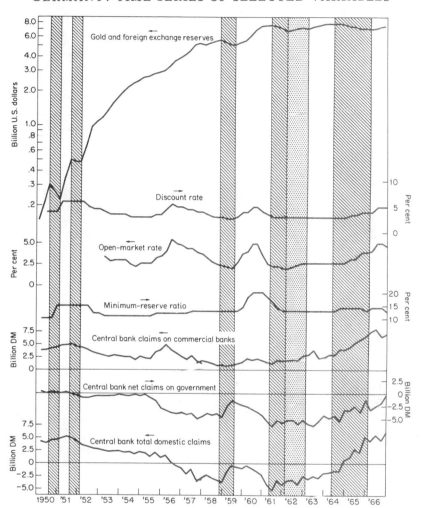

in the succeeding period, in which external reserves increased. In other instances, no such adjusting movements can be observed. Thus it may be deduced that the amount of credit (or, more precisely, its rate of expansion) was not manipulated in accordance with the requirements for balance-of-payments adjustment.

The rate of expansion of money supply (represented in column 9)

CHART 6-1 (*Concluded*)

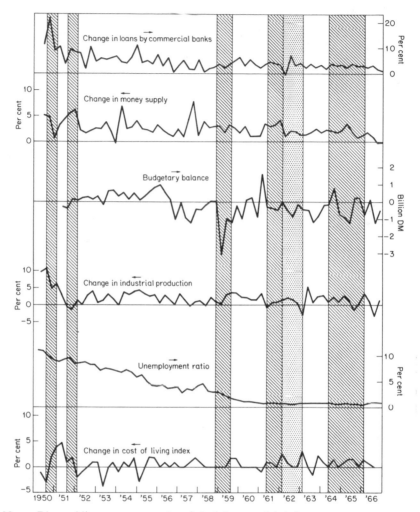

NOTE: Diagonal-line areas represent period of downward imbalances; gray areas represent stability; white areas represent upward imbalances.

gives a similar indication. This rate is quite stable most of the time, and the modest changes in it move as often in the adjusting direction as in the opposite. Thus, although it cannot be argued that money supply changed consistently in a disadjusting direction, it seems fairly obvious that this variable did not move, in any general way, in the direction required for balance-of-payments adjustment. By this yardstick too, monetary policy in Germany did not conform to the classical "rules of the game."

Turning finally to the fiscal area, the conclusions are similar. As may be seen from column 10 of Table 6-1, the budgetary (cash) balance did not fluctuate in any consistent way with imbalances of payments. Moreover, it should be added that the balances (surpluses or deficits) were in general too small, in comparision with components such as the GNP, changes in external reserves, etc., to be expected to have any appreciable effect on the economy. It is thus most probable that budgetary balances were not manipulated at all as a means of achieving either balance-of-payments adjustments or any of the other major economic targets.

We now turn to the period of continually rising external reserves, from early 1952 to the end of 1958. Let us examine a few critical policy variables for this period to see whether their behavior is consistent with the assumption that they were manipulated in accordance with the requirements of balance-of-payments adjustment. These variables are: (1) the direct monetary instruments—the discount rate, the open-market rate, and the minimum-reserve ratios; (2) the rate of expansion of money supply; (3) the budgetary balance.

To assist in balance-of-payments adjustment, the discount rate, the open-market rate, and the minimum-reserve ratio would have to move downward during a period of accumulating reserves. Such a movement did not, in fact, take place—or if it did, was only slight—as may be seen from Chart 6-1. The discount rate went down from 1952 to 1954, up from 1955 to mid-1956, and down again until mid-1959. The open-market posted rate moved in close relationship to the movements of the discount rate. The required reserve ratio was much more stable than the former two rates. It went slightly down in 1952–53; and up in 1955–57; over-all, it can probably be regarded as having been stable during the years under review. By this evidence, therefore, these three monetary variables are found to have played a neutral role, on the average, with regard to balance-of-payments adjustment: they were manipulated neither in the direction required for adjustment nor in the opposite direction.

The rate of expansion in the money supply conveys a similar impression. This rate was, on the average, much lower during 1952–58 than during 1950–51 and only slightly higher than during 1959–65. On the other hand, balance-of-payments adjustment policy would have required this rate to be particularly high during 1952–58. Taking into account the fact that the GNP's rate of increase has shown a downward trend, a fact which may account for a desire on the part of the monetary authority to slow down the expansion of money supply gradually, it cannot be argued that money supply was manipulated in a way which would conflict with the need for balance-of-payments adjustment. However, the evidence certainly would not support the opposite assumption, i.e., that the supply moved in a way consistent with the requirements for balance-of-payments adjustment during 1952–58.

The budgetary balance, as may again be seen from Chart 6-1, gives a similar indication. From 1952 to mid-1956, the budget had a consistent surplus—in fact, only in a single quarter (ii 1953) was this not the case. From mid-1956 to the end of 1958, the budget had mostly deficits. For the period under review as a whole, the budgetary balance was positive, while for the following years—1959–65—the budget had deficits during most of the time and a net deficit for those years as a whole. The substantial budgetary surplus for 1952–55—at least for most of the period—is alleged to have arisen accidentally.[1] It may well be so, but this would still not contradict the conclusion that during a period in which balance-of-payments adjustment would have required a budgetary deficit, the budget showed, in fact, mostly a surplus. It may thus be inferred that budgetary policy during the period 1952–58 was not employed as an instrument of balance-of-payments adjustment.

Thus, during 1952–58 neither monetary policy nor budgetary policy seem to have been manipulated in a way consistent with balance-of-payments requirements. The over-all finding which emerges is that monetary instruments and the budget were, by and large, not employed in Germany for balance-of-payments adjustment during the period covered in the present study.

Were these instruments used, instead, to achieve alternative targets? An attempt to analyze this question will be made with the aid of the

[1] This is the famous "Juliusturm," or the "Julius Tower" war chest. It resulted, allegedly, from the accumulation during the early 1950's of funds intended to finance Germany's participation in the planned European Defense Community—a plan which was eventually scrapped. It is hard to believe that the German authorities indeed based their policy on a rule which says that surpluses should be created during certain years in order to finance deficits in later years, without regard to the effects of the surpluses and deficits at the time in which they are manipulated. It is possible, on the other hand, that in each of these individual years actual military expenditures were lower than had been anticipated and provided for in the budget, thus leading to a surplus.

reference cycle method. Here, the "cycle" is determined by fluctuations of the policy variable; and movements of each target variable are examined separately to see whether any of them could explain the cyclical pattern of the policy variable. This will not be done for the budgetary variable; as was mentioned before, the size of the budgetary balance—surplus or deficit—appears to be rather small most of the time, and it is apparently not meaningful to discuss "cycles" of this variable. The reference cycle analysis will be confined, thus, to the direct monetary instruments: the discount rate, the open-market rate, and the minimum-reserve ratio. These show a clear "cyclical" pattern, and the question analyzed is whether this pattern can be associated with the movement of any target variable. The reference dates will therefore be determined by the turning points of these policy variables. As was mentioned before, and as may be verified again by observing Chart 6-1, these three rates fluctuated in close coordination; very rarely did they move in opposing directions. This makes it possible to define a combined reference cycle for all three instruments. The turning points, or reference dates, will be determined, whenever just one variable moves while the others are stable, by that variable which moved. The trough of such a cycle will be at the point in which the discount rate, the open-market rate, and the minimum-reserve ratio are at their lowest; while the peak will occur when they are at their highest. The results are shown in Chart 6-2, where the behavior of each of the alternative target variables —the balance of payments, the price level, the unemployment rate, and the rate of expansion in industrial production—is shown along the reference cycles. The turning points of these cycles are as follows:

Period	Trough	Peak	Trough
1950–54	IV 1950	I 1952	III 1954
1954–59	III 1954	II 1956	II 1959
1959–62	II 1959	III 1960	I 1962
1962–66	I 1962	III 1966	

Chart 6-2, Part A, shows the movement of external reserves. As could be expected from the previous analysis, no regularity can be seen here. Conformity with balance-of-payments adjustment would require this variable to fall during the trough-to-peak phase—that is, where the discount rate and the other rates are rising—and to rise during the peak-to-trough phase. In fact, nothing resembling such a pattern can be discerned.

It may be worthwhile to examine alternative definitions of the

CHART 6-2

GERMANY: PATTERNS OF TARGET VARIABLES DURING
MONETARY POLICY CYCLES

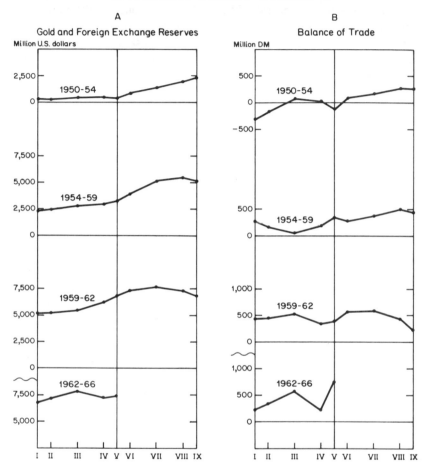

balance-of-payments target in order to see whether they can give a better clue to policy measures than the simple change in external reserves (that is, the simple balance-of-payments surplus or deficit as these are usually defined). Thus, it is conceivable that monetary measures were taken in reaction not to changes in the balance of payments as a whole, but to movements in the trade account alone. This is examined in Chart 6-2, Part B, where the balance of trade (in goods) is

CHART 6-2 (*Continued*)

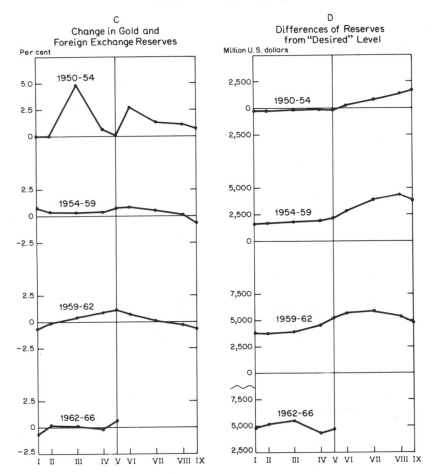

C
Change in Gold and
Foreign Exchange Reserves

D
Differences of Reserves
from "Desired" Level

represented. Again, no regular pattern appears. This balance was continuously positive after about mid-1952. An assumption that movements of this variable determined the directon of movement of the policy variables would require the balance to have been negative along the trough-to-peak phase, or at least to be lower than during the peak-to-trough phase, when it would be expected to be higher and rising. In fact, no such regular pattern could be observed.

Another possibility is that it was not the direction of change (i.e., rise or fall) of external reserves which guided policy measures, but the

CHART 6-2 (*Continued*)

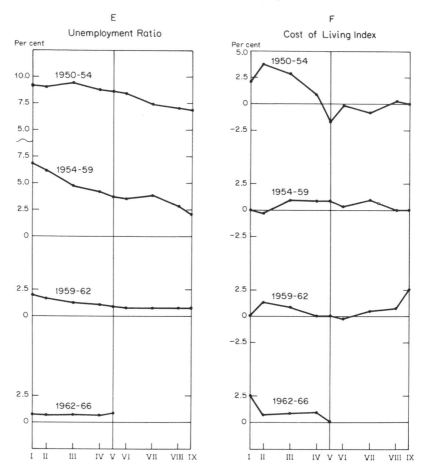

E

Unemployment Ratio

F

Cost of Living Index

rate of their change. That is, it may be assumed that whenever the rate of increase in reserves accelerated, monetary policy became restrictive. This assumption is examined in Chart 6-2, Part C. By the evidence of this chart, it must be rejected. In fact, for part of the period the opposite is true: from the peak of the 1954–59 cycle (that is, from mid-1956) the rate of increase of reserves goes down during the downward phase and up during the rising phase of the 1959–62 cycle. That is, when the rate of increase of external reserves falls, monetary policy becomes more expansive rather than more restrictive.

Still another possibility which may deserve examination is that the

CHART 6-2 *(Concluded)*

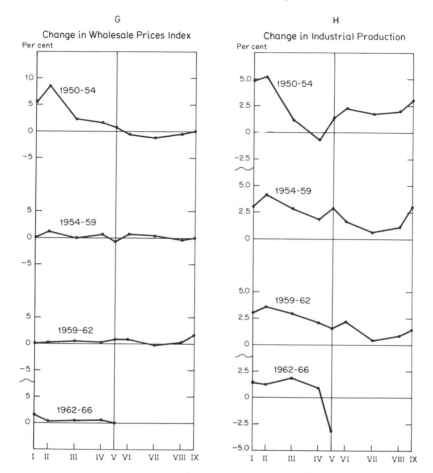

G

Change in Wholesale Prices Index

Per cent

H

Change in Industrial Production

Per cent

German authorities paid attention not to the actual movement of external reserves but to the divergence in the size of reserves from some desired level. This "desired" level could be determined by a probably infinite amount of assumptions, or models. The two simplest assumptions would be: (1) that the "desired" level is that indicated by the trend (which, in turn, can be identified in a variety of ways—a moving average, a linear or log-linear regression, etc.); or (2) that the "desired" size of reserves is a given proportion of imports (or of current transactions). The assumption of a "desired" level of reserves was tested only by the use of the latter variant. This is done in Chart 6-2,

Part D. "Desired" reserves were assumed to be a constant proportion of annual imports of goods, equal to the average of 1950–51. Discrepancies between the actual level of reserves and the "desired" level are represented in this chart.

It appears, from Chart 6-2, Part D, that in this sense, i.e., compared with "desired" level, reserves were increasing throughout most of the period; that is, the ratio of external reserves to imports increased continuously. This process went on almost without interruption until 1961. It thus cannot be maintained that monetary policy was designed to preserve a stable ratio of external reserves to imports. On the other hand, it may also be seen that until the middle of the trough-to-peak phase of the 1959–62 policy cycle—that is, until 1960—the excess of actual reserves over the "desired" level tended to rise more slowly during the trough-to-peak than in the opposite phases. This would be consistent with an assumption that during the 1950's a given rate of continuous rise in the ratio of external reserves was desired and that monetary policy became restrictive when this rate was not achieved, whereas it became expansionary when it was exceeded.

In Chart 6-2, Part E, the target of high employment is examined. The unemployment rate appears, from this chart (as from even a casual look at Chart 6-1), to be continuously and markedly falling throughout the period. However, no consistent association between this movement and the cycles of monetary measures can be distinguished. It thus does not appear that monetary policy was geared to this target. It may also be mentioned in this connection that the large budgetary surpluses observed during most of the first half of the 1950's were achieved at a time of high unemployment, so that it cannot be assumed that budgetary policy was employed in pursuance of the target of full or high employment.

In Chart 6-2, Parts F and G, the stable price level target is examined. This is done by using the rates of change in the cost of living and wholesale price indexes, respectively. These rates showed considerable fluctuations only at the beginning of the period, during the Korean crisis and shortly afterwards, while for most of the remaining period the price level appears quite stable. The rates of change in the indexes, in particular of wholesale prices, are quite close to zero and do not fluctuate greatly. What is particularly relevant, however, is the apparent lack of any cyclical regularity. Had monetary policy been intended to maintain price stability, we would expect to find a relatively high rate of price increase during the trough-to-peak phase—that is, when monetary policy becomes restrictive— and the opposite during the peak-to-trough phase. In fact, no such regularity appears at all in the two parts of the chart. Oddly, the cyclical patterns of 1954–59 and 1959–62, especially with regard to the cost of living index, even appear almost as mirror opposites of each other.

The target of a high rate of growth, as measured by the rate of increase of industrial production, is examined in Chart 6-2, Part H. Here some pattern appears, which may indicate a responsiveness of monetary policy to this target. Industrial production seems to rise faster during the trough-to-peak than during the peak-to-trough phase; that is, monetary policy would appear to be restrictive during periods of a high rate of increase of industrial production and expansive during periods of a low rate. This relationship would improve further if some time lag in responsiveness is allowed. It thus seems possible, from this evidence, that monetary policy was directed by the requirements of a high, stable rate of growth.[2]

3. Summary and Interpretation

From the preceding analysis, it seems quite safe to conclude that monetary policy—as well as budgetary policy—was not as a rule directed in Germany toward balance-of-payments adjustment, although scattered instances of possible responsiveness of monetary policy to imbalances of payments may be found.

In part, this lack of general responsiveness could probably be explained by the assignment of monetary policy to the service of other targets. Thus, the evidence seems to suggest a possible consistency of the movements of monetary policy with the requirements of high, stable rate of growth, when the latter is represented by the rate of expansion of industrial production. It should be noticed, on the other hand, that no general association of the direction of monetary policy with the unemployment position may be discerned.

It is possible, also, that part of the explanation of the mode of be-

[2] A similar impression is gained from the observation of cycles of industrial production, as they appear in a current NBER study by Ilse Mintz. These cycles were determined by the relationship of the actual level of industrial production to its trend level. Monetary policy during most of the period seems to be associated fairly well with these cycles, in a counter-cyclical direction.

havior of monetary policy could not be revealed by the present method of analysis. A potential deficiency of this method, it will be recalled, is its failure to distinguish between realized and anticipated values. Thus, if avoiding fluctuations of a certain magnitude is the purpose of policy measures, and these fluctuations are correctly anticipated and successfully averted, the data would not show correlations of policy measures with movements in the target. In the case of Germany, something of this sort may have occurred for price stability. According to frequent and emphatic statements of German policy makers, price stability has been by far the most important target of monetary policy in Germany during the period under review. The present investigation does not show this: no consistent reaction of monetary policy to changes in the degree of price stability can be detected. This may conceivably be due to the fact that price increases were anticipated accurately, and counteracting policies were taken quickly and decisively enough to prevent these anticipated increases from materializing. The virtually complete stability of prices from 1952 to 1957 might be explained in this way, for instance. It is, of course, very difficult to test such an assumption rigorously, since the process by which policy makers' anticipations were formed is not likely to be easily uncovered. It should be recalled, however, that price fluctuations were not entirely absent. On a number of occasions, price increases were large enough and persistent enough to suggest that further price rises must have been anticipated at those periods; and yet, no restrictive monetary measures are found to have been taken consistently in such periods. A prime example is the period from early 1961 to mid-1962, when monetary policy was expansive despite a relatively high rate of price increase—particularly in the cost of living.

Longer-term observations, on the other hand, lend more credibility to the opinion that price stability was indeed a prime target. In Chart 6-3 , movements of the two price levels (wholesale and cost of living) in Germany are compared with the movements of price levels (arithmetic unweighted averages) in an aggregate of eleven countries—the Group of Ten and Switzerland. It is immediately apparent that prices in Germany tended to rise considerably less than the average—although this holds true more for consumer prices than for wholesale prices, and applies more to the first half of the period studied than to the latter half. In the first half of the period, up until around 1957–58, the rate of unemployment in Germany was particularly high (though

CHART 6-3

GERMANY: COMPARISONS OF PRICE MOVEMENTS

Index (1950=100)

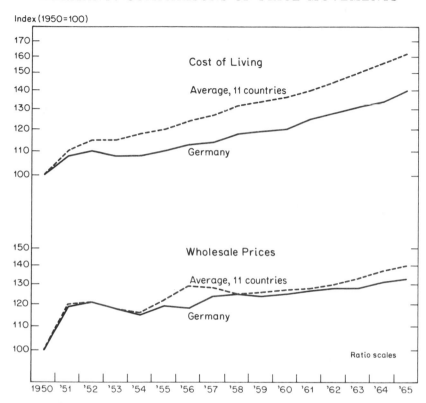

declining), and the accumulation of external reserves persisted throughout these years. Had either full employment or balance-of-payments equilibrium been the overwhelming target, expansionary monetary and fiscal measures would have been called for; the fact that such measures were not taken suggests that during these years, at least, price stability was a major target in Germany. In other words, it seems probable, by this evidence, that monetary and budgetary policy would have been more expansive throughout the 1950's had not the maintenance of price stability been a prime target for policy makers in Germany. Thus, for instance, the discount rate and other interest rates would have been expected to be generally lower had it not been for this target. At the same time, the evidence examined earlier suggests that in formulating changes in short-term monetary and budgetary policy the preservation of stable prices was not invariably, or even in the majority of instances, the guiding rule.

This analysis was carried somewhat beyond the immediate question of balance-of-payments adjustment. In the light of its mainly negative and inconclusive results, it is time to ask again what *was* the balance-of-payments policy in Germany. The probable answer seems to be, in summary form, as follows.

In the devaluation cycle of September 1949, Germany—although not devaluing the mark to the same extent as the British pound was devalued—established an exchange rate which proved later to have been higher than the rate required for balance-of-payments equilibrium. Thus, for most of the following decade, Germany's balance of payments showed a persistent surplus, and external reserves accumulated. There was no attempt to counteract this accumulation owing, presumably, to two considerations. First, starting from a low level of reserves and realizing a fast growth in the amount of trade, Germany must have regarded the increase in reserves as desirable. Second, a policy to correct imbalances of payments would have called for price increases, while the maintenance of price stability must have been regarded a prime target in view of Germany's earlier inflationary experience. At the same time, temporary downward movements of reserves in the late 1950's were not a cause for major concern in view of the large size of reserves, and thus did not call necessarily for an adjusting policy. This largely "neutral" policy was changed in the early 1960's. At that time, the relatively high level of interest rates in Germany, combined with expectations for revaluation of the mark which were formed by the persistent German surpluses, attracted large amounts of short-term capital from abroad. Monetary policy reacted first in a restrictive way, that is, in a disadjusting direction. At that stage, however, such a policy was self-defeating, since the increased interest rates acted more to increase liquidity by attracting more foreign capital than they contributed to the reduction of liquidity by reducing domestic borrowing. Also, foreign resistance to the persistent large-scale accumulation of reserves in Germany became much more severe than it had been earlier. In late 1960, as a result, monetary policy was changed in the expansive direction required for balance-of-payments adjustment. In March 1961, this was combined with an upward revaluation of the mark by 5 per cent. In the following years, policy reaction to upward disturbances mainly took the form of special measures intended to influence capital movements—that is, to discourage the flow of capital to Germany—such as the tax on income from German bonds held by foreigners, which was announced in 1964. Balance-of-payments adjustment does not appear to have been a major target in these years either: an accumulation of reserves still does not seem to be considered a disturbance, while temporary falls in reserves were not of major concern due to their high level. The assumption of policy makers in Germany appears to have been that income and price developments independent of Germany's monetary policy, and in particular developments in Germany's major trading partners, would restore equilibrium to Germany's balance of payments before an unduly large decline of reserves took place. Over-all monetary and fiscal policy thus has not been primarily tied to balance-of-payments requirements.

References

Bank for International Settlements, Monetary and Economic Department, *Germany: Monetary and Economic Developments 1955–1961,* Basle, 1965.

Boarman, Patrick M., *Germany's Economic Dilemma: Inflation and Balance of Payments,* New Haven, 1964.

Deutsche Bundesbank, *Monthly Report,* Frankfurt (Main), 1951–66. Until July 1957, issued under the bank's previous name: *Bank Deutscher Länder.*

Deutsche Bundesbank, *Report,* annual, Frankfurt (Main), 1949–66. Until 1957 issued under the bank's previous name: *Bank Deutscher Länder.*

Emmer, R. E., "West German Monetary Policy 1948–54," *Journal of Political Economy,* Vol. 63 (February, 1955), pp. 52–69.

Hein, J., "The Mainsprings of German Monetary Policy," *Economia Internazionale,* Vol. 27 (May, 1964), pp. 317–24.

———, "Monetary Policy and External Convertibility: The German Experience, 1959–61," *Economia Internazionale,* Vol. 27 (August, 1964), pp. 517–31.

Organization for Economic Cooperation and Development, *Economic Surveys: Germany,* annual, Paris. Reports for 1953–61 issued by the Organization for European Economic Cooperation.

Reuss, Frederick G., *Fiscal Policy for Growth Without Inflation: The German Experience,* Baltimore, 1963.

Robertson, W., "The Problem of Adjustment in West Germany's Balance of Payments," *Banca Nazionale del Lavoro Quarterly Review*. Vol. 10 (December, 1957), pp. 451–74.

U.S. Embassy, Germany, *Handbook of Economic Statistics, Federal Republic of Germany and Western Sectors of Berlin*, monthly, Bonn, April, 1955.

Wallich, Henry C., *Mainsprings of the German Revival*, New Haven, 1955.

CHAPTER 7  ITALY

1. Policy Instruments

The Bank of Italy, the country's central bank, is formally among the least independent of those studied in its conduct of monetary policy. All important policy decisions are made by an Interministerial Committee, chaired by the Minister of the Treasury and including other Ministers and the Governor of the Bank of Italy. But the execution of the Committee's decisions in monetary matters is then left to the Bank. And, in fact, the Governor of the Bank is reputed to have a major impact on the direction of policy, in part since, as will be noted shortly, monetary policy in Italy is conducted essentially by day-to-day decisions, made primarily by the Bank.

The Bank of Italy makes very little use of the three "classical" instruments of monetary policy—the discount rate, minimum-reserve requirements, and open-market operations. The discount rate was reduced a few times during the period from the end of World War II to 1950. From early 1950 to 1966, however, the rate was changed only once: in June 1958 it was lowered from 4 to 3.5 per cent. Minimum-reserve ratios were introduced in 1947 at the level of 25 per cent; since then, the rate has been changed only once—in early 1962, it was lowered to 22.5 per cent. The Bank of Italy rarely conducts open-market operations in the usual sense. As will be noted shortly, however, a few other instruments used by the Bank and the Treasury are similar to open-market operations, but these, too, are used only sporadically. The Bank of Italy thus relies mostly on instruments such as those described below, which most other central banks would consider subsidiary.

Bank Lending to Commercial Banks. As has just been noted, the Bank of Italy did not try to use the discount rate—which remained practically stable throughout—to affect the amount of lending to commercial banks. But the Bank is not committed to rediscount bills for the commercial banks or to make advances to them. This is left to the Bank's discretion, and it has varied the amount of lending to commercial banks according to its over-all view of monetary policy.

The amount of rediscounting done by the Bank of Italy (excluding "storage" or "crop" bills, which will be mentioned later) is usually quite small; advances against securities are larger, but still not very substantial. Total lending by the Bank to commercial banks is thus small, but variations have on occasion been large in relation to the total and may have played at least some role.

Control of Commercial-Bank Lending. The Bank of Italy's approval is required for any single loan exceeding a given proportion of a commercial bank's capital. The Bank thus maintains a certain measure of direct control over the amount of lending by commercial banks to their customers. This apparently affects mainly the smaller banks whose limited capital often makes them subject to the *fidi eccedenti* provision. It is chiefly the larger institutions, on the other hand, that are subject to the "moral suasion" exercised by the Governor of the Bank of Italy on the commercial banks, and the two approaches thus tend to complement each other. The Bank of Italy is reported to use these means on occasion to influence the development of commercial-bank lending, though in neither case can one measure the impact.

Foreign-Exchange Transactions. Since the late 1950's (and probably, to a small extent, even earlier), the Bank of Italy has used foreign-exchange transactions with the commercial banks as an instrument of monetary policy. In their effect on the banking system's liquidity, these transactions are the equivalent of open-market operations, the difference being only that the transaction is in foreign exchange rather than government securities or other domestic paper. As a means of restricting monetary expansion, the Bank of Italy offers commercial banks favorable terms for the purchase of foreign-exchange spot from the Bank against its commitment to a forward purchase from the commercial bank. The latter can then use the foreign exchange so acquired for lending in the local market or in foreign markets, for increasing its foreign-exchange holdings, or for reducing the amount of its short-term borrowings abroad. Its domestic liquid resources will decline by the amount of foreign exchange purchased—which is, in turn, equal to the improvement in its net foreign-exchange position. This may be reinforced by a direct restriction of the amount of commercial-bank borrowing from abroad.

BUDGETARY POLICY AND THE TREASURY'S FINANCIAL ACTIVITY

Besides having a larger influence, at least formally, on the central bank's conduct of monetary policy than in most other countries, the Treasury in Italy also exerts an extensive monetary impact by its own financial transactions.

The cash budget in Italy has shown a deficit almost without interruption during the period. This deficit is financed primarily by sales of government securities to all other domestic sectors—the public, commercial banks, and the Bank of Italy—and by postal savings.

Commercial banks buy two types of Treasury paper, the short-term Treasury bill and longer-term government securities. Treasury bills are held by commercial banks as part of their reserves, since the minimum reserve regulations specify either Treasury bills or deposits at the Bank of Italy as reserves; a generally smaller amount is held as "free" Treasury bills, those beyond the amount calculated as part of their reserves.

Commercial banks, along with the public, also buy longer-term government securities, which the Treasury puts on the market mostly at the beginning of the year, when banks are as a rule particularly liquid. The placement of these securities may be regarded as having, in part, the function of an open-market operation designed to eliminate excess liquidity, since in determining the amount to be sold, the Treasury is said to have weighed, on occasion, the liquidity position of the commercial banks against what the Treasury (and the Bank of Italy, which technically works as the Treasury's agent) would like it to be.

The Treasury borrows a significant amount from the Bank of Italy, and its outstanding total has been growing over the long run. It consists of several items: One is current advances, which may reach a legal maximum of 15 per cent of the budget's current expenditures. Another is the "extraordinary" advances that were created during the war and the early postwar years. The outstanding amount did not change throughout the 1950's, but from 1960 on, the government has been repaying these advances gradually. A third is advances in foreign exchange, which, technically, are received from the Foreign Exchange Office, but essentially are a form of net borrowing from the Bank of Italy.

The Bank of Italy also rediscounts "crop bills." These are issued by governmental storage agencies, which supposedly buy the crops, mainly wheat, at harvest time for storage. This is a form of government subsidy, since very often the eventual sale price is below what the storage agencies pay for the crop. While the crop bills are issued to commercial banks, which technically finance the transaction, the bills are eligible for automatic rediscounting at the Bank of Italy and as a rule are rediscounted promptly. In effect the crop bills are a means of governmental borrowing from the Bank of Italy, in which commercial banks play only an intermediary role.

Finally, the Bank of Italy buys Treasury bills as a counterpart to the deposits which commercial banks hold at the Bank as part of their legal reserves, although the two are not exactly equal—the amount of Treasury bills is normally smaller than the amount of commercial-bank deposits. The Bank of Italy may also hold Treasury bills in larger amounts and without any relationship to reserve requirements; there are no legal restrictions on the amount of Treasury bills which it may buy.

Variations in the amount of Treasury bills held by the Bank of Italy may represent merely a substitution of no real significance for monetary aggregates. Commercial banks, it should be recalled, may hold their reserves either as deposits at the Bank of Italy or in the form of Treasury bills. If they decide to switch from deposits to Treasury bills, this will induce the Bank of Italy to reduce the amount of Treasury bills which it holds as a counterpart to commercial bank deposits (which have now declined). But the reduction does not represent, in this case, any change either in governmental borrowing or in the size of commercial-bank liquidity. It merely indicates a transfer of the holding of Treasury bills from the central bank to commercial banks, and its impact is restricted to its effect on their profits. Such a process indeed took place in 1959 and 1960, when all the Treasury bills held by the Bank of Italy as counterpart for commercial-bank reserves disappeared.

2. Statistical Analysis

Chart 7-1 presents the policy variables that appear, from the foregoing discussion, to be most relevant for balance-of-payments adjustment,

CHART 7-1

ITALY: TIME SERIES OF SELECTED VARIABLES

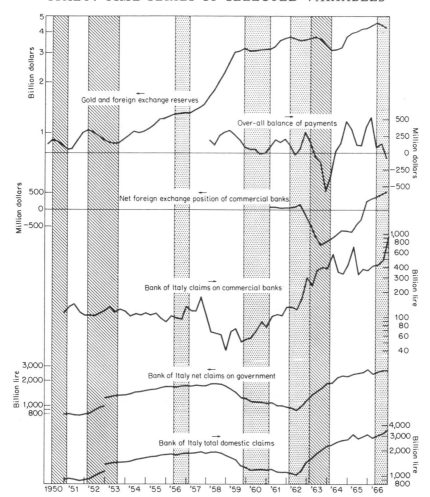

along with indicators of balance-of-payments disturbances [1] and other potential target variables. Table 7-1 provides a summary description of the behavior of policy variables during subperiods delineated by balance-of-payments developments.

[1] Since balance-of-payments movements reveal an obvious seasonal pattern, data on external reserves and the over-all balance of payments had to be seasonally adjusted.

CHART 7-1 (*Concluded*)

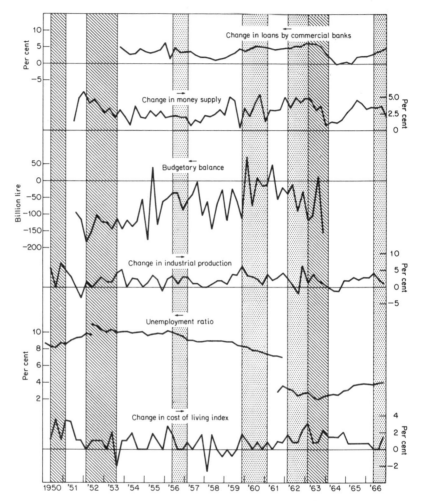

NOTE: Diagonal-line areas represent period of downward imbalances; gray areas represent stability; white areas represent upward imbalances.

It was usually not difficult to determine subperiods, since movements of external reserves show a pattern which other evidence does not contradict. For one period, however, I 1962–I 1963, the evidence is mixed; since this episode is of particular importance, as will be pointed out later, the determination of turning points within it merits some discussion. For the first quarter of 1962, all the relevant (deseasonalized) data

TABLE 7-1

ITALY: MOVEMENTS OF POLICY VARIABLES DURING SUBPERIODS OF IMBALANCES

Subperiod	External Reserve (1)	Bank-of-Italy Lending to Banks (2)	Net Foreign Exchange Position of Commercial Banks (3)	Bank-of-Italy Lending to Government (4)	Bank-of-Italy Total Domestic Claims (5)	Change in Commercial Bank Credit (quarterly average, per cent) (6)	Change in Money Supply (quarterly average, per cent) (7)	Budgetary Balance (quarterly average, in billions of lire) (8)
II 1950 – I 1951	fall	n.a.	n.a.	n.a.	n.a.	n.a.	n.a.	n.a.
I 1951 – I 1952	rise	* stable	n.a.	* stable	* stable	n.a.	+4.1	−130
I 1952 – III 1953	fall	* stable	n.a.	– rises	– rise	n.a.	(+) +3.2	(*) −126
III 1953 – II 1956	rise	* stable	n.a.	+ rises	+ rise	+4.1	(–) +2.3	(–) −87
II 1956 – I 1957	stable	rises	n.a.	stable	stable	+3.5	+1.6	−59
I 1957 – IV 1959	rise	– falls	n.a.	– falls	– fall	(–) +2.4	(+) +2.5	(*) −68
IV 1959 – I 1961	stable	rises	rises	falls	fall	+4.9	+3.3	−3
I 1961 – I 1962	rise	+ rises	* stable	– falls	– fall	(*) +4.6	(+) +3.9	(*) −15
I 1962 – I 1963	stable	rises	falls	rises	rise	+5.7	+4.7	−62
I 1963 – I 1964	fall	– rises	– falls	– rises	– rise	(+) +3.9	(+) +2.2	(–) −80
I 1964 – II 1966	rise	n.a.	– rises	+ rises	n.a.	(–) +1.1	(+) +2.9	n.a.

NOTE: For explanation of symbols, see Chapter 3, explanatory note.   n.a. = not available.

point clearly to a continuation of the balance-of-payments surpluses of 1961. In the second quarter, a small deficit occurred, and some analyses give mid-1962 as the turning point from which to date the start of the large deficit which ran through 1963. Later in 1962, however, a substantial surplus reappeared. For the year from the second quarter of 1962 to the first quarter of 1963, taken as an aggregate, the following phenomena may be noted: Foreign-exchange reserves remained about stable.[2] The balance of payments (on the "official settlements" definition explained in Chapter 2, Section 6) shows a considerable over-all surplus of about $500 million. All this surplus, however, may be explained by a deterioration of the net foreign-exchange position of commercial banks (that is, by commercial-bank short-term borrowing abroad), which amounted to some $600 million and which was most probably not regarded, by the government or by others, as a permanent feature or a "normal" source of receipts from abroad. It is thus likely that this was a period of neither a deficit nor a surplus but of approximate over-all balance.[3] In the second quarter of 1963, on the other hand, a change is obvious; external reserves are stable, but balance-of-payments data show a deficit in spite of a further deterioration in the net foreign-exchange position of commercial banks. This quarter may therefore be regarded as the beginning of the downward movement which was intensified during the next three quarters. The imbalance came to an end in the second quarter of 1964, in which external reserves remained about stable, and a slight over-all surplus appeared in the balance of payments despite a reduction of commercial-bank borrowing from abroad.

The subperiods are defined in Table 7-1, where the direction of imbalances is indicated in column 1. Changes in the Bank of Italy's lending to commercial banks are noted in column 2. As is readily apparent from Chart 7-1, this variable was rather stable and quite small until the beginning of 1957. During those earlier years, this variable seems to have been neither responsive to balance-of-payments developments nor very significant for any other purpose. In later years, the

[2] This is based on data from *International Financial Statistics,* the source of foreign-exchange reserve statistics used most often in this study. However, data from the *Bolletino della Banca D'Italia* show a substantial increase, and seem to be more consistent with balance-of-payments estimates.

[3] When the net foreign-exchange position of commercial banks is added to official reserves, a substantial decline of the combined magnitude appears during the year under consideration; this may be judged from Chart 7-1. But, once more, if the figures on reserves taken from *International Financial Statistics* are replaced by those reported in the *Bolletino,* most of this decline would disappear.

Bank of Italy's lending to commercial banks shows a tendency, although not a very consistent one, to move in a direction opposite to balance-of-payments developments, that is, in a disadjusting manner. It also assumed, toward the end of the period, a more substantial size. An examination of long periods reinforces the impression that its movements were opposite in direction to those of external reserves. From mid-1953 onward, two longer-term periods may be distinguished: until the end of 1959, a very strong rising trend in external reserves was maintained, while from then on the upward trend, although still present, was only slight. The Bank of Italy's lending to commercial banks was small and falling slightly during the first of these periods, whereas in the second it manifested a strong upward trend. It should be noted that in the subperiod from early 1963 to early 1964—the only episode of an actual, substantial fall of reserves since 1953—lending to commercial banks kept growing.

Column 3 of Table 7-1 relates to the net foreign-exchange position of commercial banks. Data for this variable are not available for years prior to 1959, a period in which the variable was apparently not very significant. Since then, this variable, too, generally moves in a disadjusting direction, but not very consistently. The subperiod of downward imbalance from I 1963 to I 1964 again deserves particular attention. In the first two quarters of this subperiod, the variable in question continued an earlier downward movement. This movement, in a direction opposite to the movement of external reserves, is in line with the general pattern of the net foreign-exchange position of commercial banks, and may be explained by the banks' desire to offset, by borrowing abroad, the effect of balance-of-payments developments on their liquid reserves. In the last two quarters of the subperiod, on the other hand, the variable rises, although not to the full extent of its decline in the first two quarters. This is explained by deliberate measures taken by the Bank of Italy to restrict borrowing abroad and to encourage the banks to hold foreign exchange. This episode, during the period of downward imbalance, is the only major occasion when the variable in question was manipulated in a direction consistent with balance-of-payments adjustment.

In column 4 movements of the Bank of Italy's net lending to the government are described.[4] Since these are found to be very similar, in

---

[4] In addition to a series of the government's net indebtedness to the central bank defined in a way similar to that applied in other cases, two other series have been constructed. One excludes the Treasury bills held by the Bank of Italy as counterpart to commercial-bank deposits at the Bank. Going in the opposite

direction of movement, whether or not Treasury bills obtained as a "counterpart" to commercial-bank deposits are included, only the former alternative is represented in Chart 7-1. It appears that no general, clear association of movements of this variable with balance-of-payments movements may be established. As may be seen from Chart 7-1, the amount of this lending tended to rise, slightly but consistently, from 1951 to mid-1958; to fall from then to mid-1962; and to rise quite strongly from that point to the end of the period. Each of these three periods included episodes of surpluses, deficits and stability of the balance of payments, without any apparent effect of these fluctuations on the trend of development of the debt. From the evidence of column 4, some tendency of the variables in question to move in a disadjusting direction may be detected; but the evidence is not very strong.

When Treasury bills held by commercial banks are added to the government's debt to the Bank of Italy (a series not represented in Chart 7-1), the trends of developments are found to be slightly different; the variable seems now to be stable, rather than to fall, between 1958 and 1962. But the conclusion that movements of this variable appear to be generally unrelated to balance-of-payments developments, or probably tend only slightly to move in a disadjusting direction, remains valid.

This is also largely true of the Bank of Italy's total domestic assets, as may be seen from column 5. This variable is dominated by the Bank's lending to the government and moves in much the same way. The inclusion of the Bank's lending to commercial banks—which, as has been noted, tends to move in a disadjusting direction—matters little for the movements of the Bank's total assets. The latter reveal, at best, a slight tendency to move in a direction opposite to movements of the balance of payments.

The rate of expansion of commercial-bank lending to the public is given in column 6. There and in Chart 7-1, it may be seen that, while the rate fluctuated during the period surveyed, these fluctuations cannot be associated in any consistent way with those of the balance of

direction, a series is also constructed which includes *all* Treasury bills, whether held by the Bank of Italy or by the commercial banks. While the fraction which is held by commercial banks does not, of course, form a part of the government's indebtedness to the Bank of Italy, it has an effect identical with central-bank lending in its impact upon commercial-bank reserves. As an indication of the influence of government finance on commercial-bank reserves, the observation of this combined magnitude may be helpful.

payments. Only during the downward disturbance from 1 1963 to 1 1964 did the movement of the rate, which declined considerably, conform closely to the requirements of balance-of-payments adjustment. The rate remained very low, however, after this episode, apparently not as a result of any policy decision but due to a lack of demand for bank credit.

On the other hand, as may be seen from column 7 of Table 7-1 and from Chart 7-1, money supply did move in an adjusting direction as required by balance-of-payments developments. The association is not perfect, but its existence seems certain, and it is consistent over the period as a whole. Every deterioration of the balance-of-payments position is accompanied by a clear tendency of the rate of expansion of money supply to fall; and with almost every upward turning of the country's external reserves, an upward movement appears also in the rate of expansion of money supply.

Finally, none of the budgetary variables—revenues, expenditures, or the budgetary balance—appear to be associated with the balance of payments. For the budgetary balance this may be seen from Chart 7-1, and from column 8 of Table 7-1. The budgetary deficit is rather stable during 1951–54; it then declines gradually, to the point of complete disappearance, between 1955 and 1960, and rises again between 1961 and 1963, the latest year for which data on this variable are available. None of these trends can be explained by balance-of-payments developments.

The general lack of association between most policy variables and balance-of-payments tendencies probably cannot be explained by assuming that these policy instruments were used to achieve some other major economic targets—price stability, high employment, or a high rate of growth. The price level appears not to be increasing throughout most of the time, at least from 1951 to 1961; this holds true both for the cost-of-living index, which is shown in Chart 7-1, and even more so for the index of wholesale prices, which actually declined during these years. The unemployment ratio appears to be rather high, declining gradually but only slightly, until mid-1959, and then somewhat more rapidly until mid-1963. Here, too, none of these developments seem to have any consistent effect on movements of policy variables. From mid-1963 to the end of 1965 unemployment was rising—and the discussion will shortly return to this experience. The index of industrial production, plotted in Chart 7-1, appears to have been rising at a fairly steady and high rate. Significant dips in the rate of increase of production may be observed only for the periods from mid-1951 to mid-1952, from mid-1957 to mid-1958, and from mid-1963 to late 1964. For the first of these periods information about most policy variables is missing; the second appears to leave no impact on policy variables; and the third will now, again, be discussed separately.

The period extending from early 1963 to mid-1964 seems, from the foregoing review, to be an episode of major interest for an examination of the conduct of policy in Italy. During that episode all trend lines were broken: the balance of payments turned from surplus to deficit; prices, stable at most other times, rose considerably; unemployment changed its course and started climbing; and the rate of expansion of industrial production, stable and high most of the time, not only declined but even became negative for a brief period. These are, of course, developments of a contradictory nature, with opposite claims on the use of policy instruments: the first two targets, balance-of-payments equilibrium and price stability, would call for restrictive policies; while the other two—high employment and high growth—would call for expansionary measures. The timing of these conflicting developments did not coincide precisely, but at least for part of this period, during late 1963 and early 1964, the contradiction is clear. It may be interesting to note, therefore, in which directions the different policy variables moved in response to these conflicting demands.

On the whole, financial policy seems to have been restrictive during this episode, as would be required for balance-of-payments equilibrium and price stability. But the pattern is far from clear-cut. As the major restrictive movement, the drop in the rate of expansion of money supply may be cited. This would have been the outcome of the fall in external reserves alone, but it was also helped by a very substantial decline of the rate of expansion of credit. The latter, again, would have resulted merely from the fall in commercial-bank reserves due to the fall of the country's external reserves; but it was also affected by other policy variables—and here the evidence is mixed. On the one hand, the net foreign-exchange position of commercial banks improved significantly, most probably due to the Bank of Italy's specific actions; this is a restrictive measure, which reduces banks' reserves and lending capacity. On the other hand, lending by the Bank of Italy to commercial banks increased. Similarly, lending by the Bank to the government, which affects both money supply directly and commercial-bank reserves, also expanded. From this evidence, it is not clear at all whether the Bank of Italy (and the government) tried to reinforce the restrictive impact of the balance-of-payments deficit on money and credit supply, or to neutralize it. It is conceivable that the conflicting demands of the various targets pulled monetary policy in both directions and led to inconsistencies. Unfortunately, data for the budgetary variables are missing for part of this crucial period. From the available evidence, the budgetary balance appears to have tended during this episode toward increasing deficits—an expansionary measure. This may be, again, part of a general inconsistency. But it may also be due to a decision to use monetary measures in a restrictive way, to serve the needs of balance-of-payments and price stability, and, at the same time, to use budgetary policy in the opposite way, to combat unemployment and the slack in production. This would also explain the increase in the Bank of Italy's lending to the government. But the nature and duration of the evidence would make such an explanation, at best, speculative.

3. Summary and Interpretation

Italy appears to be a country in which monetary policy was subject, to a larger extent than in most other countries, to automatic mechanisms. The reserve ratio for commercial banks and the discount rate were maintained virtually unchanged throughout the period. Other policy variables employed by the monetary authorities, though not stable, do not appear to have been used in accordance with some overriding rules —either in order to adjust the balance of payments or to serve other major policy targets. As a result, money supply (that is, its rate of expansion) was, by and large, allowed to fluctuate in the same direction as foreign-exchange reserves. The impact of the latter on the former tended to be neutralized, to some extent, by an offsetting recourse of commercial banks to borrowing from the central bank when reserves fell, and by the redemption of the debt when reserves rose. But this tendency was much less consistent, and much less important, than in most other countries. Another partly offsetting factor was the tendency of commercial banks to increase their short-term borrowing from abroad as a substitute for the liquidity acquired by external reserves, when the latter failed to rise. This was quantitatively more important than the former factor; but it, too, was not very consistent, and played a part only from the late 1950's.

From mid-1953 to the end of 1959, the balance of payments was consistently in surplus, often a very substantial one. Evidently, the automatic impact of external reserves on the money supply was not sufficient to lead to a full adjustment during this period. Had this adjustment been desired, a reinforcing of the automatic mechanism would have been called for. The lack of a deliberate policy in that direction would thus indicate that the accumulation of reserves was considered a desirable feature rather than a disturbance calling for correction.

This impression gains support from the single major episode in which external reserves declined—namely, the period from early 1963 to early 1964. Although the level of reserves was by that time very high in relation to earlier years and to other relevant economic magnitudes (such as the level of imports, or the GNP), deliberate policy measures were taken this time in an adjusting direction. This was done by a reduction, directed by the Bank of Italy, of the commercial banks' foreign indebtedness and of the rate of increase in their credit to the public. During at least the greater part of this episode, the restrictive policy measures were taken in spite of a slack in domestic activity. It would thus seem that, in a time of deficit, the requirements for balance-of-payments adjustment were given priority over domestic targets.

Other analyses of the Italian economy indicate that budgetary policy was considered a major tool in the service of long-term growth, used to increase the proportion of saving and investment and to affect the direction of investment. But this policy does not appear, from available data, to react to short-term fluctuations in the rate of expansion. The absence of the use of budgetary policy for balance-of-payments adjustment thus does not seem to be due to the appropriation of this policy instrument for the control of domestic activity. The only episode for which such an interpretation would seem plausible is that of 1963, when the budgetary deficit increased, while monetary policy was restrictive. This may have been due to the wish to use budgetary policy to combat the slack in economic activity, while monetary policy was assigned the role of adjusting the balance-of-payments deficit.

References

Baffi, P., "Monetary Analysis in Italy," *International Monetary Fund Staff Papers,* Vol. 5 (February, 1957), pp. 316–23.

————, "Monetary Developments in Italy from 1961 to 1965," *Banca Nazionale del Lavoro Quarterly Review,* Vol. 19 (March, 1966), pp. 18–41.

————, "Monetary Stability and Economic Development in Italy, 1946–1960," *Banca Nazionale del Lavoro Quarterly Review,* Vol. 56 (March, 1961), pp. 3–30.

Banca D'Italia, *Abridged Version of the Report,* annual, Rome, 1931–66.

Bank for International Settlements, Monetary and Economic Department, *Italy; Monetary and Economic Situation 1949–1958,* Basle, 1959.

Brovedani, Bruno, "On the Implementation of Monetary Programs: The Italian Case," *Banca Nazionale del Lavoro Quarterly Review,* Vol. 17 (June, 1964), pp. 130–59.

Carli, G., "The Italian Balance of Payments Problem," *Banca Nazionale del Lavoro Quarterly Review,* Vol. 6 (July–September, 1953), pp. 151–58.

Gambino, Amedeo, "The Control of Liquidity in Italy," *Banca Nazionale del Lavoro Quarterly Review,* Vol. 52 (March, 1960), pp. 3–23.

Hildebrand, George H., *Growth and Structure in the Economy of Modern Italy,* Cambridge, Mass., 1965.

Istituto Centrale di Statistica, *Bolletino Mensile di Statistica,* monthly, Rome, 1925–66.

Masera, F., "International Movements of Bank Funds and Monetary Policy in Italy," *Banca Nazionale del Lavoro Quarterly Review,* Vol. 19 (December, 1966), pp. 328–45.

Menichella, Donato, "The Contribution of the Banking System to Monetary Equilibrium and Economic Stability," *Banca Nazionale del Lavoro Quarterly Review,* Vols. 36–37 (January–June, 1956), pp. 5–21.

Modigliani, F., and La Malfa, G., "Inflation, Balance of Payments Deficit and Their Cure through Monetary Policy: The Italian Example," *Banca Nazionale del Lavoro Quarterly Review,* Vol. 20 (March, 1967), pp. 3–47.

Organization for Economic Cooperation and Development, *Economic Surveys: Italy,* annual, Paris. Reports for 1953–61 issued by the Organization for European Economic Cooperation.

Pietranera, G., "The Crisis in the Italian Balance of Trade," *Banca Nazionale del Lavoro Quarterly Review,* Vol. 6 (January–March, 1953), pp. 44–61.

U.S. Embassy—Rome Economic Section, *Statistical Bulletin,* annual, Rome, 1965–66.

CHAPTER 8  JAPAN

1. Policy Instruments

Monetary policy is conducted primarily by the Bank of Japan in cooperation with, or subject to the approval of, the Ministry of Finance. Commercial banking institutions in Japan are of various types; some private, others established and run by the government; some of a general nature, others fulfilling specialized functions. The most important category of banks is that known as "All Banks," consisting of "City Banks," "Trust Banks" and "Long-Term Credit Banks"; in terms of the amount of loans or the size of deposits, these constitute over 80 per cent of the commercial banking system. Other categories of bank-type financial institutions are usually restricted in nature to rather narrow purposes. They include such institutions as agricultural or industrial cooperatives, credit associations, or investment corporations. Monetary policy is concerned, by and large, although not exclusively, with the category of "All Banks"—where, in turn, it affects primarily the large (and heavily concentrated) "City Banks." The following are the actual or potential instruments at the disposal of the Bank of Japan.

The Discount Rate. This is the major instrument used in the conduct of monetary policy in Japan. The rate, or rates, apply to bills discounted at the Bank of Japan and to advances against collateral from the Bank to commercial banks (there are usually no overdrafts on the Bank). These loans and discounts have been very important in Japan not only as a means of bridging temporary gaps in banks' reserves, as is customary elsewhere, but also as a major long-term (in effect) source of liquidity for the banking system. Since, as will be mentioned later, the government's budget has been approximately balanced for reasonably long periods of time and open-market operations are of minor importance, borrowing from the central bank is the only major source of additional banking liquidity beside the accumulation of foreign exchange reserves.

During most of the period under survey, the Bank of Japan applied a system of multiple discount rates. This was known as the "higher-interest-rate system." Each bank was allocated a quota of loans from the Bank of Japan, for which a low "basic" discount rate was in force. Above this quota a higher rate—the "first penalty rate"—came into effect. Sometimes a second margin of Bank of Japan lending was established, beyond which a still higher rate—the "second penalty rate"—was applied. Until August 1955, the basic discount rate was of practically no significance for monetary policy: loans to all the banks considerably exceeded their rationed quotas so that the first penalty rates, and very often the second, were the relevant rates for decisions at the margin. In August 1955, the basic rate was increased considerably and quotas were changed. From that date on, the basic rate became indeed the usually meaningful figure. Higher penalty rates were still applied even at later dates, but sparingly and in exceptional cases. In 1962, the system of "higher interest rates" was abolished altogether.

In addition to influencing the amount of banks' borrowing through changes in the discount rate, the Bank of Japan sometimes determines actual ceilings of the amounts lent to each individual bank. This is done in connection with rationing the credit granted by commercial banks to their customers, a practice which will be mentioned shortly.

Reserve Requirements. The minimum-reserve requirement instrument has been used only for the last few years and is still of minor significance. Traditionally, commercial banks in Japan have held practically no reserves beyond the cash used in day-to-day operations and small deposits at the Bank of Japan required for interbank clearing. In 1957, a law was passed which enabled the Bank of Japan to require the banks to hold reserves, in the form of deposits at the Bank of Japan, at a ratio not exceeding 10 per cent of the banks' deposits. In fact, reserve requirements were laid down for the first time in September 1959; the reserve ratios varied then according to the type of bank and the type of deposit, but they were all very low—around 1 per cent of bank deposits. Minimum-reserve ratios were raised slightly in October 1961 and again in December 1963; on the latter date, they reached .5 per cent of time deposits and 3 per cent of sight deposits. Apparently, these increases, besides being slight, were not considered as monetary measures intended to affect current monetary developments. As a rule, reserve requirements have thus not played any significant role; although toward the end of 1965, a reduction of legal reserve ratios (to virtually zero) was undertaken apparently as a means of encouraging monetary expansion.

Open-Market Operations. The instrument of open-market operations, as this term is normally understood, was not employed in Japan until recent years. This has been attributed to a number of factors, chief of which were the lack of a substantial organized capital market and a low pegging of rates on government securities. Occasionally, the Bank of Japan conducted a transaction in securities with a commercial bank, but this was usually a bilateral, ad hoc transaction—with a specific bank, in a specific security, and for a specified period. It was usually motivated by the desire to bail the bank concerned out of a particular difficulty or, conversely, to provide it with an outlet for a particularly large accumulation of reserves. It was not used as an instrument of over-all monetary policy.

Toward the end of the period (since 1963), open-market operations became more significant in size and probably a more integral part of over-all monetary policy; they are still, however, conducted in a bilateral manner rather than strictly in the open market.

Direct Credit Control. The Bank of Japan has maintained, with varying degrees of severity, a direct control on the amount of credit granted by each individual bank. In general, this has been an important instrument—in fact, the only significant tool of monetary policy aside from discount rate manipulations. Naturally, the use of this control is limited to periods when the banks wish to expand their loans more than the Bank of Japan is willing to allow: it cannot be used to encourage an expansion of credit. By and large, therefore, this instrument was relevant primarily when the monetary authorities were trying to limit, rather than encourage, the expansion of credit.

The control system was adopted in its present form in 1954. It operates not on a formal, legal basis but through "moral suasion" by the Bank of Japan and is known as the "discount-window operation," or "official guidance." Despite its informal character, it is extensive and rather detailed, particularly with regard to the few large "City Banks," and the "Long-Term Credit Banks." The Bank of Japan, in consultation with the banks, determines—at least at certain periods—the amount of credits that each can extend to the public in a month's time; it sometimes follows the actual development of the banks' accounts on a day-by-day basis. The Bank of Japan imposes its views both by moral suasion and by pressure and sanctions, either threatened or actually practiced. Sanctions include primarily a restriction of the amount of Bank of Japan lending to the "delinquent" bank; or, insofar as the banking system as a whole is concerned, a threat that discount rates will be further increased if the "voluntary" control proves to be ineffective.

FISCAL POLICY

The central government's budget consists of various accounts. The most important among these is the general account, which encompasses most of the normal government activities, both of a current and a capital nature. In addition, there are about forty "special accounts." These have widely different functions, sources of income, and types of expenditure. Some of them channel savings accumulated by governmental savings institutions or by the social security system into capital expenditures. A major "special account," from the standpoint of size, is the foodstuffs control program, which is essentially a form of subsidization of mass-consumed (and mass-produced) foodstuffs, primarily rice. Another major "special account" is the foreign exchange account. Strictly speaking, this is not a legitimate part of the government's budget but a reflection of the movement of foreign exchange in the country's foreign transactions. In Japan, as frequently happens in other countries with foreign exchange control, these transactions are handled formally through the Treasury.

In principle, the government adheres to a balanced-budget policy, and has indeed maintained a roughly balanced budget over the period as a whole. As a rule, the general account provides a surplus, which is transferred to some of the special accounts, thus maintaining an over-all balance. Over short periods, however—sometimes of a few years—deficits or surpluses do show up.

The budgetary procedure in Japan apparently does not allow a large measure of administrative flexibility. Supervision of the budgetary performance by the parliament (the Diet) is tight; rules are determined in advance for the annual budget without leaving much leeway in actual execution.

The government does not, as a rule, borrow much from the public (including the commercial banks). As mentioned earlier, interest rates on government bonds are pegged at a low level, considerably below comparable rates in the market. Likewise, the government does not normally deal in short-term borrowing from (or lending to) foreign countries. Budgetary cash surpluses and deficits are expressed, thus, mainly in changes in the government's indebtedness to the Bank of Japan.[1] The Bank is not restricted by law in its extension of credit to the government. It is, moreover, obligated to underwrite the government's short-term securities. The government itself, on the other hand, is legally denied the right to borrow at long term from the Bank of Japan or to sell long-term securities to it. In effect, the Bank of Japan's obligation to "underwrite" government securities implies that it has actually to buy these securities, since the public would not buy them under the conditions of their issuance; some securities are resold, however, to governmental agencies. In the earlier years of the period, a sizable portion of the government's indebtedness to the Bank of Japan took the form of loans. These later declined, and from about 1954 to 1961 loans to the government were nil or negligible in comparison with the amount of government bonds at the Bank. Since 1962, however, loans—this time in the form of debentures rather than advances—again became prominent.

2. Statistical Analysis

Data on changes in policy and target variables are presented in diagrammatic form in Chart 8-1. It appears that the series (not shown in the chart) of balance-of-payments surpluses and deficits since 1958 gives almost the same impression, so far as turning points in directions of movements are concerned, as the series of gold and foreign exchange reserves. It was therefore decided to take the latter—with minor modifications suggested by the former—as the indicator of imbalances of payments. An upward movement of this magnitude is considered an upward imbalance (that is, a balance-of-payments surplus), and a

---

[1] The word "cash" should be emphasized. "Accrued" obligations of the public to the government, or vice versa, are certainly widespread. It may also be mentioned that from time to time the government becomes indebted to commercial banks due to the latter's assumption of deferred government payments. For instance, food sudsidies may first be paid out by commercial banks, which are later reimbursed by the government.

CHART 8-1

JAPAN: TIME SERIES OF SELECTED VARIABLES

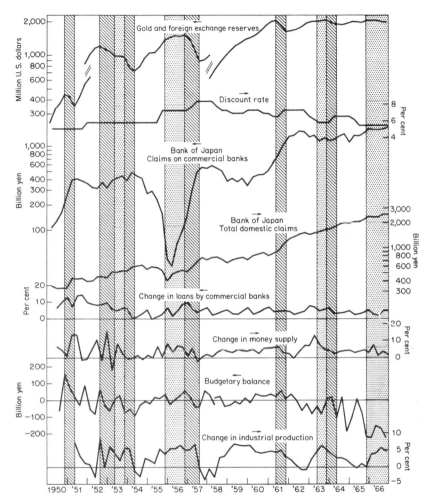

NOTE: Diagonal-line areas represent period of downward imbalances; gray areas represent stability; white areas represent upward imbalances.

downward movement is considered a downward imbalance. The subperiods are presented in the first column of Table 8-1.

Looking, first, at the discount rate (column 2 of Table 8-1), it is immediately apparent that this variable moved consistently—indeed with no exception—in an adjusting direction: the rate was raised when

TABLE 8–1

JAPAN: MOVEMENTS OF POLICY VARIABLES DURING SUBPERIODS OF IMBALANCES

Subperiod	External Reserves (Indication of Disturbance) (1)	Discount Rate (2)	Bank of Japan Claims on Commercial Banks (3)	Bank of Japan Total Domestic Claims (4)	Commercial Bank Lending to Public (quarterly rate of increase, per cent) (5)	Money Supply (quarterly rate of increase, per cent) (6)	Budgetary Balance (quarterly average, in billions of yen) (7)
II 1950 – IV 1950	rise	a	+ rise	* stable	11.5	3.0	+48
IV 1950 – II 1951	fall	a	– rise	– rise	(*) 10.5	(–) 14.4	(*) +46
II 1951 – III 1952	rise	a	* stable	+ rise	(**) 9.9	(–) 3.0	(+) –3
III 1952 – II 1953	fall	a	– rise	– rise	(+) 7.0	(–) 5.8	(–) –19
II 1953 – IV 1953	stable	a	stable	rise	6.2	.9	–20
IV 1953 – II 1954	fall	a	– rise	– rise	(+) .5	(+) .6	(–) –72
II 1954 – IV 1955	rise		– fall	– fall	(–) 3.0	(+) 2.7	(–) –2
IV 1955 – III 1956	stable	stable	rise	rise	6.2	(+) 4.6	(+) 13
III 1956 – IV 1957	fall	+ raised	– rise	– rise	(+) 4.8	.9	(–) –18
IV 1957 – II 1961	rise	++ reduced	* no trend	+ rise	(**) 4.4	(+) 4.1	(–) +8
II 1961 – IV 1961	fall	++ raised	– rise	– rise	(**) 4.7	(+) 2.8	(+) +33
IV 1961 – II 1963	rise	++ reduced	* no trend	+ rise	(**) 4.9	(+) 6.4	(+) –28
II 1963 – IV 1963	stable	stable	fall	rise	6.0	4.5	–38
IV 1963 – II 1964	fall	+ raised	– rise	– rise	(+) 3.1	(+) 2.7	(*) –40
II 1964 – IV 1965	rise	+ lowered	* no trend	+ rise	(*) 3.8	(*) 3.6	(+) –93
IV 1965 – IV 1966	stable	stable	stable	rise	3.4	3.5	(–) 193

NOTE: For explanation of symbols, see Chapter 3, explanatory note.   a = not applicable.

a downward imbalance of payments took place, and lowered in opposite instances.[2] The evidence thus suggests the tentative conclusion that discount-rate policy was used by the Bank of Japan as an instrument of balance-of-payments adjustment.

Next, in column 3 of Table 8-1, Bank of Japan lending to commercial banks is examined. Here a consistent pattern again appears, but in the opposite direction. These loans move regularly upward at times of a downward imbalance, and vice versa; these are, of course, movements which could augment imbalances rather than correct them. In the few exceptions to this pattern, the variable in question merely did not move, instead of moving in a disadjusting direction; only in one instance, the upward imbalance of 1950, did the variable actually move in a way consistent with balance-of-payments adjustment.

The fact that commercial bank borrowing from the central bank increased, as a rule, when the discount rate was raised, and diminished when the rate was lowered, may seem somewhat surprising. This relationship may be explained, however, in the light of concurrent changes in other variables. I will come back to this relationship after examining the other related variables.

The other component of the Bank of Japan's domestic claims is its net claims on the government. Unfortunately, the amount of such claims as they appear in the data is misleading, because the size of these claims is heavily affected, in a biased way, by foreign exchange movements. A decline in foreign exchange reserves, for instance, would usually, but not necessarily always, mean a (net) sale of foreign exchange (not drawn, most often, from the Bank) by the government's foreign exchange fund to the public. This, in turn, would increase the government's deposits at the Bank, or be used to redeem government debt to the Bank, thus reducing the government's net indebtedness to the Bank. An impression of a movement in an adjusting direction may thereby be created. But, in fact, the adjusting impact is that of the movement of foreign exchange itself, and recording its reflection in the government's accounts at the Bank would amount to double counting.[3]

[2] It should be recalled that data on discount rate variations are relevant, so far as the "basic" rate is concerned, only from August 1955 onward. Partial information on the manipulation of the "penalty rates" indicates, however, that discount rate variations were employed in an adjusting direction also during the downward imbalance of the first half of 1954 and of the following upward imbalance of mid-1954 to the end of 1955.

[3] From published sources, there does not seem to be a reliable way of separating the effect of the government's foreign exchange transactions from its other transactions.

In an indirect way, however, some conception of this variable can be gained by looking at the movements of the budgetary balance. As will be be recalled, the government conducts its financial transactions (other than those in foreign exchange) primarily with the Bank of Japan rather than with the public or with commercial banks. Movements of the variable under consideration are, thus, primarily the mirror reflection of the government's cash balance. It will be observed later that this balance does not show a consistent reaction to imbalances of payments throughout the period, and during the 1950's it may be regarded as having been changed most often in a disadjusting direction.

Due to the deficiency of the data on the Bank's net claims on the government, for the purpose at hand, the recorded magnitude of total domestic assets of the Bank may also be biased. However, it is not difficult to guess what an unbiased record would have shown. The budgetary balance, as has just been mentioned, usually did not tend to move in a way which would offset the movements of the Bank's claims on commercial banks: on the contrary, the two moved most often together in a disadjusting direction. It may therefore be quite safely assumed that had bias-free data on the Bank's total domestic claims existed, they would have shown consistent movements in a disadjusting direction. Moreover, even without the necessary correction (that is, including movements biased in an adjusting direction), the data give the same indication. This is shown in column 4 of Table 8-1, in which the frequency of movements in a disadjusting direction appears to be only slightly less than in column 3.

Loans of commercial banks to the public are represented in column 5 of Table 8-1. They increased continuously at a rather fast pace throughout the period under review, and the rate of increase appears to be rather stable over the subperiods of imbalances of payments. The rate does not seem to vary much among these periods; in the few instances where it does, the variations show no consistent tendency either in the adjusting direction or in its opposite.

Money supply, on the other hand, which may be observed in column 6, does seem to react to imbalances of payments in an adjusting direction at least from the beginning of 1954. From that period on, the rate of increase in money supply most of the time was less during periods of downward imbalances of payments, and greater during periods of upward imbalances.

Turning to the fiscal variables, it appears much more difficult to distinguish any consistent reaction to imbalances of payments. Both gov-

TABLE 8-2

JAPAN: REFERENCE DATES OF CYCLES
OF EXTERNAL RESERVES

Cycle	Trough	Peak	Trough
1951–54	II 1951	III 1952	II 1954
1954–57	II 1954	IV 1956	III 1957
1957–61	III 1957	II 1961	IV 1961
1961–64	IV 1961	IV 1963	III 1964

ernment revenues and expenditures show a clear long-term expansionary trend, as should be expected. However, the rate of increase, although not quite stable, does not seem to be associated with balance-of-payments fluctuations.[4] The budgetary cash balance, or the government's excess demand, is represented in column 7 of Table 8-1.[5] It appears that, for the period as a whole, no clear-cut pattern may be distinguished. However, during the 1950's, movements of the balance in a disadjusting direction do seem to dominate.

Let us now turn from the examination of subperiods of imbalances to the application of reference cycle analysis. External reserves indeed manifest, as may be observed from Chart 8-1, rather clear cyclical movements. The reference dates will be determined by the turning points of these cycles, which will be defined from trough to trough. An expansionary phase (from trough to peak) will thus be the phase of the cycle in which external reserves rise; and the contractionary phase, its opposite. The reference dates are shown in Table 8-2.

The positions of the policy variables during the reference-cycle stages are presented in Chart 8-2. In Part A, it may be seen that the discount rate moves almost invariably in a consistent pattern—it falls when external reserves rise (that is, along the stages from trough to peak), and rises when reserves fall. Bank of Japan claims on the public

[4] To save space, these variables are not shown in Table 8-1 and in Chart 8-1.

[5] Revenues and expenditures, and thus the budgetary balance, are compiled *net* of the foreign exchange account of the budget. The latter, as has been pointed out earlier, does not form a part of the government's excess demand; its inclusion would not only have distorted the budgetary accounts for the purpose at hand but also clearly introduced a bias in favor of movements in an adjusting direction.

From 1958 on, the budget is presented in this way in the source (International Financial Statistics). For earlier years, the exclusion of revenues and expenditures in the foreign exchange account was done by us.

CHART 8-2

JAPAN: PATTERNS OF POLICY VARIABLES DURING
BALANCE-OF-PAYMENTS CYCLES

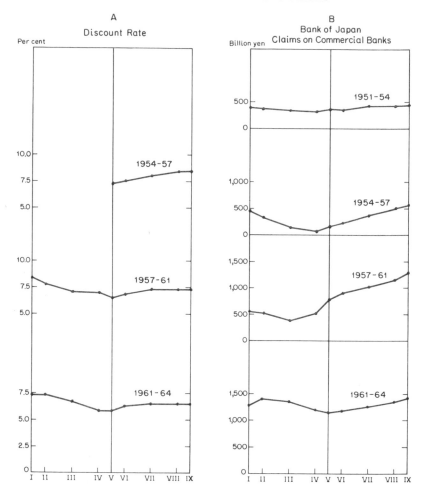

(i.e., on commercial banks), represented in Part B, also follow a generally consistent pattern—falling during the expansionary phase of the
cycle, and rising during the contraction. Total domestic assets of the
Bank of Japan, shown in Part C, reveal a weaker pattern: [6] during the

[6] But, here, the distorting effect of the inclusion of foreign exchange transactions of the government should be recalled.

CHART 8-2 (*Continued*)

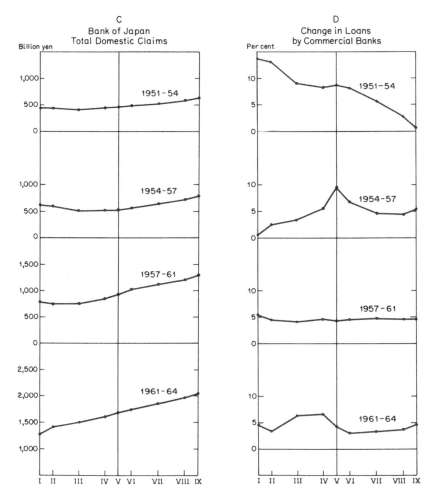

C
Bank of Japan
Total Domestic Claims
Billion yen

D
Change in Loans
by Commercial Banks
Per cent

expansionary phase, their level appears, as a rule, to be either falling or rising less fast than during the contractionary phase.

Commercial bank lending to the public, shown in Part D, shows a probably slight dependence on the stage of the foreign-exchange reserves cycle. Only during the cycle of II 1954–II 1957 does this manifest itself as clear-cut cyclical behavior—namely, an increase in the rate of expansion of credit when reserves rise, and a reduction of this rate when reserves fall. A similar but much weaker pattern appears

CHART 8-2 (*Concluded*)

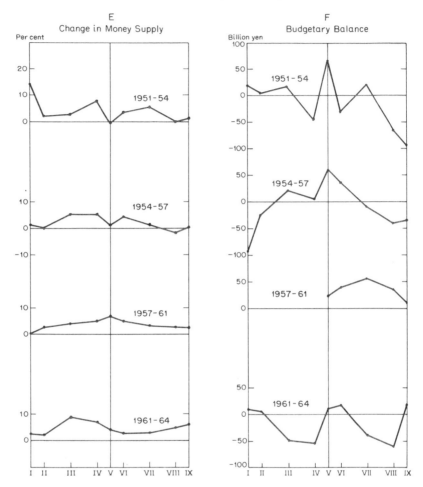

also during the cycle of IV 1961–III 1964. It is thus apparent that this variable did occasionally respond in an adjusting direction, but that such response was far from being a general rule.

The rate of increase of money supply, drawn in Part E, appears as a rule to be higher during the expansionary phase than during the subsequent contraction. This observation conforms, of course, to the tentative conclusion reached earlier. However, the pattern of behavior of this variable throughout each of these two phases is rather weak. Only once, in the 1957–61 cycle, does a neat, perfect pattern appear—that of a gradual rise during the expansion, and a gradual decline during the contraction. In the 1954–57 cycle this pattern is approached, though not perfectly matched, while in the other two cycles no such patterns can be found at all.

The positions of the budgetary balance, presented in Part F, do not reveal any consistent pattern. No regular contrast appears, either with regard to the sign of the balance (surplus or deficit) or its form of movement between stages of rising and falling foreign-exchange reserves. This evidence tends to indicate that budgetary policy was not directed, as a rule, toward adjusting balance-of-payments disturbances.

Before trying to interpret these findings, we must ask whether the policy measures which were identified by this analysis as being taken to adjust balance-of-payments disturbances may not in fact be related to other economic targets, movements of which happened to be associated in a consistent manner with balance-of-payments disturbances. We turn now to the examination of this possibility.

As will be recalled, alternative competing targets are represented in the study by three variables: the rate of unemployment, the rate (and direction) of price changes, and the rate (and direction) of changes in industrial production. The unemployment rate, at least as it appears in available data, has been very low throughout the period under consideration. It is therefore assumed here, without further confirmation, that these changes could not, as a rule, have explained the policy measures taken. Even if this assumption is not fully warranted, it should be realized that the more significant changes in unemployment, at least, would not disappear from the analysis altogether, since these changes must be reflected in the rate of change of industrial production.

Two variables, standing for two targets, are left. One is the rate of change of the price level; the other, the rate of change in industrial production. Since the index of wholesale prices and the cost of living index (in Tokyo) give substantially the same indications of price movements, the latter index alone will be used to represent this variable. The target of maintaining a stable price level will be considered violated here not when prices move, since prices moved upward almost continuously, but when their movement deviates from the price level's short-term trend (which is measured, in turn, by a three-year moving average).

The question posed is, thus, whether the manipulations of the discount rate and the budgetary balance could not be explained by either the wish to maintain a stable (movement of) price level or the wish to achieve a high rate of expansion of industrial production, rather than by the requirements of balance-of-payments adjustment. Again, more than one method will be used to test this hypothesis.

Take first the discount rate. In Table 8-3, each change in this variable is shown for the period from 1957 onward (the change in early 1957 being the first since August 1955 when the "basic" discount rate became meaningful). The position of each of the three alternative target variables—external reserves, the price level, and industrial production—is examined in each quarter in which the discount rate moved.

TABLE 8-3

JAPAN: CHANGES IN THE DISCOUNT RATE AND
POSITIONS OF TARGET VARIABLES

Discount Rate	External Reserves (1)	Cost-of-Living Index (compared with trend) (2)	Industrial Production (rate of increase) (3)
Raised:			
I 1957	+ fall	* stable	+ high
II 1957	+ fall	+ rises	+ high
IV 1959	− rise	+ rises	+ high
III 1961	+ fall	+ rises	+ high
I 1964	+ fall	− falls	+ high
Lowered:			
II 1958	+ rise	− rises	+ low
III 1958	+ rise	+ falls	* average
I 1959	+ rise	+ falls	− high
III 1960	+ rise	− rises	* average
I 1961	+ rise	− rises	− high
IV 1962	+ rise	* stable	+ low
I 1963	+ rise	− rises	* average
II 1963	+ rise	− rises	− high
I 1965	+ rise	− rises	+ low
II 1965	− fall	− rises	+ low

+ indicates that the change in the target variable would justify the direction of change in the discount rate.

− indicates that the change in the target variable would justify the opposite direction.

* indicates that the change in the target variable would call for no change in the discount rate.

It appears immediately that the movements of the discount rate are consistent with the assumption that this instrument was used for balance-of-payments adjustment—not a surprising finding, of course, at this stage of the analysis, since a similar finding was the starting point of the present test. Table 8-3 also shows, on the other hand, that changes in the discount rate are not, as a rule, compatible with the assumption that they were intended to maintain a stable rate of change in the price level. This assumption is, indeed, so obviously contradicted by the data that it will not be subject here to further investigation. The assumption that discount rate policy was motivated by a desire to maintain stability on a high level in the rate of expansion of industrial production does not fare too well either. It is true that in no case was the discount rate raised when industrial production was low; but many of the instances of reductions of the discount rate cannot be explained by the position of the target of industrial production. Additional evidence on this is provided in Table 8-4, in which subperiods of imbalances of payments

TABLE 8-4

JAPAN: THE DISCOUNT RATE AND INDUSTRIAL PRODUCTION DURING SUBPERIODS OF IMBALANCES

Subperiod	External Reserves (1)	Industrial Production (rate of change) (2)	Discount Rate (3)
IV 1955 – IV 1956	stable	high	+ stable
IV 1956 – III 1957	fall	normal	+ raised
III 1957 – II 1961	rise	normal	+ reduced considerably
II 1961 – IV 1961	fall	normal	+ raised
IV 1961 – II 1963	rise	fluctuates	+ reduced considerably
II 1963 – IV 1963	stable	high	+ stable
IV 1963 – II 1964	fall	normal	+ raised
II 1964 – IV 1965	rise	low	* lowered
IV 1965 – IV 1966	stable	high	+ stable

+ indicates that the policy variable changes in the direction required for balance-of-payments adjustment; no change would be justified by the movement of industrial production.

* indicates that the policy variables' movement is consistent with the positions of both the balance of payments and industrial production.

serve again as units of observation. It may be seen immediately that the movements of the discount rate in each of these subperiods could be explained by a wish to correct imbalances of payments, but not—with a single exception—by the desire to maintain a high rate of expansion in production. This evidence seems to provide another strong basis for rejecting the assumption that discount rate policy was intended to promote a high rate of growth. The assumption, on the other hand, that this policy was manipulated in the interest of balance-of-payments adjustment is strongly supported by these tests.

Table 8-5 describes the two alternative target variables—external reserves and industrial production—during periods in which the budget displayed clearly either surpluses or deficits. It may be seen, from column 2, that the assumption that budgetary policy was used to adjust imbalances of payments could not be sustained by this evidence: it is supported by only a single episode—that of the budgetary deficit of III 1962–III 1963—out of the six listed in Table 8-5. The alternative assumption, that budgetary policy was used to serve the target of a high rate of expansion of industrial production, fares much better; it is supported by four episodes (out of five), and clearly rejected by none.

TABLE 8–5

JAPAN: THE BUDGETARY BALANCE AND MOVEMENTS
OF POLICY TARGETS

Period	Budgetary Balance	External Reserves	Industrial Production (rate of increase)
	(1)	(2)	(3)
IV 1950 – II 1951	surplus	* stable	n.a.
IV 1953 – I 1955	deficit	* no trend	+ low
II 1955 – I 1957	surplus	– rise	+ high
II 1960 – I 1961	surplus	* no trend	* normal
III 1962 – III 1963	deficit	+ rise	+ low
II 1964 – IV 1966	deficit	* stable	+ low

NOTE: See Table 8-3 for explanation of symbols.   n.a. = not available.

3. Summary and Interpretation

From all the evidence presented, it appears that budgetary policy in Japan did not usually serve as an instrument for adjusting balance-of-payments disequilibria. It seems possible that, insofar as budgetary policy was regarded as a tool to be used in the pursuance of economic policy, it was allocated to the target of preserving a high rate of expansion of economic activity.

Monetary developments, on the other hand, definitely appear to respond to the movements of the balance of payments, and monetary policy may be viewed as being geared to the needs of balance-of-payments adjustment. Imbalances of payments lead to changes in monetary variables in accordance with the following typical pattern.

In a downward imbalance, that is, a downward tendency of external reserves, the Bank of Japan invariably reacts by raising the discount rate. From information available, it also seems likely that the Bank would use "moral suasion," or "discount-window guidance," in an effort to restrict the amount of credit extended by commercial banks to their customers. At the same time, however, the change in the public's demand for this credit would be expected to move in the opposite direction. This is a period in which the amount of liquidity available to the economy from the (net) acquisition of foreign-exchange reserves is falling, that is, the loss of reserves tends to diminish the amount of liquid means. As a result, demand for bank credit by the public must rise. In the end, the rate of credit expansion may tend to show a slight tendency to fall during downward imbalances, although this tendency is far from being consistent. This seems to be an indication that the aforementioned restrictions on the supply of credit are effective. To what extent this may be attributed to cost restrictions (through the increase of the discount rate), or how much of it may be due to direct quantitative restrictions ("window guidance"), is impossible to tell on the basis of available information.[7]

[7] The increase in the discount rate would act as a cost restriction in either of two ways. If the rates charged by banks on loans to their customers remain unchanged, the increased cost incurred by the banks themselves on their borrowing from the central bank would act as a deterrent to their borrowing and relending (or lending and rediscounting). If, on the other hand, the banks "pass on" the increase in their cost by raising the interest rates charged on their lending, the amount of credit demanded by the public should tend to decline. As a rule,

But even when the rate of credit expansion does fall, this tendency is only slight. To maintain the expansion of credit, commercial banks must take some compensatory action with regard to their own liquidity or reserves. Bank liquidity is affected by three major factors (disregarding the possibility of changes in the public's desired currency ratio): changes in the amount of external reserves, changes in the amount of central bank lending to the government, and changes in central bank lending to the commercial banks themselves. Information about the second factor is deficient; but it does not seem likely that it operates with enough force even nearly to offset the operation of the first factor, changes in external reserves. Thus, in order to resist the downward pressure on their liquidity, the banks resort to increased borrowing from the central bank. They do so despite the increased cost of this borrowing—presumably, as has been explained, as a result of increased demand by the public for the bank credit.

The rate of expansion of money supply tends to move in an adjusting direction—to fall when external reserves fall—somewhat more clearly than the variable of credit supply. But here, too, the tendency is not strong or fully consistent.

In a period of an upward imbalance, this pattern is reversed; and Bank of Japan lending to the government most often tends to increase. Commercial banks use the added liquidity acquired by them not to increase the rate of expansion of their lending to the public but to repay debts to the Bank of Japan—despite the fall in the latter's discount rate, which is a practically invariable consequence in this situation. The rate of expansion of bank credit remains stable, or tends to rise, and the rate of expansion of money supply tends to accelerate.

To sum up: the discount rate responds consistently to imbalances of payments. At times of downward imbalances the discount rate is raised, whereas in episodes of upward imbalances it is lowered. With less consistency, the rate of expansion of money supply tends to move in the same direction as the movement of external reserves. These, of course,

the former channel was probably more important in the Japanese case. The rates charged by banks were subject to legal ceilings; usually, the rates found in effect were the ceiling rates. Thus, changes in the discount rate were not transformed into changes in the various rates charged by the banks, but acted through the reduction of profitability of the bank's lending. This, in turn, should presumably lead the banks, in such a time, to increase the proportion of favored, less risky loans in their total lending. The special difficulties realized in fact by Japan's small business sector during such periods may be an indication that this indeed was the process.

arc tendencies consistent with the assumption that monetary policy was used to adjust the balance of payments.

References

Allen, G. C., *Japan's Economic Recovery,* London, 1958.

The Bank of Japan, *Annual Report,* Tokyo, 1962–66.

The Bank of Japan, *The Bank of Japan, Its Function and Organization,* Tokyo, 1964.

The Bank of Japan, Statistics Department, *Economic Statistics of Japan,* annual, Tokyo, 1949–66.

The Bank of Japan, Statistics Department, *Economic Statistics,* monthly, Tokyo, January, 1947–66.

Ezekiel, H., and Patel, C., "Fluctuations in Japan's Balance of Payments and the Role of Short-Term Capital Flows, 1959–66." *International Monetary Fund Staff Papers,* Vol. 14 (November, 1967), pp. 403–30.

Japan, Bureau of Statistics, Office of the Prime Minister, *Monthly Statistics of Japan,* Tokyo, Japan Statistical Association, July 1961–66.

Japanese Government. Economic Planning Agency. *Economic Survey of Japan,* annual, Tokyo, The Japan Times, Ltd., 1945–66.

Japan, Ministry of Finance, *Quarterly Bulletin of Financial Statistics,* Tokyo, 1926–66.

Japan, Ministry of Foreign Affairs, *Statistical Survey of Economy of Japan,* annual, Tokyo, 1953–66.

Koizumi, A., "Foreign Exchange Reserves as a Buffer in Japanese Countercyclical Policy," Tokyo, *Hitotsubashi Academy Annuals,* Vol. 9 (April, 1959), pp. 255–66.

Narvekar, P. R., "The 1954–55 Improvement in Japan's Balance of Payments," *International Monetary Fund Staff Papers,* Vol. 6 (November, 1957), pp. 143–69.

———, "The Cycle in Japan's Balance of Payments," *International Monetary Fund Staff Papers,* Vol. 8 (December, 1961), pp. 380–411.

Organization for Economic Cooperation and Development, *Economic Surveys: Japan,* annual, Paris.

Patrick, Hugh T., *Monetary Policy and Central Banking in Contemporary Japan,* Bombay, 1962.

CHAPTER
9

THE NETHER-
LANDS

1. Policy Instruments

The Netherlands Bank, the central bank in the Netherlands, has gradually changed in character. Some acts affecting the Bank's structure, powers, and functions have been adopted since World War II. The Bank's constitution and the definition of its functions are incorporated primarily in legislation enacted in 1948.

The Netherlands Bank is almost entirely independent of the government. Its Board of Managers and its President are appointed by the Crown for periods of seven years. Representatives of the government participate in meetings of the larger Bank Council in an advisory capacity. The Finance Minister may formally give instructions to the Board of Managers; the latter is entitled, in this case, to present its objections to the Crown, which then has to make public both the arguments and counter-arguments and the final decisions it reaches. In effect, no such instructions have ever been given since the 1948 Act, and the Bank may thus be regarded as independent of the Ministry of Finance.

Banking institutions in the Netherlands vary widely in functions and structure. The greater part of banking transactions are conducted by regular commercial banks. These are highly concentrated: a few large banks, each with a large number of branches (up to 200 or 250), play a dominant role. The assets of the four largest banks amount to some 60 per cent of the total assets of commercial banks, and those of the thirty-three "representative" banks to 95 per cent. The high measure of concentration and the ease of communication may be important reasons for the tendency of the Netherlands Bank to act as much as possible by agreement with the banks rather than by directives and coercion; these factors also contribute to the high level of mutual under-standing which is found between the Bank and the commercial banks.

The Netherlands Bank employs primarily the three classical instru-ments of monetary policy: changes in the discount rate, changes in minimum-reserve ratios of the banks, and open-market operations. To a lesser extent, it also applies quantitative credit controls.

The Discount Rate. Lending by the Netherlands Bank to commercial banks takes three forms. First, it may be done by discounting at the Bank. Eligible for discounting is short-term paper, such as Treasury bills or commercial bills of not over 105 days to maturity. More often, banks will resort to the second possibility, which is receiving advances on current account against the pledge of collateral—usually of Trea-sury bills. The rate charged by the Bank on these advances is one-half of 1 per cent above the discount rate. Finally, the Bank may buy Treasury paper from the banks with a repurchase stipulation. Tech-nically, the Netherlands Bank regards such a transaction as the equivalent of a lending operation rather than an open-market operation.

In general, lending by the Bank to the commercial banks is very slight, and so are the absolute fluctuations in the amount of lending. Borrowing from the Bank is considered an emergency act, intended for the shortest duration, rather than one intended to add reserves to the borrowing bank for any length of time.

Changes in the discount rate thus have a very slight impact on the size of the banking system's reserves, since the amount of borrowing from the Bank is generally insignificant in relation to the size of reserves. However, the discount rate is considered an important yard-stick. Changes in it are supposed to reflect the intentions of the Nether-lands Bank, thus giving a directive to the commercial banks with regard to the tightening or relaxation of credit supply. A conventional semi-automatic relationship exists between the discount rate and the commercial banks' interest on their lending. Usually, the rate charged on lending to prime borrowers from the banks is about 2 per cent above the discount rate, although it could not fall below the level of 5 per cent.

Minimum-Reserve Ratios. Minimum-reserve policy was, most often, the major tool of the Netherlands Bank after 1954. Although the Bank was empowered by law to impose minimum-reserve ratios on the bank-ing system, it preferred to do so by agreement. In February 1954, a gentlemen's agreement was concluded between the Bank and some forty commercial banks, which in their aggregate constituted the overwhelming majority of the banking system. According to the agreement, the participating banks were required to maintain balances at the Netherlands Bank at a ratio to their deposits determined by the Bank. Subject to this requirement were all sight and time deposits, excluding saving deposits and deposits in foreign currency. The ratio is the same for all types of banks and deposits covered by the agreement. It was not, however, to exceed 15 per cent, and the Netherlands Bank undertook not to raise it above 10 per cent without first selling Treasury paper in the open market on a large scale. In fact, the ratio has always stayed within the 10 per cent limit. The lower limit of fluctuations in the ratio was 4 per cent for most of the time. During 1963, however, it was reduced to zero and has stayed at that level since; that is, the minimum-reserve ratio has not been used as a policy instrument since mid-1963. Before that, on the other hand, changes in the ratio had been rather frequent.

The gentlemen's agreement was concluded at a time when commercial banks were extremely liquid due to an influx of foreign exchange. Market rates of three-month Treasury bills came down to as low as .4 per cent, and the Netherlands Bank was not equipped to eliminate liquidity to the desired extent by open-market operations. The reason for the highly liquid position of the banks is well reflected in the agreement itself. Given its importance, this part of the agreement deserves to be quoted:

> In view of the desire of the Netherlands Bank that the commercial banks should make a contribution towards financing the greatly increased stock of gold and foreign exchange the undersigned [name of bank] is prepared to enter into a gentlemen's agreement with the Netherlands Bank, directed to the maintenance at the Netherlands Bank of a cash reserve adaptable in relation to the movement in the stock of gold and foreign exchange.[1]

This relationship was explained by the Netherlands Bank in terms of equity:

> . . . the central bank must be supplied with . . . resources for the purpose of holding [stock of gold and foreign exchange]. Unless it is desired that these resources shall be provided by the Treasury, that is to say at the cost of the taxpayer, they will have to come from the banks—which in our modern national economy provide a part of the money in circulation, just as much as the Netherlands Bank does, and enjoy the resulting benefits in

[1] Preamble to the gentlemen's agreement, *Netherlands Bank Report,* 1953, p. 176.

the form of interest. It is no more than reasonable that, as against these benefits, the banks should also contribute towards providing the means for carrying the international cover for the country's money.[2]

The exceptions to the rule of behavior indicated in these passages are also explained in terms of equity. Suppose credit supply increases thanks to some autonomous factor. As a result of this expansion, external reserves fall. There would be no need under these circumstances to increase commercial bank profits by increasing their lending capacity, since the banks already had their credit raised at the beginning of the process. For such reasons, the Netherlands Bank stated that the relationship of the reserve ratio to gold and foreign-exchange reserves should not be entirely rigid, but that the Bank would investigate the reasons for the movements of foreign-exchange reserves in each case.

Open-Market Operations. Until 1952, open-market operations were conducted by the Treasury. In July 1952, an agreement between the Treasury and the Netherlands Bank specified that the former would limit itself to issuing new Treasury paper when old paper falls due, and since that time open-market operations have been conducted by the Netherlands Bank. But this does not rule out other financial operations by the Treasury, which, as will be noted later, have the same effect as open-market operations.

Although the Bank is empowered to deal in a variety of papers, its stock—and its operations—have been restricted to Treasury paper. These are mainly Treasury bonds with a maturity of one to five years. The stock of this paper held by the Bank at the beginning of its operations, in 1952, was later replenished by converting part of the Treasury's book debt to the Bank into Treasury paper, as well as by the transfer—against Treasury paper—of claims on the EPU from the Bank to the Treasury.

Open-market operations are not transacted with commercial banks. They are handled by special brokers, who buy and sell both for their clients and on their own account, financing the latter transactions by borrowing on the call-money market and, on occasion, by resorting to rediscounting at the Netherlands Bank. While the greater part of the Treasury paper which serves as instrument in open-market operations is held by banking institutions, a substantial proportion is also held by others, such as institutional investors, corporations, or households.

Open-market operations appear most of the time to be periodic

[2] *Ibid.,* p. 79.

rather than continuous: they are usually concentrated within short periods and not conducted gradually in small amounts.

Quantitative Controls. The Netherlands Bank is entitled by law to impose quantitative (as well as qualitative) restrictions on credit. In 1954, the Bank also concluded a gentlemen's agreement with the banks to that effect. The provisions of this agreement were not implemented; but on one occasion, between the fall of 1957 and the spring of 1958, the Bank tried to impose credit ceilings by charging penalty rates on the amounts by which the Bank's lending to commercial banks exceeded specified ceilings. In 1960, a new gentlemen's agreement was concluded by which quotas may be imposed on each bank's credit according to a uniform formula relating the size of credit to its size at some base period. A commercial bank which exceeds its quota would have to deposit at the Netherlands Bank, interest-free, an amount equal to the excess. In July 1961, the banks were directed under the stipulations of this agreement not to let the size of their lending exceed that of the base period (which was either the last quarter of 1960 or the corresponding month of the previous year) by more than 15 per cent. After that date, the banks were allowed to increase lending by .5 per cent per month. Since August 1962, it was found that this restriction was not effective; the actual size of credit was below the size permitted. The restrictions were removed altogether in January 1963. In September 1963, however, they were renewed and remained in effect until the end of the period investigated. The average amount of each bank's credit during the first half of 1963 was taken as the base. By the end of September 1963, the amount of the banks' lending should not have exceeded the base amount by more than 5 per cent; from that month on, expansions of credit by 1 per cent or .5 per cent per month were allowed, for a total of 3 per cent (of the base amount) during the last quarter of 1963, 9 per cent in 1964, and 10 per cent in 1965. In 1966, credit expansion was restricted to 8 per cent of the outstanding amount at the end of 1965; this rate represents a total, however, of a few imposed ceilings, which became gradually more restrictive.

In the last few years of the period, the Netherlands Bank thus appears to have used quantitative restrictions of credit to a significant extent. The Bank has also, on a few occasions, exercised its authority to restrict certain types of credit.

Occasionally, the Bank tried to prevent what it considered an excessive credit expansion by "moral suasion." Due to the close relationship between the Bank and commercial banks, this may have had some effect. However, in general, the Bank did not rely on this means as an important policy instrument.

FISCAL AND DEBT POLICY

The central government's budget consists of an ordinary, and an extraordinary, section. The latter always shows a large deficit—its expenditures may be as much as five or six times larger than its revenues. In the ordinary budget, on the other hand, a surplus is normally maintained. Most of the time, the surplus in the ordinary budget is smaller than the deficit in the extraordinary budget, so that total expenditures exceed total revenues. The difference is usually financed by borrowing from the public.

The central government maintains a strong influence on local budgets. The major source of the municipalities' normal revenue is transfers from the central government, which assigns 12 per cent of its tax revenues to the Municipalities Fund and, in addition, finances major local expenditures such as the costs of police and education. Borrowing by the municipalities in the form of general quantitative ceilings, ceilings on the rate of interest, and requirements for ad hoc approval of borrowing by the government.

The Treasury's cash balances are held exclusively at the Netherlands Bank, while those of local authorities are held outside it. According to the 1948 Bank Act, the Treasury is entitled to automatic advances from the Bank within fl. 150 million; beyond that, current advances to the Treasury may be given at the Bank's discretion. In effect, such advances have been negligible, usually nonexistent. The Bank extends credit to the government, instead, by purchasing Treasury bills. Variations in the size of this credit too are usually not considerable. In the earlier years of the period the Bank held a substantial book claim on the Treasury. From early 1952, this was gradually diminished until it disappeared completely by the beginning of 1958. On the other hand, in the earlier part of the period, the government maintained "special deposits" at the Bank, representing the counterpart funds of foreign aid. These grew considerably until early 1952, but declined continuously from then on until they too disappeared in early 1958.

Thus, until 1958, the movement in the government's net indebtedness to the Netherlands Bank was dominated by the movement of the Treasury's book debt and "special deposits," and to some extent by the movement of Treasury bills. Since then, the major sources of variations in the size of this indebtedness are the Treasury bills and, even more often, the government's deposits. The latter are a highly fluctuating category: weekly or monthly changes in them are very large in comparison with long-term movements.

Besides financing budgetary deficits, the government very often conducts financial transactions with the public for the exclusive purpose of affecting monetary conditions. It may, for instance, borrow from the public and deposit the proceeds at the Netherlands Bank. Changes in the government's net indebtedness to the Bank thus reflect not only the cash balance of its budgetary operations but also its financial transactions with the public. To an extent, therefore, the government conducts financial operations which have the same effect as, and may be regarded as a substitute for, open-market operations of the Bank.

2. Statistical Analysis

Movements of external reserves in the Netherlands do not give evidence of any cyclical pattern. An attempt to divide the whole period into cycles and use cyclical analysis does not, therefore, seem to be very useful. However, though a strong upward trend of reserves is apparent, a substantial number of episodes in which reserves declined, or rose with particular rapidity, make the analysis of policy reactions to balance-of-payments disturbances possible.

In Table 9-1, the period is divided into subperiods according to the fluctuations of the balance of payments. This division is based, until 1958, on the movements of external reserves and, from 1958 onward, on the IMF data of surpluses and deficits in the balance of payments, which series almost invariably gives results similar to those provided by the series of external reserves.

It may be seen that the discount rate is changed most often in the direction that would be required for balance-of-payments adjustment. Only in one subperiod—during 1950—is an opposite movement found; while in a few other cases the discount rate remained stable when balance-of-payments adjustment would have required some change. This relationship is further examined in Table 9-2, which gives the direction of balance-of-payments movements during all quarters in which changes were made in the discount rate. It appears, again, that

discount rate changes were consistent with balance-of-payments requirements. This is true particularly with regard to all the changes
made before 1962. Out of fourteen such discount rate movements, only
one was in the opposite direction to the requirements of adjustment;
three took place when no balance-of-payments adjustment was required; and ten could be explained by the requirements for balance-of-
payments adjustment.

To help test this association still further, Table 9-2 also gives the
movements of alternative target variables. It appears that the price
stability target performs, in general, about as well as the balance-of-
payments adjustment target—and better from 1962 on. On the basis
of this evidence, one could not assert that the discount rate was used
exclusively for balance-of-payments adjustment. It is evident that the
requirements of the two targets—balance-of-payments equilibrium and
price stability—coincided most of the time, so that the discount rate
changes were consistent with both. This coincidence of the two targets
may be expected in a country whose share in world trade is not very
large, and the share of whose trade in its own economy is substantial.
Changes in conditions abroad are likely to have only small impact on
the trade of such a country; while inflationary or deflationary pressures
within the economy, which are likely to be reflected in price movements,
may be expected to have an immediate and substantial effect on the
country's trade balance.

Movements of the other two targets examined in Table 9-2—industrial production and employment—do not reveal any consistent pattern
in relation to discount rate changes. It appears from the evidence of
this table that these two were not usually regarded as the targets at the
service of which the discount rate is employed.

Column 3 of Table 9-1 shows the changes in another short-term
interest rate, which is often quoted in the Netherlands: the rate (yield)
of three-month Treasury bills. As may be seen from Chart 9-1, the
movements of this rate and of the discount rate are highly correlated.
It is thus not surprising that Table 9-1 shows this variable also moving
in a way which is, by and large, consistent with the requirements for
balance-of-payments adjustment.

In column 4 of Table 9-1, movements of the minimum-reserve ratio
are described for 1954 through 1963, the period during which this
instrument was used. It appears that, throughout these years, this variable was changed mostly in a direction opposite to the requirements of

TABLE 9-1

THE NETHERLANDS: MOVEMENTS OF POLICY VARIABLES DURING SUBPERIODS
OF IMBALANCES

Subperiod	External Reserves (1)	Discount Rate (2)	Market Rate for Three-Month Treasury Bills (3)	Reserve Ratio Requirements (4)	Open-Market Operations (net) (5)	Netherlands Bank Claims on Commercial Banks (6)
I 1950 – IV 1950	rise	– raised	* stable	a	a	n.a.
IV 1950 – III 1951	fall	+ raised	– falls	a	a	– rise
III 1951 – II 1954	rise	+ lowered	+ falls	a	– sales	– fall
II 1954 – I 1956	stable	stable	rises	stable	no trend	stable
I 1956 – III 1957	fall	+ raised	+ rises	– lowered	* no operations	– rise
III 1957 – I 1959	rise	+ lowered	+ falls	– raised	– sales	– fall
I 1959 – IV 1959	stable	raised	rises	lowered	purchases	0
IV 1959 – IV 1961	rise	* stable	+ falls	– raised	* no trend	0
IV 1961 – I 1963	stable	no trend	no trend	lowered	purchases	0
I 1963 – IV 1963	rise	* stable	* stable	+ lowered	* no operations	0
IV 1963 – II 1964	fall	+ raised	+ rises	a	+ sales	0
II 1964 – IV 1964	rise	* stable	* stable	a	* no operations	0
IV 1964 – IV 1966	stable	raised	rises	a	no operations	rise

Subperiod	Netherlands Bank Net Claims on Government (7)	Netherlands Bank Total Domestic Claims (8)	Commercial Bank Lending to Public (quarterly rate of increase, per cent) (9)	Money Supply (quarterly rate of increase, per cent) (10)	"Primary and Secondary Liquidity" (quarterly rate of increase, per cent) (11)	Budgetary Balance (quarterly average, in millions of guilders) (12)
I 1950 – IV 1950	– fall	n.a.	(*) 4.6	(–) –2.0	n.a.	(–) +109
IV 1950 – III 1951	* no trend	– rise	(–) 7.2	(+) –.4	n.a.	(*) +116
III 1951 – II 1954	– fall	– fall	(–) 2.9	(+) 2.2	n.a.	(*) +119
II 1954 – I 1956	rise	rise	4.2	1.1	.9	–11
I 1956 – III 1957	– rise	– rise	(+) 3.0	(+) –.8	(+) .4	(–) –52
III 1957 – I 1959	– fall	– fall	(–) –1.2	(+) 2.3	(+) 3.0	(*) –50
I 1959 – IV 1959	no trend	no trend	4.7	.5	1.0	+225
IV 1959 – IV 1961	– fall	– fall	(*) 4.4	(+) 1.8	(+) 1.5	(+) +11
IV 1961 – I 1963	no trend	rise	3.3	1.9	2.2	–122
I 1963 – IV 1963	– fall	– fall	(*) 3.2	(*) 2.4	(–) .2	(–) –79
IV 1963 – II 1964	– rise	– rise	(–) 5.8	(*) 1.9	(–) 1.8	(–) –159
II 1964 – IV 1964	– fall	– fall	(–) 1.8	(*) 2.1	(+) 3.1	(+) –213
IV 1964 – IV 1966	rise	rise	3.3	2.1	2.3	–355

NOTE: For explanation of symbols, see Table 8-3.   n.a. = not available.   a = not applicable.

TABLE 9-2

THE NETHERLANDS: CHANGES IN THE DISCOUNT RATE
AND POSITION OF TARGET VARIABLES

Discount Rate	External Reserves (1)	Cost-of-Living Index (compared with trend) (2)	Industrial Production (rate of increase) (3)	Unemployment (4)
Raised:				
III 1950	* stable	* stable	+ high	+ high
II 1951	+ fall	+ rises	− low	* stable
I 1956	* stable	* stable	* normal	* stable
IV 1956	+ fall	* stable	* normal	* stable
III 1957	+ fall	+ rises	− low	− rises
IV 1959	* stable	+ rises	+ high	+ falls
II 1962	− rise	+ rises	* normal	* stable
I 1964	* stable	+ rises	* normal	* stable
II 1964	* stable	+ rises	* normal	* stable
II 1966	* stable	+ rises	* normal	* stable
Lowered:				
I 1952	+ rise	− rises	+ low	+ rises
III 1952	+ rise	+ falls	+ low	+ rises
II 1953	+ rise	+ falls	− high	− falls
III 1956	− fall	* stable	* normal	− falls
I 1958	+ rise	+ falls	+ low	+ rises
II 1958	+ rise	+ falls	+ low	+ rises
IV 1958	+ rise	+ falls	− high	+ high
I 1959	+ rise	+ falls	* normal	− falls
I 1963	* stable	− rises	+ low	* stable

NOTE: For explanation of symbols, see Table 8-3.

balance-of-payments adjustment. This relationship is examined in greater detail in Table 9-3, which lists all the quarters in which the reserve ratio was changed.[3] The impression which emerges from this

[3] Excluded from this table are the changes through the first half of 1954. When reserve requirements were first introduced, by the gentlemen's agreement of February 1954, the rate was determined at 5 per cent, and was then increased each month by 1 per cent, until it reached the level of 10 per cent. These increases, however, should be regarded as part of the gradual process of establishing a starting ratio of 10 per cent.

CHART 9-1

THE NETHERLANDS: TIME SERIES OF
SELECTED VARIABLES

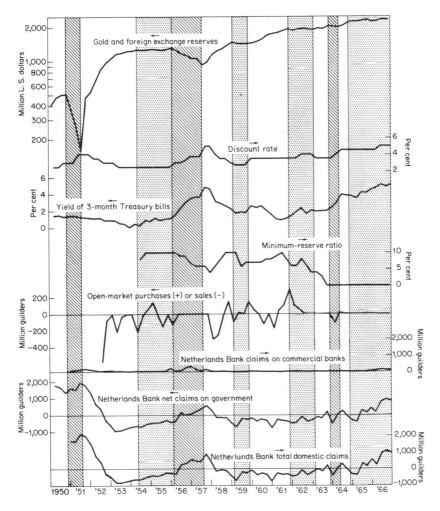

NOTE: Diagonal-line areas represent period of downward imbalances; gray areas represent stability; white areas represent upward imbalances.

CHART 9-1 (*Concluded*)

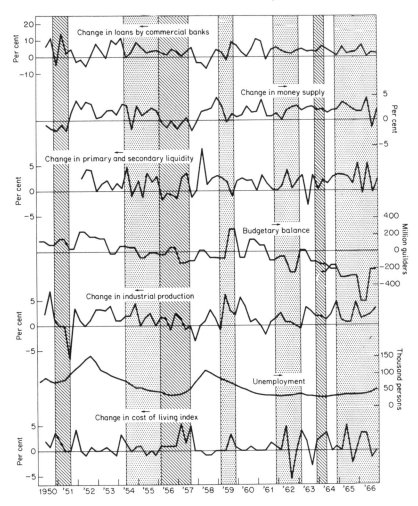

table is very clear: the minimum-reserve ratio was changed, with only a few exceptions, in the direction opposite to balance-of-payments requirements. This happened in thirteen of eighteen quarters in which the ratio was changed, while the opposite happened only four times. The association is even more striking for the period prior to mid-1961. This relationship might have been expected, of course, from the very justification given to concluding the gentlemen's agreement, which

TABLE 9-3

THE NETHERLANDS: CHANGES IN THE MINIMUM-
RESERVE RATIO AND POSITION OF TARGET
VARIABLES

Quarter	Minimum-Reserve Ratio	External Reserves	Cost-of-Living Index (compared with trend)	Industrial Production (rate of increase)	Unemployment
	(1)	(2)	(3)	(4)	(5)
II 1956	lowered	− fall	* stable	* normal	− falls
IV 1956	lowered	− fall	* stable	* normal	* stable
I 1957	lowered	− fall	− rises	* normal	* stable
IV 1957	lowered	+ rise	− rises	+ low	+ rises
I 1958	raised	− rise	− falls	− low	− rises
II 1958	raised	− rise	− falls	− low	− rises
III 1958	raised	− rise	− falls	* normal	− rises
II 1959	lowered	− fall	+ falls	− high	+ high
III 1960	raised	− rise	− falls	+ high	+ falls
I 1961	raised	− rise	− falls	* normal	+ falls
II 1961	raised	− rise	− falls	− low	* stable
III 1961	lowered	+ rise	* stable	− low	* stable
IV 1961	lowered	+ rise	− rises	* normal	* stable
II 1962	raised	− rise	+ rises	* normal	* stable
III 1962	lowered	* stable	+ falls	* normal	* stable
IV 1962	lowered	− fall	+ falls	+ low	* stable
II 1963	lowered	+ rise	− rises	+ low	* stable
III 1963	lowered	− fall	+ falls	− high	* stable

NOTE: For explanation of symbols, see Table 8-3.

established and governed the instrument under consideration, and the
mode of operations which the agreement specified. As will be remembered, the agreement stated that movements of the minimum-reserve
ratio should, as a rule, be positively correlated with movements of
foreign-exchange reserves: when the latter rise, the ratio should be
raised, and vice versa. This, of course, is a policy which works in the
opposite direction from what balance-of-payments adjustment would
require. The agreement did not call for a strict adherence to this rule,

and the Netherlands Bank was always careful to point this out. Yet, throughout the 1950's, this was virtually an airtight rule.[4] Only in the 1960's did this practice change, and exceptions to it became as frequent as observance of it.

The competing targets are also observed in Table 9-3. It appears that the minimum-reserve ratio was definitely not used to maintain price stability; the ratio was changed in the direction opposite, as a rule, to that which price stability would require—a relationship which must be attributed to the correlation between price movements and imbalances of payments noted earlier. Once more, this seems to change during the 1960's. From 1962 on (to the effective abolition of the use of this instrument toward the end of 1963), changes in the reserve ratio were mostly consistent with the requirements of price stability, and might be explained by this target. On the other hand, no consistent relationship appears between changes in the minimum-reserve ratio, on the one hand, and either the level of unemployment or the level of industrial production, on the other. It appears quite safe to conclude that, like the discount rate, the minimum-reserve ratio was not generally employed either to serve the ends of high industrial production or high employment.

The third monetary instrument, open-market operations, is shown in column 5 of Table 9-1. It appears to move less often in the direction required for balance-of-payments adjustment than it does in the opposite direction; but, over all, the relation between this instrument and the movements of external reserves seems to be much weaker than that between either the discount rate or the minimum-reserve ratio and movements of external reserves. Open-market operations were taken, we recall, rather sporadically. They seemed to have been intended most of the time to "stabilize the market"—that is, to help maintain an existing level of interest rates. Apparently, they were considered a secondary tool rather than a major one and were not universally employed in pursuit of one of the major global targets.

Commercial-bank borrowing from the Netherlands Bank is described in column 6 of Table 9-1. It will be recalled that, as a rule, the amount

[4] Just a single exception is found, in the last quarter of 1957: while external reserves were rising, the minimum-reserve ratio was lowered, rather than raised, as was the normal practice. This, however, may perhaps be ascribed to a time lag and imperfections of knowledge and measurement. The ratio was lowered in October 1957; external reserves were falling until September 1957, and then started rising only just before the ratio was lowered.

of this borrowing was very small; hence changes in it were of no quantitative significance either. In only two instances did the amount of borrowing rise to considerable proportions—during the two discernible episodes of substantial declines of external reserves in 1951 and 1956–67. In both instances it dropped back to its normal low level in the subsequent periods of rising external reserves. These, of course, are movements in a direction opposite to the requirements of balance-of-payments adjustment. It should also be noted that they are in a direction opposite to that which movements of the discount rate should engender: that is, in both episodes, commercial-bank borrowing increased when the discount rate was lowered.

The net indebtedness of the government to the Netherlands Bank (excluding changes due to open-market operations) is illustrated next, in column 7 of Table 9-1. It appears immediately that its movements were usually in a direction opposite to the requirements of balance-of-payments adjustment: the indebtedness rises, most often, when external reserves fall, and falls when reserves rise. A glance at column 12, which describes the budgetary balance, will show that this pattern is quite similar to that of the movements of the budgetary balance, but is even more consistent in its negative relationship to the balance of payments. This greater consistency must be attributed to the government's financial transactions with the public—in distinction to the "real" transactions which find expression in the budget. In other words, the government must have conducted its equivalent of open-market operations —borrowing from the public and depositing at the central bank, or repaying (lending to) the public by drawing on deposits at the Bank —in a direction opposite to balance-of-payments requirements. To some extent, this seems to have been due to public initiative. When external reserves fall and reduce the economy's liquidity, banks (and other potential buyers) are less likely to increase their lending to the government (i.e., to buy Treasury bills or bonds), and more likely to reduce the amount of these assets held by them; and the opposite is true when the economy's liquidity increases by an accumulation of external reserves.

Total domestic claims of the Netherlands Bank, the combination of the last three elements (Bank lending to the commercial banks, Bank acquisition of government paper in the open market, and other net lending of the Bank to the government), is illustrated in column 8 of Table 9-1. The net claim on the government was usually the main component of this category and accounted for most of the changes in it. Since it (as well as Bank lending to the banks) moved in the opposite direction to the requirements of balance-of-payments adjustment, it is, of course, not surprising to find that so did the combined category. Indeed, this pattern was even more consistent for the total than for each of its components: only a single exception—the period from mid-1953 to mid-1954—appears to violate this inverse relationship.

Lending by commercial banks to their customers, described in column 9 of Table 9-1, appears to move in the disadjusting direction. It rises faster than usual when external reserves fall, and falls (or rises only much less than the trend) when reserves rise. This inverse relationship seems to be clearly indicated, although there are a few exceptions to it.

Quite the opposite pattern applies to changes in money supply, as is shown in column 10 of Table 9-1. It moves almost invariably in the direction which balance-of-payments adjustment would require. Money supply and external reserves appear clearly to rise together and fall together. Essentially, this is true also with regard to another measure of the economy's liquidity, to which much attention is given in the monetary analysis of the Netherlands Bank: the magnitude of "primary and secondary liquidity," [5] which is described in column 11 of Table 9-1. Like money supply, which is itself, of course, a major component (roughly two-thirds) of "primary and secondary liquidity," this moves most of the time in the direction indicated by the need for balance-of-payments adjustment, that is, in the same direction as external reserves.

Budgetary policy is described in column 12 of Table 9-1. As has been mentioned before, it appears to run most often in a direction contrary to the requirements of balance-of-payments adjustment. When external reserves rise, the government's excess demand falls (that is, its deficit turns to surplus, or becomes smaller in absolute magnitude, or a surplus gets bigger); and when reserves fall, the government's excess demand rises. This pattern has its exceptions, but they are few.

To test the budgetary policy further, Table 9-4 analyzes the episodes in which the budget was clearly either in a surplus or in a deficit position. Movements of external reserves are given in column 2 of the table. It appears, as before, that the budgetary balance behaved

[5] The "primary" liquidity is money supply, defined in the conventional way. "Secondary" liquidity includes: (1) claims on the government; (2) claims on the local authorities; and (3) claims on money-creating institutions, i.e., time deposits and day-to-day loans, foreign-currency balances of residents, and balances in savings accounts.

TABLE 9-4

THE NETHERLANDS: THE BUDGETARY BALANCE AND
POSITION OF TARGET VARIABLES

Period	Budgetary Balance	External Reserves	Cost-of-Living Index (compared with trend)	Industrial Production (rate of increase)	Unemployment
	(1)	(2)	(3)	(4)	(5)
I 1950 – II 1953	surplus	– rise	* stable	* normal	– rises
IV 1956 – IV 1957	deficit	– fall	– rises	+ low	+ rises
II 1960 – II 1961	surplus	– rise	– falls	– low	+ falls
II 1961 – IV 1962	deficit	* rise slightly	* stable	* normal	* stable
II 1963 – IV 1966	deficit	+ rise	* stable	– high	* stable

NOTE: For explanation of symbols, see Table 8-3.

most of the time—but not consistently—contrary to what balance-of-payments adjustment would require. The price stability target does not appear to be generally served by budgetary policy, which seems to be "neutral" to these targets. In general, budgetary imbalances (surpluses or deficits) were rather small and apparently played only a minor role in pursuit of short-term targets. During one episode only, from the beginning of the period surveyed to the middle of 1953, were budgetary surpluses large and consistent. As can be seen from Table 9-4, none of the targets represented there could explain the surpluses during the period of the early 1950's. External reserves were rising rapidly. Price increases were normal, that is, not exceeding their long-term trend, or even slightly below it. Industrial production was also rising at its normal rate, while employment was even falling. The large surpluses must be explained either by other targets or as an accidental phenomenon. One explanation sometimes suggested is that budgetary policy was aimed at encouraging long-term growth by accumulating capital through government saving. Another possibility is that the surpluses resulted, as in Germany, from the planning of military expenditures which did not in fact materialize.

Another interesting episode of budgetary imbalances is that of 1957.

During that year, there was an obvious contradiction between the requirements of the targets of balance-of-payments equilibrium and price stability, on the one hand, and employment and output on the other. In this year changes in circumstances abroad were, apparently, particularly important and must have played a significant part in the Netherlands' balance-of-payments situation. While most often, as has been pointed out before, balance-of-payments deficits were accompanied by domestic expansions, this episode was an exception. External reserves were falling and prices were rising rapidly, while unemployment was rising and industrial production falling. The budgetary policy during those years appears to be expansive, as would be required by the targets of employment and production. Monetary policy, on the other hand, if judged by the movements of money supply and interest rates, was restrictive—as would be required by the balance-of-payments equilibrium and price stability targets.

3. Summary and Interpretation

From the preceding analysis it seems clear that, at least during the 1950's, monetary policy was strongly associated with the balance of payments—although in a somewhat intricate manner, which, on the surface, appears to involve contradictory tendencies.

A point of major importance is the extremely high share of foreign trade in the economy of the Netherlands. Foreign trade in proportion to national income is higher in the Netherlands than anywhere in Europe (save Luxembourg, which for economic purposes may in effect be considered a region of Belgium). Any change of a given proportion in exports or imports carries thus a heavier weight in the Dutch economy than in most other countries. Since the ratio of external reserves to trade is not particularly low in the Netherlands, the large trade means also a large size of reserves in relation to income or to money supply. A given proportional change in reserves thus has a particularly large monetary impact there.

Any imbalance of payments has thus a very large automatic impact on the economy of the Netherlands in comparison with other countries; and this inflationary or deflationary impact seems to have been judged too large by the Netherlands' policy makers—that is, the impact, by itself, gives too much weight to balance-of-payments adjustment and too little to other targets. Therefore, policy has been directed at counteracting this automatic impact. Thus, the discretionary monetary policy runs counter to the requirements of balance-of-payments adjustment. However, the counter-action is not complete, so that some adjustment is still allowed to take place.

Let us consider an imbalance in which external reserves fall. The typical pattern of monetary policy would be as follows: the fall of reserves is, by itself, a factor which tends to diminish money supply and commercial bank reserves. The lending capacity of banks is thus reduced—a factor which, if not offset, would tend to lead to a further reduction of money supply through reduced lending. At the same time, demand for credit by the banks' customers probably tends to rise, due to the drain on their liquidity caused by an imbalance in transactions with the outside world.[6] In effect, commercial-bank credit to the public increases in such instances more often than it diminishes. This is accommodated by replenishing the lending capacity of banks in three principal ways. First, the minimum-reserve ratio of the commercial banks is reduced; this is quantitatively of major importance. Second— and this is normally much less significant—banks increase their borrowing from the Netherlands Bank, despite an increase in the Bank's discount rate. Third, net indebtedness of the government to the Netherlands Bank increases, thus raising the liquidity of the economy in general and bank reserves in particular. To some extent, as has been mentioned earlier, this is an automatic reaction: lending by the public (including commercial banks) to the government—in the form mainly of acquisition of Treasury bills and bonds—falls, thus automatically raising the government's indebtedness to the central bank. In other words, some substitution takes place: the commercial banks increase their lending to private customers at the expense of their lending to the government. Yet even when an increase in commercial-bank credit occurs, and is combined with the increased indebtedness of the government to the Bank, the expansionary impact on money supply is not sufficient to offset fully the initial effect of the decline in external reserves. In the end, the amount of money does go down from its level in the period prior to the disturbance (or, more often, rises significantly less than the trend). Interest rates thus go up—as indicated, for instance, by the yields of short-term Treasury bills. The discount rate is raised, presumably for three interrelated purposes: one is to prevent

---

[6] It could also happen, however, that the increased demand for credit preceded the balance-of-payments deficit, and was the cause of it.

the banks from increasing their borrowing from the Netherlands Bank to an even larger extent than they actually do; the second is to "follow the market"—namely, some market rates (such as the yield of Treasury bills) which rise through the aforementioned process of diminished liquidity and reduced demand for the bills; and third—and this is probably a most important consideration—to indicate the trend of policy. The discount rate is regarded in the Netherlands, as in many other places, as a major weather vane of the government's intentions. Moreover, interest rates on commercial-bank lending are traditionally tied to the discount rate. As mentioned before, the rates on prime loans are usually 1.5 to 2 per cent above the discount rate; they move with the latter—as do other interest rates—in a semi-automatic way. Since in the final analysis money supply is diminished and interest rates should rise, the increase of the discount rate is thus called for.

This resolves the apparent contradiction between the movements of the two major monetary instruments employed—the minimum-reserve ratio and the discount rate. Minimum-reserve ratios are reduced in order to offset the automatic effect of a fall in external reserves. Yet this is only a mitigation and not a full counteraction. Eventually, money supply would fall and interest rates should rise—hence the increase of the discount rate. Whether this whole pattern of monetary measures should be called "restrictive" or the opposite is an open question. Likewise, it may be debated whether this should be called an "adherence" to the classical "rules of the game" or its opposite. According to the definition suggested and defended earlier in this study, this should indeed be regarded a compliance with the "rules of the game."

Similarly, when external reserves rise, the process runs in the opposite direction. In general, no asymmetry shows up in the conduct of monetary policy in the Netherlands. It appears to be equally consistent in adhering to the pattern described here, both in the course of balance-of-payments surpluses and deficits.

Compliance with this pattern was almost uniform during the 1950's, but from 1961 or 1962, this no longer holds true. From this point to the end of the period surveyed, the level of external reserves was rather stable in comparison with earlier years. Fluctuations in the level were rather weak; and the existing slight upward trend was apparently regarded as a desirable feature, not strong enough to be considered a disturbance. Monetary policy during these later years appears, thus, to be less concerned with balance-of-payments developments. It is now employed in the service of other targets as well—to a large extent, probably, the target of price stability.[7] It is important to note that the change in pattern came at a period of generally rising—albeit slowly—external reserves. An element of asymmetry may be indicated by this; however, it would be necessary to contrast a long period of slightly and gradually declining reserves with this period in order to check this indication, and such cannot be found.

Budgetary policy was oriented in a direction contrary to the requirements of balance-of-payments adjustment more often than it was in the direction which adjustment would require. This may be consistent with the hypothesis that automatic income effects of the trade balance were considered more than sufficient to achieve the necessary adjustment, so that some counteraction was called for. In view of the generally small size of either budgetary surpluses or deficits, however, a conclusion that budgetary policy was indeed fashioned in this way may not be justified. It seems that this policy was usually intended to be "neutral," not only in relation to balance-of-payments developments, but also with regard to other major targets. It would be even less correct to conclude that the combined pattern of monetary-fiscal policy adhered to the well-known policy mix, assigning monetary policy to the pursuance of balance-of-payments equilibrium and fiscal policy for "domestic" targets. Only one episode—1956–57—might be explained in this way. In this case, restrictive monetary policy could have been intended to adjust the balance of payments and expansionary fiscal policy, to counteract unemployment and slack production. In the two other episodes of significant budgetary deficits, increases in the discount rate are again found; but on these occasions the opposite movements could not be explained by the requirements of balance-of-payments equilibrium, on the one hand, and domestic targets on the other.

The rate-of-exchange instrument was used on only one occasion, March 1961, when the rate was lowered (and the currency appreciated) by 5 per cent. During the preceding period, external reserves

---

[7] This impression is supported by the observation of quantitative credit restrictions. Their introduction in 1961 came at a time of rising external reserves; their relaxation during 1962–63, at a time of stable reserves; and their reintroduction, in 1963, again at a period of accumulating reserves. This would be consistent with the pattern of the 1950's, of a counteracting policy. Yet the quantitative restrictions since 1963 do not seem to be affected by the balance-of-payments position. On the other hand, these years are characterized by substantial price rises, which could explain the introduction and preservation of credit restrictions.

were rising, and the economy was showing inflationary tendencies. This, indeed, is a combination in which currency appreciation would be a proper measure. However, the development of reserves and prices prior to the revaluation does not seem to be radically different in size or other circumstances than it was on many other occasions. The use of currency revaluation in this instance may thus presumably be explained, as, indeed, was insistently argued by policy makers when the measure was taken, only by the fact of the similar German measure. Since Germany is a major trading partner of the Netherlands, the appreciation of the mark could be expected to intensify strongly the trends of rising external reserves and rising prices in the Netherlands. Speculation could have contributed to it even further. It was thus not so much actual developments as the anticipations of strongly intensified trends which led to the Dutch measure. The fact that a change in the exchange rate could be represented as following the lead of another country must have also been a strong contributing factor. An additional explanation could be the realization that a long-term accumulation of external reserves may be an indication of fundamental disequilibrium. Despite this episode, it is obvious that during the period surveyed changing the exchange rate was not considered a proper instrument for balance-of-payments adjustment in the Netherlands.

References

Amsterdam-Rotterdam Bank N.V., *Economic Quarterly Review*, Amsterdam, September, 1924–66.

De Nederlandsche Bank N.V., *Report*, annual, Amsterdam, 1913–66.

Holtrop, M. W., "Method of Monetary Analysis Used by De Nederlandsche Bank," *International Monetary Fund Staff Papers*, Vol. 5 (February, 1957), pp. 303–16.

Organization for Economic Cooperation and Development, *Economic Surveys: The Netherlands*, annual, Paris.

Reports for 1953–61 issued for Benelux by the Organization for European Economic Cooperation.

CHAPTER 10  SWEDEN

1. Policy Instruments

MONETARY POLICY

The Sveriges Riksbank, Sweden's central bank, is legally independent of the government, and is directly responsible to the parliament. Most members of the Board of Directors (except its chairman, who is a government appointee) are nominated by—and are members of—the parliament, which provides general guidance to the Riksbank's operations. In the actual conduct of policy, a large measure of cooperation exists between the Riksbank and the government. Yet, the former has been known to have on occasion acted independently, even without prior consultation with the government.

The discount rate is the most significant of the monetary instruments employed by the Riksbank. Left almost untouched until 1955, the discount rate has been changed regularly (about once a year, on the average) since the beginning of that year. As in most other countries, these changes had little direct impact on the amount of commercial-bank borrowing from the Riksbank. Although not restricted to emergency situations, this borrowing was nevertheless quite limited and was used primarily as a device for smoothing out short-term fluctuations rather than as a long-term source of funds. In recent years the average amount of this borrowing has increased, but changes in the discount rate still do not play a major role in determining the size of borrowing. During a few recent periods (mid-1961 to early 1962; early 1964 to mid-1966), penalty rates were imposed on borrowings beyond given quotas—a measure which apparently did have a large impact on the amount of borrowing. In general, however, changes in the discount rate were important primarily as a major signal of changes in over-all policy. Rates of interest, both on bank deposits and on commercial-bank lending, tended to change with the discount rate, although the association was not rigid or automatic, and on a few occasions the order of change was reversed: the discount rate followed market rates rather than the other way around.

In addition to discount policy, the Riksbank uses a variety of other monetary instruments. Open-market operations are undertaken on occasion, but not continuously. The government, which regularly sells large amounts of its securities in the market, in fact carries out most of the open-market operations by its debt policy. However, the National Debt Office, which carries out these operations, works in close coordination with the Riksbank. Minimum-liquidity ratios are also regulated by the Riksbank. Actual formal changes in the ratios have been rare, and most of the time the minimum requirements have been of little relevance. But at the time of its introduction in 1952, the system of minimum ratios was used as a restrictive measure. Later, on a few occasions, the system was again used for this purpose, but more by agreement with the banks and by persuasion than by the strict legal enforcement of the schedule of liquidity ratios. Another and probably more important instrument was the direct regulation by the Riksbank of the amount of commercial-bank lending. A few times this took the form of "moral suasion." From mid-1955 to mid-1957, however, banks were actually instructed to reduce their credit by specific amounts (gradually, the reduction reached 5 per cent of the amount outstanding in mid-1955). The use of these various instruments, though by no means unimportant, was sporadic and often cannot be quantified. As a rule, they were applied in conjunction with changes in the discount rate, though not necessarily at precisely the same time. Movements of the discount rate may thus be taken to indicate the thrust of other policy instruments as well.

BUDGETARY POLICY

Sweden, unlike many other countries, does not aim at a regular balance in the government's budget. It is assumed that a rough balance in the budget should be attained over a number of years, but that for each year, or for even longer periods, the budget may yield a deficit or surplus. In other words, the budgetary balance—as well as specific components of the budget—is regarded as an important instrument in the conduct of short-term policy. The declared task of this policy is to counteract cycles in domestic economic activity.

In order to facilitate the fulfillment of this task, several devices have been introduced to make budgetary performance more flexible than in most other countries. Thus, the amount of expenditures authorized in the budget is only a ceiling, and the government may use its discretion in deciding whether or not to spend it fully. The government has an inventory of public work projects, which may be activated or terminated on a few months' notice when the need arises. Another important device is the "investment fund," a semibudgetary instrument that allows considerable tax concessions to firms that refrain from investment in boom times, depositing their allocations to the fund in a blocked account, while spending for investment in slack times. It is relevant to note that the time schedule for the operation of this device —that is, the decision on when is the proper time to save and when to spend—is determined by the government's Labor Market Board; the use of this tool is thus directly associated with the employment situation.

As has been noted, the government borrows on a large scale in the market. It also borrows from the Riksbank, which faces no legal limitations on the amount or form of its lending to the government.

2. Statistical Analysis

The postwar record of Sweden is marked by an almost complete absence of balance-of-payments deficits of long duration or significant size. The only exception is the period between the third quarter of 1959 and the first quarter of 1960; but even this brief deficit was not very substantial in proportion to the country's trade, or even to its customarily quite small external reserves. Except for this episode, a graph of the level of the country's external reserves (as in Chart 10-1) has the form of long plateaus, interrupted by a few brief and quite steep upward steps. The first—and steepest—rise occurs from mid-1951 to early 1952, when reserves (which had been almost stable since 1947) more than doubled. The second upward movement took place between early 1960 and mid-1962, when reserves again nearly doubled; the last episode, a brief one, occurred between mid-1964 and early 1965.

A statistical analysis of the pattern of policy responses to balance-of-payments developments in Sweden must therefore be very limited in the number of observations covered. The summary presented in Table

CHART 10-1

SWEDEN: TIME SERIES OF SELECTED VARIABLES

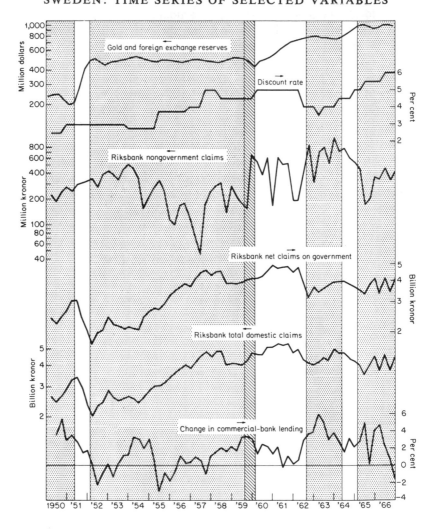

10-1 is confined to the three periods of surplus just noted, the single deficit episode of 1959–60, and several longer periods of stability. Starting with the discount rate (column 2), it seems clear that its movements do not conform to an assumption which would make them dependent on the balance-of-payments position. The discount rate is found to be stable in the first surplus period; almost stable in the sec-

CHART 10-1 (*Concluded*)

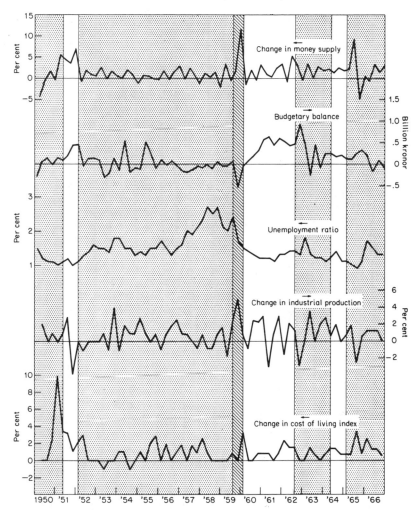

NOTE: Diagonal-line areas represent period of downward imbalances; gray areas represent stability; white areas represent upward imbalances.

ond—except for a lowering of the rate in mid-1962, toward the end of this relatively long period; and rising during the third. A response to the balance-of-payments position, however, would require the lowering of the rate during these periods. In the deficit period of III 1959–I 1960 the discount rate was raised, as balance-of-payments adjustment would require.

TABLE 10-1

SWEDEN: MOVEMENTS OF POLICY VARIABLES DURING SUBPERIODS OF IMBALANCES

Subperiod	External Reserves (1)	Discount Rate (2)	Riksbank Claims on Commercial Banks (3)	Riksbank Net Claims on Government (4)	Commercial-Bank Lending to Public (quarterly rate of increase, per cent) (5)	Money Supply (quarterly rate of increase, per cent) (6)	Budgetary Balance (quarterly average, in millions of kronor) (7)
I 1950 – II 1951	stable	raised	rise slightly	rise	3.7	2.2	+17
II 1951 – I 1952	rise sharply	* stable	* rise slightly	– fall	(–) 1.1	(+) 3.3	(–) +426
I 1952 – III 1959	stable	raised	fluctuate	rise	.8	.8	+10
III 1959 – I 1960	fall	+ raised	– rise sharply	* stable	(–) 2.3	(–) 5.1	(–) –180
I 1960 – III 1962	rise	* mostly stable	* fluctuate	– fall	(–) 1.6	(*) 2.0	(–) +425
III 1962 – II 1964	stable	fluctuates	fluctuate	rise	3.7	1.7	+293
II 1964 – I 1965	rise	– raised	* fall slightly	* stable	(–) 2.7	(*) 2.1	(+) +166
I 1965 – IV 1966	stable	raised	fluctuate	fluctuate	2.2	1.6	+96

NOTE: For explanation of symbols, see Table 8-3.

Similar conclusions hold for all the other monetary variables—the Riksbank's nongovernment claims (column 3); the Bank's net claim on the government (column 4); the Bank's total domestic claims (not represented in Table 10-1, but very similar to the Bank's claim on the government, which is the chief component of the Bank's total domestic claims); the rate of expansion of commercial-bank credit (column 5); and the rate of expansion of money supply (column 6). In the examination of all these variables, the same pattern is repeated: when balance-of-payments movements (predominantly upward) take place, the variables either show no response (remaining stable) or move in the direction opposite to that which balance-of-payments adjustment would require.

Examination of the budgetary balance (column 7) leads to a similar conclusion with regard to this major fiscal variable. By and large, it moves in the direction opposite to that which the target of balanced external transactions would call for and in no single instance is a movement in the adjusting direction found. It is therefore safe to conclude that the budgetary instrument was not used in Sweden as a means of maintaining stability in the balance of payments.

It thus appears that none of the monetary and fiscal instruments examined were used for balance-of-payments adjustment. Tables 10-2, 10-3, and 10-4 are intended to investigate the possible relation of three major variables—the discount rate, the credit supply and the budgetary balance, respectively—to major economic targets. This may indicate whether the lack of use of these instruments for balance-of-payments adjustment might have been due to the assignment of the instruments to other targets, whose claims conflicted with those of the balance of payments. The only conclusion which emerges at all firmly from observation of these tables is that the budgetary balance changed regularly in a manner consistent with the target of high employment (column 4 in Table 10-4). This conforms, of course, with the announced target of budgetary policy, which is supposed to follow an anticyclical pattern where the "cycle" refers mainly to the employment situation. The two monetary variables (the discount rate and the rate of expansion of money supply) give some indication—as may be seen from column (5) in Tables 10-2 and 10-3, respectively—that they were intended to be used to maintain price stability. But the evidence is not very firm: the pattern is not entirely consistent, and the variations in price movements between periods of "high" and of "low" price increases are not very large—usually the differences are only in the order of 1 to 1.5

TABLE 10-2

SWEDEN: THE DISCOUNT RATE AND POSITION OF TARGET VARIABLES

Subperiod	Discount Rate (1)	External Reserves (2)	Industrial Production (rate of increase) (3)	Level of Unemployment (4)	Rise of Cost-of-Living Index (compared with trend) (5)
I 1950 – I 1955	stable	rise, stable	normal	fluctuates	slow (since 1952)
I 1955 – III 1957	raised	* stable	* normal	– rises	+ fast
III 1957 – I 1962	stable	fluctuate, rising trend	normal	falls	normal
I 1962 – I 1963	lowered	+ rise, stable	+ low	+ rises slightly	* normal
I 1963 – II 1966	raised	– rise	+ high	+ low	+ fast

NOTE: For explanation of symbols, see Table 8-3.

TABLE 10-3

SWEDEN: CREDIT SUPPLY AND POSITION OF TARGET VARIABLES

Subperiod	Credit Supply (rate of expansion) (1)	External Reserves (2)	Industrial Production (rate of increase) (3)	Level of Unemployment (4)	Rise of Cost-of-Living Index (compared with trend) (5)
II 1950 – IV 1951	high	* mostly stable	+ low	– low	– fast
IV 1951 – IV 1953	low (negative)	* stable	– low	– rises	– slow
IV 1953 – IV 1954	high	* stable	* normal	– falls	+ slow
IV 1954 – IV 1957	low (negative)	* stable	* normal	– rises	+ fast
IV 1957 – I 1961	high	* fluctuate	– high	+ high	* normal
I 1961 – I 1962	low	– rise	– low	+ falls	+ fast
I 1962 – II 1966	high	* mostly stable	* normal	– low	– fast

NOTE: For explanation of symbols, see Table 8-3.

TABLE 10-4

SWEDEN: THE BUDGETARY BALANCE AND POSITION OF TARGET VARIABLES

Subperiod	Budgetary Balance (1)	External Reserves (2)	Industrial Production (rate of increase) (3)	Level of Unemployment (4)	Rise of Cost-of-Living Index (compared with trend) (5)
I 1950 – I 1953	surplus	– rise	– low	+ low	+ fast
I 1953 – IV 1956	nil	* stable	– high	+ moderate	+ slow
IV 1956 – I 1960	deficit	* stable	+ normal	+ high	– fast
I 1960 – I 1963	large surplus	– rise	* normal	+ low	– slow
I 1963 – I 1966	moderate surplus	– rise	+ high	+ low	– fast
I 1966 – IV 1966	small deficit	* stable	* normal	+ moderate	– fast

NOTE: For explanation of symbols, see Table 8-3.

per cent per annum. It also seems that monetary policy was not tied to price developments until the mid-1950's; during these earlier years the discount rate was practically stable, while credit supply—which did fluctuate substantially—does not seem to have responded to the needs of price stability. It is possible, though, that the pattern of changes in credit supply during these earlier years was motivated by price developments, but with a quite considerable time lag.

3. Summary and Interpretation

Sweden entered the 1950's with an unusually low level of external reserves in relation to its volume of international trade. From 1950 to the end of the period surveyed, the absolute level of reserves increased about fourfold in a few relatively short episodes interrupting long periods of stable reserves. Yet this increase only more or less kept pace with the rising volume of the country's trade. Such an increase of reserves could well have been regarded as desirable, rather than as a disturbance which should be counteracted. Yet, the stability of the absolute size of reserves during most of the period was also apparently not considered a source of anxiety and a disturbance calling for adjustment through restrictive policies. Thus balance-of-payments developments appear not to have played a role in determining broad policy patterns in Sweden. Major policy instruments were reserved for the achievement and maintenance of other primary targets. Budgetary policy, which appears to be more flexible than in most other countries, was regarded as the major instrument to employ in counteracting cyclical fluctuations in the domestic economy, and, in particular, cycles in the labor market. Monetary policy does not appear to have followed the same consistent pattern. It seems likely that, part of the time, monetary instruments were used in the same way as fiscal policy, that is, for countercyclical adjustment. At other times—either by coordinated design or, not implausibly, due to a high degree of independence of the central bank—monetary policy must have been intended to prevent substantial price increases.

Only a single episode of an actual absolute fall of reserves of some significance may be distinguished: it took place during late 1959 and early 1960. During this time, the target of high employment appears to have been given preference in budgetary policy over the target of balance-of-payments stability. Unemployment at that time was still high, although declining, and the budget recorded an unusually large deficit. Indications are less clear-cut for the monetary instruments. The discount rate, the major instrument and the directional signal of monetary policy, was raised, as balance-of-payments equilibrium would require. In addition, "recommended" liquidity ratios of commercial banks were raised. But commercial bank borrowing from the central bank increased markedly, despite the higher discount rate—as is quite usual under similar circumstances in other countries; and both commercial-bank credit and money supply increased at a fast rate. The evidence of this episode is thus inconclusive in the monetary sphere. Needless to say, this review cannot suggest what the country's policy patterns, in both the monetary and the budgetary areas, would have been, had the country realized periods of substantial balance-of-payments deficits rather than a succession of periods of stability and of surplus. It is thus relevant to point out that the apparent disregard of the needs of balance-of-payments adjustment is confined to a period in which balance-of-payments deficits were, by and large, absent.

References

Nordisk Udredningsserie, *Yearbook of Nordic Statistics,* annual, Stockholm, 1962–66.

Organization for Economic Cooperation and Development, *Economic Surveys: Sweden,* annual, Paris. Reports for 1954–61 issued by the Organization for European Economic Cooperation.

Statistiska Centralbyrån, *Allman Månadsstatistik* (Monthly Digest of Swedish Statistics), Stockholm, 1963–66.

Stockholms Enskilda Bank, *Some Data about Sweden,* Stockholm, 1962.

Svenska Handelsbanken, *Economic Survey,* annual, Stockholm, 1951–66.

Sveriges Riksbank, *Yearbook,* annual, Stockholm, 1909–66.

Thunholm, L. E., "Monetary Policy in Sweden," *Banca Nazionale del Lavoro Quarterly Review,* Vol. 5 (October–December, 1952), pp. 195–200.

1. Policy Instruments

MONETARY POLICY

The present structure of the Bank of England was established by the Bank-of-England Act of 1946, which entitles the Treasury to issue directives to the Bank and to guide its operations.[1] The conduct of monetary policy is not regarded as independent of economic policy as a whole. The Chancellor of the Exchequer is ultimately responsible for monetary policy, and is, in fact, involved in major policy decisions. While theoretically the executive organ for implementing decisions made in the monetary sphere, the Bank is left with considerable leeway in carrying out monetary policy, and its advice is largely heeded in policy decisions. The Chancellor of the Exchequer and the Governor of the Bank thus share in the direction of monetary policy.

The regulation of commercial banking activity by the Bank of England is done mostly by conventions, advice, and "moral suasion," rather than by legal stipulation. Nonetheless, this control is effective and on occasion consists not merely of broad directives but also of rather detailed instructions.

Commercial banks in the United Kingdom are highly varied in structure and function. For purposes of monetary policy, the most important of them are the clearing banks, which are dominated by the "Big Five." The clearing banks fulfill the essential functions of holding the public's deposits and making loans to the public, although a substantial fraction of their assets consists also of claims on the government, in the form of government securities. In the statistical analysis, commer-

---

[1] This section draws heavily upon the "Radcliffe Report": Committee on the Working of the Monetary System, *Report* (London: Her Majesty's Stationery Office, Cmnd. 827, 1959), *passim*.

cial banks will usually be represented by clearing banks.[2] With one exception, the functions of other banks are, by and large, peripheral to over-all monetary policy. The exception, discount houses, act largely as an intermediary between the clearing banks and the government (although clearing banks also directly maintain substantial investments in government securities). The discount houses are provided with funds mostly by borrowing on call from the clearing banks (and to some extent from other types of banks) and also partly from overseas banks. These funds are invested mainly in Treasury bills, and to a smaller extent in gilt-edged securities. Only discount houses are entitled to borrow from the Bank of England. The largest twelve houses form the London Discount Market Association. Members of the Association share one commitment—to cover the weekly tender of Treasury bills— and enjoy one privilege—the right to unlimited borrowing from the Bank of England (other discount houses can borrow only at the Bank's discretion).

Bank Rate. Among the instruments used by the Bank of England, the bank rate is undoubtedly regarded as the most important. From late 1951, when this instrument was reactivated, to early 1967, the rate was changed twenty-nine times—that is, about twice a year. The range of the rate, which fluctuated between 3 and 7 per cent,[3] was also considerable.

The bank rate is the rate at which the Bank stands ready to make loans to the discount houses, either by rediscounting or by lending against securities. The fact that the Bank stands ready to act, in this way, as lender of last resort, and the rate at which it is willing to do so, are of the utmost importance. But actual borrowing is quite limited both in average level and the extent of fluctuations. Borrowing from the Bank of England by the discount houses is considered a way of temporarily replenishing resources when short-term money is recalled from the houses, rather than a source of long-term, permanent finance. The actual size of Bank-of-England lending to the banking system cannot be considered as one of the variables of monetary policy.

The bank rate is the foundation, by convention, of the whole structure of short-term interest rates. The rate of interest on advances of clearing banks to their customers is almost completely determined by

[2] The Scottish banks have a somewhat different structure from that of the clearing banks, but for the most part they fulfill the same functions. In view of the relatively small total assets of the Scottish banks, however, they are omitted from most of the statistics given here.

[3] In November 1967, the rate was raised to the unprecedented level of 8 per cent.

the bank rate: the former is normally (except for advances to a few choice customers, or to nationalized industries) 1 per cent above the bank rate, provided it is not below 5 per cent. As long as the bank rate is 4 per cent or above, as it has been since early 1955, movements of interest rates on commercial-bank credit are strictly linked with movements of the bank rate. The link to the bank rate is also strong, although somewhat less rigid, for the interest rate on three-month Treasury bills. Since members of the London Discount Market Association are committed to cover the tender of Treasury bills at a rate fixed by the Association, the interest rate thus set is usually determined in accordance with the discount houses' anticipation of the level of the bank rate during the lifetime of the bill—that is, during the thirteen weeks from the day of its issue. The rate is set at this level because the discount houses bear continuously in mind the possibility that they may find themselves forced to apply to the Bank of England as lender of last resort, in which case the bank rate would represent the cost of their borrowed money. The existing bank rate at the time of issue would normally have, it may be assumed, a most prominent role in determining such anticipations.[4]

Changes in the bank rate also signify, probably even more in the United Kingdom than in any other country, the general direction of monetary policy. They not only help determine expectations and general mood, but may also be interpreted as directives for action. Due to the largely informal manner in which commercial-banking activity is regulated, banks have come to consider an increase in the bank rate as a call upon them to be restrictive. This may lead to a restriction of advances to customers even beyond the effect of the increase in the interest cost on demand for such advances.

Open-Market Operations. The Bank of England operates regularly in the markets for both short-term and long-term government debt instruments. The operations are carried out daily, in considerable amount. But their function is primarily to smooth the market for these instruments, to prevent undue fluctuations in the money market, and to ensure the effectiveness of the bank rate as a regulator of the Treasury-bill rate and other interest rates. They are not regarded, by

[4] In early 1963, the Bank of England informed the discount houses that on its lending to them it may charge a rate higher than the bank rate. In this way, the semi-automatic link between the bank rate and the Treasury-bill rate no longer exists. In fact, a difference between the bank rate and the bank's lending rate occurred only once, in March 1963, when the latter exceeded the former by ½ per cent.

and large, as an independent instrument of monetary policy. Available evidence suggests that open-market operations are intended normally to be "neutral"—that is, they are taken in order to smooth the operation of the money market according to an existing interest rate structure, rather than to lead to changes in interest rates. In view of this evidence, and of the lack of data about them,[5] open-market operations will be disregarded in the statistical analysis.

Liquidity Requirements. Until 1960, clearing banks were not bound by law or regulation to hold any specified reserve of liquid assets. Two liquidity ratios have existed by convention, however, one dating from many years back and one from the postwar period. The Bank of England and the commercial banks treat these ratios as binding. First, the banks maintain a minimum ratio of "cash" to total deposits, where "cash" consists of deposits at the Bank of England and of cash in vault. Second, the banks are expected to maintain a minimum ratio of "liquid assets" to deposits. These "liquid assets" include, primarily, "cash" and Treasury bills and loans on call to the discount houses (which, in turn, finance mainly the purchase of Treasury bills). The cash ratio has remained at 8 per cent throughout the period here studied, and the liquid assets ratio has been changed only once during this time, when it was reduced in 1963 from 30 to 28 per cent. These ratios may thus not be regarded as instruments which are used, in fact or potentially, in the conduct of monetary policy, but their existence is still relevant to the reaction of monetary developments to balance-of-payments fluctuations, as will be noted shortly.

Since 1958, the Bank of England has been entitled to impose a requirement upon the clearing banks to maintain "special deposits" at the Bank of England, beyond the already existing liquidity requirements. These deposits are not considered part of the banks' "cash" or "liquid assets." Unlike the two other ratios, the ratio of "special deposits" (to bank deposits) is flexible. The requirement was first imposed in mid-1960, when the ratio was set at 1 per cent; after a few variations of the rate, the requirement was discontinued at the end of 1962. It was reimposed at the beginning of 1965. From its first imposition to the end of 1966, the ratio was changed six times; that is, on the average about once a year.[6]

---

[5] Although the Bank of England publishes no information on open-market operations, a few partial estimates may be found. For the years 1952–57, an estimate is constructed by Peter B. Kenen, *British Monetary Policy and the Balance of Payments, 1951–57.* Cambridge, Mass., 1960, Appendix C.

[6] In early 1968, a "Cash Deposits Scheme" was introduced to help in the control of credit granted by nonclearing banks.

Direct Control of Credit. The Bank of England, it can be seen, does not, in the main, try to control the credit supply by affecting the lending capacity of banks. Open-market operations are "neutral"; reserve ratios are constant, except for changes in the "special deposits" ratio during the 1960's; and changes in the bank rate, while probably affecting (through changes in other rates) the demand for credit, do not affect bank reserves, since commercial-bank borrowing from the Bank of England is small. Instead of controlling lending capacity by these means, the Bank of England has resorted very often to direct regulation of the size of advances from clearing banks to their customers. Due to the special relationships within the banking community, this regulation has been done by appeals from the Governor of the Bank, rather than by regulation or law; but such appeals were considered by the clearing banks to be binding. This method of control varied from the use of general statements calling for a restrictive policy to the issuance of (in effect) specific instructions as to the size of advances which the Bank regards as adequate. Credit control has apparently been regarded by the Bank of England as the most important instrument of monetary policy after the bank rate.

The guidance provided by the Bank has often been qualitative instead of, or in addition to, quantitative. Credit for specific purposes was often cited as being particularly due for contraction. In a few episodes during the 1950's, credit for hire purchase (i.e., installment credit) was thus singled out, in conjunction with changes made by the Board of Trade in the terms allowed (minimum down payment and maximum duration of payments) in hire-purchase transactions. The quantitative reflection of these hire-purchase regulations in the statistics is, however, quite small: total lending of clearing banks to hire-purchase finance companies is not very significant in comparison with total advances, and this is also true with regard to the extent of fluctuations in the amount of this lending.

BUDGETARY AND DEBT POLICY

The budget is divided into two parts, "above the line" and "below the line." [7] The former is by far the larger, and covers primarily the government's transactions of a current nature (current expenditures and normal revenues). Expenditures "below the line" are mostly of a capital nature, and consist primarily of loans to nationalized indus-

[7] This form of the budgetary presentation was changed toward the end of the period surveyed.

tries, the Public Works Board, and other public corporations. These are financed partly by a customary surplus "above the line," which is transferred "below the line." The difference between expenditures and this surplus is provided for by government borrowing.

In earlier years, a substantial fraction of lending to the government came from the outside world, within the framework of postwar aid programs. During most of the period surveyed, however, government borrowing was done primarily in the domestic market. A few major forms of borrowing may be distinguished. First, a permanent source of lending to the government is the Issue Department of the Bank of England, which increases its stock of government securities to the extent that the fiduciary note issue increases. While the size of the note issue has increased continuously, and may be expected to do so normally, it is not determined by the government; hence, the size of borrowing from this source cannot be affected by the government. Borrowing from the Banking Department of the Bank of England is, on the contrary, quite flexible but not permanent. It comprises current ("ways and means") advances, which are given for a very short time (a day or less) to cover cash gaps, and are on the average very small, and the purchase of Treasury bills. Holdings of the latter by the Banking Department do not increase over the long run, and are thus not considered a permanent source of finance of government expenditures. But the size of these holdings may vary considerably over short periods.

The main source of finance of the over-all budgetary deficit is borrowing from the commercial-banking system and the public. This takes almost entirely the form of sales of long-term government (or government-guaranteed) securities. The amount of Treasury bills (which are held primarily by the London clearing banks, the discount houses, and overseas holders) fluctuates considerably over short periods. But, as in the case of holdings by the Bank of England, this is not considered a permanent form of government borrowing.[8]

An important short-term source of lending (positive or negative) to the government, which appears in the statistics as an "external source," is the Exchange Equalization Account. Due to the importance of this item for the nature of response of financial policies to balance-of-

---

[8] Over the years, the amount of outstanding market Treasury bills even shows a slight downward trend. This reflects the desire of the government to "fund" the national debt. In absolute magnitudes, most of the funding took place before the start of the period surveyed. In terms of the ratio of short-term debt to total debt, however, this funding was also considerable during the years under review.

payments fluctuations, it deserves a somewhat more detailed discussion.

Exchange Equalization Account. The Exchange Equalization Account, which is administered by the Bank of England, holds the official reserves of gold and foreign exchange, as well as domestic assets in the form of "top" Treasury bills.[9] The total size of the Account's assets is constant.[10] Any increase in the holding of reserves is compensated for by an equivalent reduction in the holding of Treasury bills; and any decline of reserves, by an increase of Treasury bills. When, for instance, the Account acquires foreign exchange, it finances this acquisition by reducing its lending to the Exchequer, and, thus, reducing its holdings of Treasury bills. In the Exchequer's accounts, this is recorded as payment to (or negative receipt from) the Exchange Equalization Account. In fact, this does not lead to a decline in the amount of resources available to the government, since the Exchequer's practice is to sell in the market an equivalent amount of Treasury bills (a necessary practice in view of the Exchequer's custom of holding only a very small cash balance). The end result of this process is, therefore, that total borrowing by the Exchequer is unaffected, but the holding of "top" Treasury bills by the Exchange Equalization Account is replaced by the holding of "market" Treasury bills by the commercial banks (the clearing banks and the discount houses). The banks are left, at the end of the process, with the additional asset of Treasury bills against the additional liability of deposits of their customers, which resulted from the original sale of foreign exchange to the banks.

The secondary repercussions of this process are not clear-cut. If the cash ratio limitation is effective—that is, if before the accumulation of foreign-exchange reserves banks did not hold cash in excess of the required 8 per cent—the banking system will now find that its cash reserves are short (since deposits have risen without a change in the amount of cash). Clearing banks will have, therefore, to contract credit. This means that the secondary repercussion will be in a restrictive direc-

---

[9] During the period surveyed, the Account's assets also included some claims on foreign countries which were not counted as official reserves. These were foreign long-term securities (stocks and bonds), which had been surrendered to the government following the imposition of foreign-exchange control during World War II. In February 1966, assets valued at over 880 million dollars were sold out of this portfolio, thus augmenting the amount defined as official holdings of foreign-exchange reserves.

[10] This does not refer to changes due to fluctuations in the market value of foreign assets which were mentioned in the last footnote; however, these fluctuations do not find expression in the Account's records.

tion, contrary to the direct impact of the accumulation of foreign assets. If, prior to the disturbance, expansion of credit was restricted by the amount of liquid assets held by banks, while banks had excessive cash, then the increase in holdings of Treasury bills would make possible an expansion of credit. But this possibility is probably remote, since there is no reason for banks to prefer the holding of zero-yielding cash— beyond the required 8 per cent—to the holding of other liquid assets with positive yields.

It may, thus, be assumed that, in general, due to the form of operation of the Exchange Equalization Account and the Exchequer, the secondary repercussion of the accumulation of foreign assets is restrictive, contrary to its direct impact; and expansive for a decline of foreign-exchange reserves. The operation of the Exchange Equalization Account seems to imply the existence of an automatic mechanism which leads to at least some neutralization, or "sterilization," of the effect of foreign-exchange fluctuations on the monetary system.[11]

2. The Determination of Imbalances

In one sense, the determination of balance-of-payments turning points is comparatively easy for the United Kingdom. It is evident from the series on gold and foreign-exchange reserves in Chart 11-1 that there is no discernible long-term trend that is significant in relation to the size of periodical fluctuations in the level of these assets.[12] These fluctuations, in turn, are numerous enough that a substantial number of subperiods with clear upward or downward movements may be established.

In another sense, however, the case of the United Kingdom is more complicated than most. This is because it serves as a "reserve country"; that is, one in which the outside world holds substantial sterling claims. A considerable amount of attention is usually paid to these claims, making it evident that this factor will have to be considered in an attempt to determine the country's external position.

There are undoubtedly very many combinations of different assets

[11] For a similar conclusion, see the discussion of the British experience during the 1930's in William Adams Brown's chapter on Exchange Stabilization Funds, *International Currency Experience, op. cit.,* particularly pp. 150–54.

[12] A calculation of the trend factor, made for the purpose of the analysis in the first part of this study, confirms this impression.

and liabilities which may be worth observation. Here, however, the four will be used which, on the basis of the literature and of *a priori* reasoning, seem the most promising.

First, we shall look at the series most often used in this study, the gross external assets (gold and foreign-exchange reserves) held by the government. In official publications, official reserves include only gold and short-term liquid dollar assets held by the Exchange Equalization Account. When, however, the size of reserves is affected by transactions with the IMF, this is usually mentioned at the time the figures are released, with the indication that calculation of the "true" change in reserves would have to take these transactions into account. This series is defined here, therefore, as in the studies of other countries, to include the net IMF position (and, until 1958, the EPU position) among the external assets.

Another possible variable is *net,* rather than gross, external official assets. This net is obtained by deducting sterling short-term liabilities to official monetary institutions abroad from the United Kingdom's official external assets. Observing changes in this magnitude is useful when the government is indeed indifferent between changes in official net assets brought about by changes in gross assets and changes created by movements of liabilities in the opposite direction; that is, for instance, if the government considers an increase of external assets and a reduction of sterling liabilities to be of equal benefit. The observation of changes in this net magnitude as indicative of imbalances amounts, in effect, to defining the balancing item in the balance of payments by the "official settlements" approach.

Still another possibility is to derive net figures in which not only *official* foreign holdings of sterling, but also private short-term sterling claims by foreigners are deducted from the country's official external reserves. (This method would correspond to the "liquidity" approach employed in the United States.) While the arguments advanced in the United States against this approach would apply in the United Kingdom, it seems that at least some attention may have been paid by the British government to the behavior of net assets defined in this way.

Finally, since the United Kingdom is a reserve country, it might be assumed that the government views its external assets the way a commercial bank treats its reserve of liquid means—that is, as being held to assure the conversion of foreign sterling claims into other assets (gold or dollars), to which the holders of the sterling assets have the ultimate claim. If this is so, it would then be useful to observe the ratio of the United Kingdom's official external assets to its official sterling liabilities: the higher this ratio, the more "sound" is the country's external position, and the more secure are foreign holders of sterling about the possibility of conversion. An increase of this ratio would then be an improvement, and a decline would be a deterioration. Again, there are indications of at least some tendency by the government to pay attention to this ratio.[13]

In Chart 11-1 these series are represented by the top four lines. To facilitate observation of these series, the direction of movement indicated by each is given in Chart 11-2. A black line for a given period indicates a downward movement (a "deterioration," or a "deficit"). The absence of a black line indicates either the opposite or (much less often) a period of relative stability.

It is immediately apparent from Chart 11-2 that all the series yield very similar indications. The only extensive length of time in which considerable divergence among the series is found is between the beginning of 1963 and the middle of 1964, which is explained by a substantial rise, at that time, of sterling liabilities to both foreign monetary authorities and other foreigners. Apart from this episode, there seems to be an almost complete agreement among the four series.

Accordingly, it was decided to determine turning points in balance-of-payments developments by the indications provided by all four series together, the disagreements among the series being too minor to justify experimentation with more than one division into subperiods. This division is shown by the bottom line in Chart 11-2 and appears also in column 1 in Table 11-1.[14] As has been mentioned, periods of stability (only insignificant upward or downward movements) were rare. Thus, only two subperiods of stability are indicated in Table 11-1. One of these—the subperiod from III 1962 to III 1963—is indicated as "stable" not only because the relevant movements were not large but also because of the conflicting evidence of the various series.

---

[13] ". . . the relationship between reserves and liabilities was clearly far from satisfactory throughout the postwar period and remains so. Treasury witnesses told us that it had been the main aim of policy to improve this relationship by increasing the reserves and reducing the liabilities; they appeared to be comparatively indifferent which form the improvement took." *Radcliffe Report, op. cit.,* p. 231.

[14] In Table 11-1, as very often in the text, a period of deterioration will be designated as one in which "reserves fall," and a period of improvement as one in which "reserves rise." This should be understood simply as a short-cut device; a period of deterioration will indeed be usually one in which official reserves fall, but there are a few minor exceptions; this goes, similarly, for periods of improvement.

CHART 11-1
UNITED KINGDOM: TIME SERIES OF SELECTED
VARIABLES

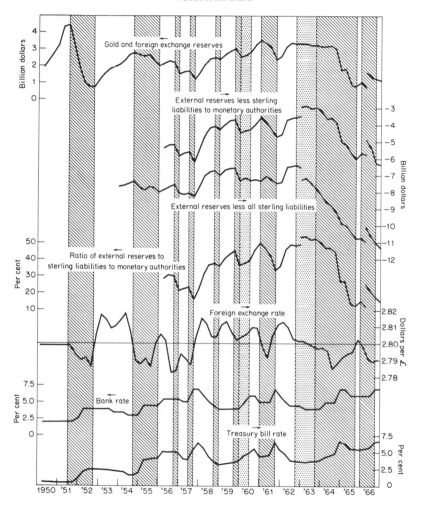

CHART 11-1 (*Continued*)

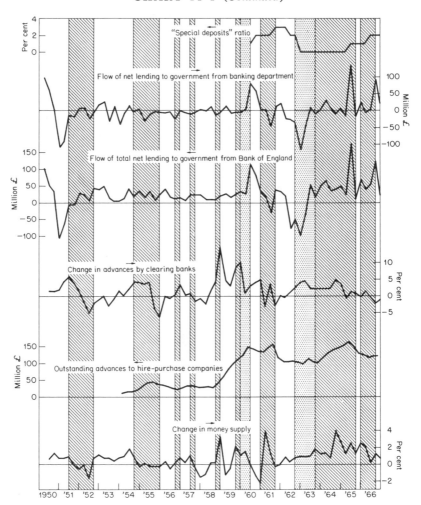

NOTE: Diagonal-line areas represent period of downward imbalances;

CHART 11-1 (*Concluded*)

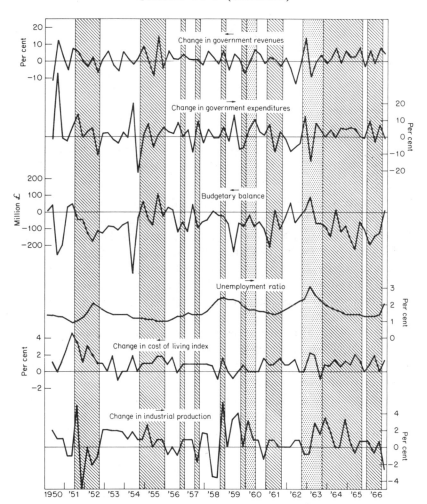

gray areas represent stability; white areas represent upward imbalances.

CHART 11-2

UNITED KINGDOM: ALTERNATIVE BALANCE-OF-
PAYMENTS INDICATORS AND COMPOSITE INDEX

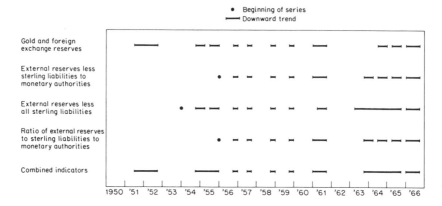

It may be worthwhile to investigate still another possible indicator of the country's external position: the rate of exchange. Although the rate is basically fixed, a small range of fluctuations, between 2.78 and 2.82 dollars per pound, was allowed.[15] While fluctuations within this range can hardly be expected to correct imbalances of payments—certainly not in the current account—they may have served as indicators of these imbalances: there is no doubt that movements of the rate of exchange in the United Kingdom attract wide attention, and may conceivably have signified to the government a need for policy action.

By and large, the level of the rate of exchange appears to be positively correlated with the country's external position.[16] The correlation of the two improves considerably if the series depicting the rate of exchange is shifted to the right one quarter. This is done in Chart 11-3, which compares movements of official gold and foreign-exchange reserves with movements of the rate of exchange, the latter being moved by one quarter. The two series appear in this chart to be moving in close unison, particularly since the beginning of 1954. The correlation

[15] When, in November 1967, the formal rate was changed to $2.40 per pound, a similar range was allowed around the new rate.

[16] In this connection, the term "rate of exchange" is used according to the normal practice in the United Kingdom, rather than as in most of the literature or in the rest of this study; a "low rate," for instance, means here a low price of the home currency (i.e., dollars per pound).

CHART 11-3

UNITED KINGDOM: EXTERNAL RESERVES AND
RATE OF EXCHANGE

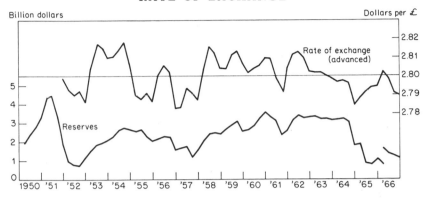

seems to be weak during the most recent years covered, 1965 and 1966; but if these two years are disregarded, it is strong indeed. From 1952 to 1964, reserves changed in forty-two of the fifty-two quarters (while in the other ten quarters the movement of reserves was slight enough to be disregarded). In thirty-four of these forty-two quarters, changes in the rate of exchange were in the same direction as the changes in reserves. This association between changes in reserves and changes in the rate of exchange may be explained in two ways. First, it is possible that the foreign-exchange market anticipates changes in reserves, expects a response of the rate to these changes, and reacts accordingly. Another, perhaps more plausible, explanation is that both the change in the rate and the following change in reserves are due to the same factor. Take, for instance, a decline of demand for sterling. The rate will tend to move down; but as long as it does not approach the floor of 2.78 dollars per pound, no intervention (or very little intervention) by the Exchange Equalization Account will take place. If the change in demand is persistent, however, the rate will gradually decline toward the floor; intervention by the Account will start, and the Account's external reserves will decline. The fall of reserves will thus follow, with some time lag, the fall of the rate. Similarly, movements in the opposite direction will take place when demand for sterling increases.

Whatever its possible explanation, the association is relevant in the present context. First, because it indicates that, if the government's

TABLE

UNITED KINGDOM: BALANCE-OF-PAYMENTS

Subperiod (end of quarters)	External Reserves	Bank Rate	Clearing-Bank Advances (quarterly rate of change, per cent)
	(1)	(2)	(3)
IV 1949 – II 1951	rise	* stable	+3.0
II 1951 – III 1952	fall	+ raised	(+) −.6
III 1952 – III 1954	rise	+ lowered	(+) +.5
III 1954 – IV 1955	fall	+ raised	(*) +.4
IV 1955 – III 1956	rise	− raised	(−) −.1
III 1956 – IV 1956	fall	* stable	(−) +3.7
IV 1956 – II 1957	rise	+ lowered	(−) +.6
II 1957 – III 1957	fall	+ raised	(+) −1.6
III 1957 – III 1958	rise	+ lowered	(−) −.6
III 1958 – IV 1958	fall	− lowered	(−) +1.0
IV 1958 – III 1959	rise	* stable	(+) +5.5
III 1959 – IV 1959	fall	* stable	(−) +10.7
IV 1959 – II 1960	stable	raised	+2.0
II 1960 – IV 1960	rise	+ lowered	(+) +4.8
IV 1960 – III 1961	fall	+ raised	(+) +1.3
III 1961 – III 1962	rise	+ lowered	(−) +.9
III 1962 – III 1963	stable	lowered	+3.4
III 1963 – III 1965	fall	+ raised	(+) +2.1
III 1965 – IV 1965	rise	* stable	(−) 0
IV 1965 – III 1966	fall	+ raised	(+) −.2
III 1966 – I 1967	rise	+ lowered	—

NOTE: For explanation of symbols, see Table 8-3.

target were stability of the exchange rate, the timing of policy reactions would be similar to that called for by stability of the balance-of-payments target, as indicated by the series in Chart 11-2. Second, if the target is the latter, but the association under discussion was recognized by the government, movements of the rate of exchange would be interpreted as giving an advance warning of impeding imbalances of payments, and could thus be expected to shorten the time lag involved in policy reactions to balance-of-payments disturbances.

11-1

POSITION AND MOVEMENTS OF POLICY VARIABLES

Outstanding Advances to Hire-Purchase Companies (4)	Money Supply (quarterly rate of change, per cent) (5)	Government Revenues (quarterly rate of change, per cent) (6)	Government Expenditures (quarterly rate of change, per cent) (7)	Budgetary Balance (quarterly average, in millions of pounds) (8)
—	+.9	+2.1	−7.8	−50
—	(+) −.3	(−) −.3	(−) +2.4	(−) −85
—	(+) +.9	(−) +.8	(−) 0	(+) −118
− rise	(+) −.1	(+) +2.4	(−) +2.5	(+) +11
− fall	(*) +.1	(*) +2.2	(+) +4.7	(+) −19
+ fall	(−) +.9	(+) +4.1	(+) +.7	(−) −57
+ rise	(−) +.6	(+) +1.1	(−) −2.4	(−) −30
* stable	(+) −.5	(*) +.7	(−) +9.4	(−) −88
− fall	(−) −.5	(*) +1.3	(−) +.2	(−) −29
− rise	(−) +3.3	(+) +6.3	(−) +6.3	(*) −19
+ rise	(−) +.2	(+) +.3	(−) +1.2	(+) −147
− rise	(−) +1.1	(−) −7.0	(+) −6.2	(+) −78
rise	+.8	+3.1	+7.8	−45
− fall	(−) −1.8	(+) +1.6	(−) +1.9	(+) −75
+ rise	(−) +1.8	(−) +.2	(+) +.3	(−) −94
− fall	(−) +.5	(+) −4.1	(−) −5.0	(−) −13
stable	+1.2	+2.1	+2.6	−7
− rise	(−) +2.0	(+) +3.5	(−) +3.2	(−) −105
− fall	(+) +2.5	(+) −3.0	(−) −.7	(*) −105
* stable	(+) +1.2	—	—	—
—	—	—	—	—

3. Pattern of Policies

The first policy instrument shown in Table 11-1 is the bank rate (column 2). Its indication is quite clear, and is supported by a relatively large number of observations: in the large majority of cases, the bank rate responds in an adjusting direction to balance-of-payments fluctuations. In a small number of instances the bank rate remains unchanged, while reserves move either up or down; only in a single subperiod does the bank rate move in a direction opposite to that which balance-of-payments adjustment would have required.[17] The response of the bank rate to balance-of-payments fluctuations seems to be about as consistent during periods of upward, as during periods of downward, imbalances.

The evidence thus suggests strongly that the bank rate was used in the service of balance-of-payments adjustment. To check further the validity of this conclusion, a few other methods of observation will be attempted.

Chart 11-4 presents a reference-cycle analysis in which reference dates are determined by balance-of-payments developments: a trough-to-peak phase is a period of increasing reserves; and a peak-to-trough phase, a period of declining reserves. The reference dates are as follows:

Cycle	Trough	Peak	Trough
1950–52	i 1950	ii 1951	iii 1952
1952–57	iii 1952	iii 1954	iii 1957
1957–61	iii 1957	iv 1960	iii 1961
1961–66	iii 1961	iv 1962	iii 1966

Essentially, these phases are similar to the subperiods of imbalances distinguished in Table 11-1, but they disregard minor changes of brief duration, admitting only phases of at least a few quarters. Part A of Chart 11-4 depicts the position of the bank rate during the phases of balance-of-payments developments. It appears clear that movements in the rate approach the V-shape which balance-of-payments adjustment would require—the rate falls during upward movements of reserves, and rises during downward movements. This method of observation gives, therefore, the same results as that provided by Table 11-1.

Table 11-2 is designed to test whether the apparent association between the balance-of-payments and movements of the bank rate can be explained by responses of the rate to other targets. Column 1 lists the increases and all the reductions in the bank rate. The remaining columns record the movements of each of the major target variables—

[17] This is the subperiod from iv 1955 to iii 1956, in which the bank rate was raised although reserves were rising. In Table 11-1 another such period is indicated—the fourth quarter of 1958—in which the bank rate was lowered despite a balance-of-payment deterioration. But this seeming contradiction is due to the use of quarterly data, which in this case (a very brief movement) yield misleading results: when the rate was lowered in November 1958, reserves were still rising.

CHART 11-4

UNITED KINGDOM: PATTERNS OF POLICY VARIABLES
DURING BALANCE-OF-PAYMENTS CYCLES

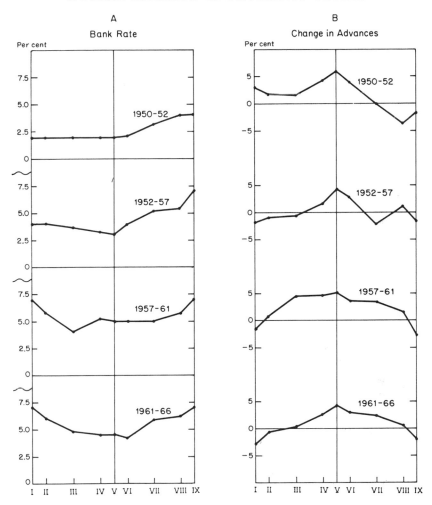

reserves, employment, industrial production, and the price level—during the last quarter before each respective change in the rate.[18] It appears, again—from column 2—that almost all changes in the bank

[18] A similar analysis has also been made taking the record of each target variable during the last *two* quarters, rather than the last quarter alone. But the results were generally very close to those obtained by the use of a single quarter.

CHART 11-4 (*Continued*)

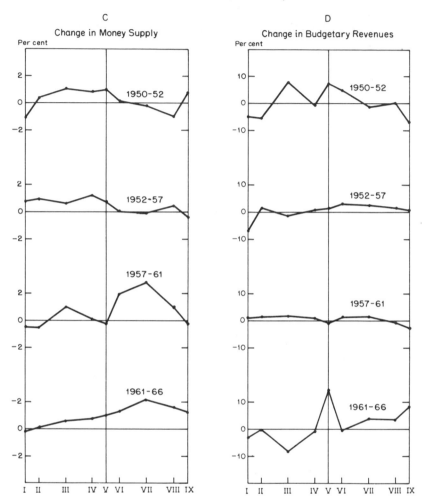

rate could be explained by the requirement for balance-of-payments adjustment. The single exception was a reduction of the rate in June 1965, during a period of substantial loss of reserves.

From column 3 it appears that an assumption that changes in the bank rate were intended to counteract fluctuations in unemployment cannot be dismissed altogether. But the association of the bank rate with the target of high employment seems to be much weaker than its association with the target of balance-of-payments stability. Moreover,

CHART 11-4 (*Concluded*)

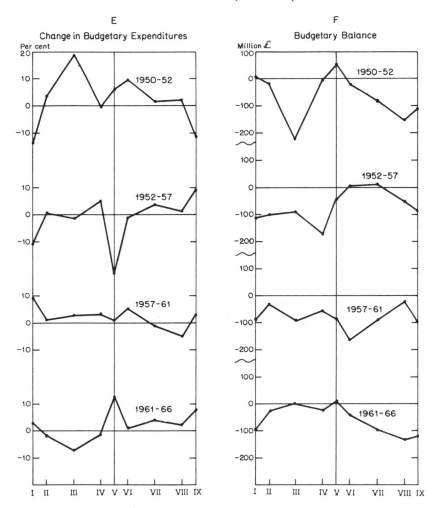

for all the episodes in which the targets of balance-of-payments stability and high employment require opposite policy responses, priority appears to be assigned to the balance of payments: in two instances (November 1951 and March 1952) a fall of reserves was accompanied by an increase in the bank rate despite a rise in unemployment; while in two other episodes (February 1957; November and December 1960) the rate was lowered when reserves were rising and the unemployment ratio was low and falling.

TABLE 11-2

UNITED KINGDOM: CHANGES IN BANK RATE AND POSITION OF TARGET VARIABLES

Change in Bank Rate	External Reserves	Ratio of Unemployment	Industrial Production (rate of increase)	Cost-of-Living Index (rate of increase)
(1)	(2)	(3)	(4)	(5)
Raised:				
November 1951	+ fall	− rises	− low	+ high
March 1952	+ fall	− rises	− low	+ high
January 1955	+ fall	− falls	* normal	* normal
February 1956	+ fall	+ low	− low	+ high
September 1957	+ fall	* stable	− low	* normal
January 1960	+ fall	− high	− low	* normal
June 1960	* stable	* stable	* normal	− low
July 1961	+ fall	+ falls	* normal	* normal
February 1964	+ fall	− high	+ high	* normal
November 1964	+ fall	+ falls	+ high	+ high
July 1966	+ fall	+ low	− low	+ high
Lowered:				
September 1953	+ rise	* stable	− high	+ low
May 1954	+ rise	− falls	* normal	+ low
February 1957	* fluctuate	+ rises	* normal	* normal
March 1958	+ rise	+ rises	− high	* normal
May 1958	+ rise	+ rises	+ low	* normal
August 1958	+ rise	+ rises	+ low	+ low
November 1958	+ rise	+ rises	− high	− high
November 1960	+ rise	− falls	+ low	− high
December 1960	+ rise	− falls	+ low	− high
October 1961	* stable	+ rises	+ low	* normal
November 1961	* stable	+ rises	+ low	* normal
April 1962	+ rise	+ rises	* normal	* normal
June 1962	+ rise	+ rises	* normal	− high
January 1963	* stable	+ rises	+ low	+ low
June 1965	− fall	− low	+ low	* normal
January 1967	+ rise	+ rises	+ low	* normal
April 1967	+ rise	+ rises	−	−
May 1967	+ rise	+ rises	−	−

+ indicates a position of the target variable which would justify the change in the bank rate.

− indicates the opposite position.

* indicates a position which requires no change in the bank rate.

The target of industrial production fares even less well than that of employment. There is but little association between increases of the bank rate and fluctuations in the rate of expansion of production. Most bank rate reductions could be explained by slack developments of industrial production; but there are a few exceptions. Again, in almost all cases of conflict between the requirements of high industrial production and stability of the balance-of-payments—and these include a large number of instances of slack production accompanied by a loss of reserves—the movement of the rate must be interpreted as resulting from assigning priority to the balance of payments. The single exception to this interpretation is the instance of June 1965, mentioned earlier, in which a reduction of the rate while reserves were falling could be explained by a low rate of expansion of industrial production.

The target of price stability, measured by the cost-of-living index, does not perform very well either. Fluctuations of the rate of increase of prices usually could not explain the movements of the bank rate. Once again, in time of conflict (November and December 1960; June 1962), the target of balance-of-payments adjustment seems to win; the rate is lowered when reserves rise, despite a high rate of increase of the price level.

Chart 11-5 performs, by reference-cycle analysis, an examination similar to that based on Table 11-2. The reference dates are determined this time by the cycle of the bank rate and the Treasury-bill rate.[19] At the trough of this cycle, the rate is low; it increases toward the peak, where it is highest; and falls during the peak-to-trough phase. The dates of the reference cycles of bank rate are as follows:

Cycle	Trough	Peak	Trough
1950–54	III 1950	III 1952	II 1954
1954–57	II 1954	III 1956	II 1957
1957–58	II 1957	IV 1957	IV 1958
1958–61	IV 1958	III 1960	I 1961
1961–63	I 1961	III 1961	I 1963
1963–65	I 1963	I 1965	IV 1965
1965–66	IV 1965	IV 1966	

Parts A, B, C, and D of Chart 11-5 show, respectively, the positions of the variables of external reserves, the unemployment ratio, the rate of change of industrial production, and the rate of change of the cost-

[19] Whenever the time series of the bank rate is flat, the turning point was selected by the movement of the Treasury-bill rate.

CHART 11-5

UNITED KINGDOM: PATTERNS OF TARGET VARIABLES DURING BANK–RATE CYCLES

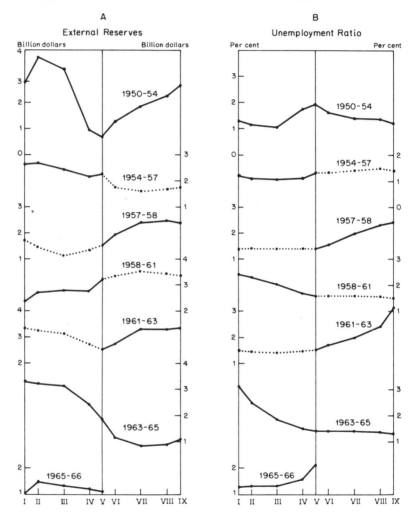

A — External Reserves

B — Unemployment Ratio

CHART 11-5 (*Concluded*)

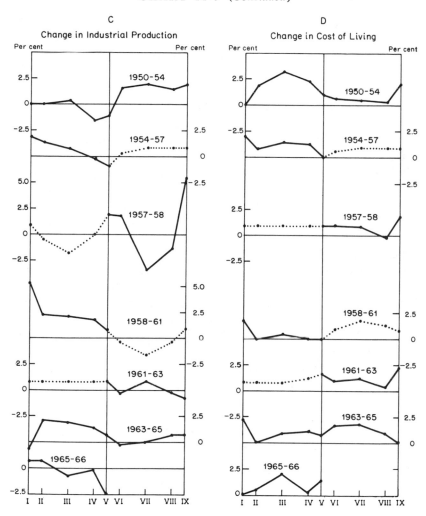

C

Change in Industrial Production

D

Change in Cost of Living

of-living index during the bank rate's reference cycles.[20] To be consistent with the assumption that the rate was manipulated in response to the need of the target in question, Parts A and B would have to be V-shaped; that is, the rate would have to go up when foreign reserves go down, or when the unemployment rises. The other two variables (the rates of change of industrial production and of the price level) would, on the contrary, have the shape of an inverted V if the bank rate were employed to serve these targets.

Observation of Part A of the chart shows that, by and large, the expected V-shape is found for the variable of external reserves. It is clearest in the 1950–54 rate cycle, but is found also on most other occasions. The important exception to it is the first half of the contraction phase of the 1963–65 cycle—that is, about the first half of 1965. From Part B it appears that the V-shape occurs less often for the variable of unemployment: it is found regularly from the peak of the 1957–58 cycle to the peak of the 1963–65 cycle—that is, from about the end of 1957 to the beginning of 1965—but not in other periods. Parts C and D, on the other hand, do not approach at all the expected inverted V-shape; nor, in fact, do they exhibit any other consistent shape. By this evidence, it must be concluded that the bank rate was not tied in any regular way to the needs of the targets of high industrial production or stable prices, and that the rate seems most likely to have been used for balance-of-payments adjustment, although the possibility that during part of the time it was used to secure high employment cannot be entirely dismissed. These conclusions conform, by and large, to those derived by earlier methods.

Chart 11-6 presents the movements of policy variables during cycles of unemployment—the reference dates are selected by observation of the ratio of unemployment, the trough determined at a point of low unemployment and the peak at a point of high unemployment. Three such cycles may be clearly distinguished, with the following dates:

Cycle	Trough	Peak	Trough
1951–55	II 1951	II 1952	IV 1955
1955–61	IV 1955	IV 1958	II 1961
1961–66	II 1961	I 1963	II 1966

In Part A of Chart 11-6 movements of the bank rate are represented. If these movements respond to the need to maintain high employ-

[20] The phases of III 1956 to II 1957, II 1957 to IV 1957, and I 1961 to III 1961, are probably too short to display any reliable pattern of behavior of variables. This is indicated in Chart 11-5 by dotted lines for these periods.

CHART 11 6

UNITED KINGDOM: PATTERNS OF POLICY VARIABLES
DURING UNEMPLOYMENT CYCLES

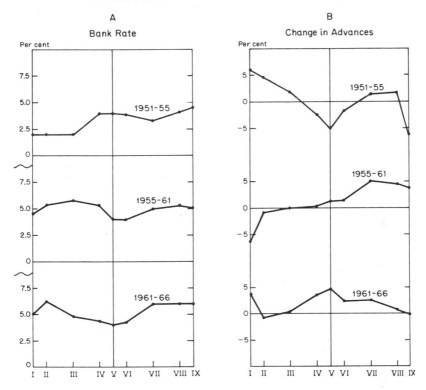

ment, they should have a V-shape, a high bank rate when unemployment is low, and vice versa. Some resemblance to this shape may be
detected during part of the time; but it is considerably less consistent
than the pattern indicated in Part A of Chart 11-4, where the movements of the bank rate were examined during cycles of external
reserves.

The results from all these methods of observation agree roughly with
one another and support the same conclusion—movements of the bank
rate were closely associated with the position of the balance of payments, and could be interpreted as intended to adjust imbalances of
payments; and it is unlikely that these movements were in fact intended,
by and large, to achieve one of the other major alternative targets.

CHART 11-6 *(Continued)*

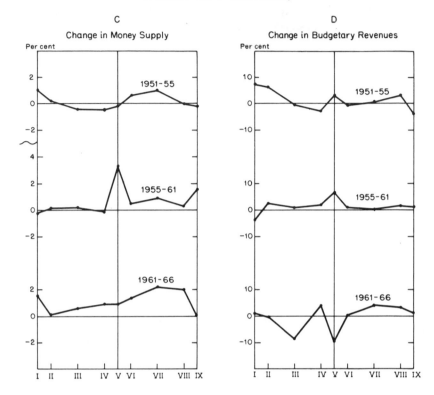

C

Change in Money Supply

D

Change in Budgetary Revenues

The only other direct and comprehensive instrument used by the Bank of England is the "special deposits" ratio. Since it was introduced only in 1960, the period of its operation has been too short to permit reliable generalizations. But the experience thus far does not, as may be seen from Chart 11-1, indicate a close relationship between the use of this instrument and the position of the balance of payments. The ratio appears to have been raised from the time of its introduction, in mid-1960, to the end of 1961—a period in which the balance-of-payments position fluctuated. It was reduced between the second quarter of 1962 and the end of that year, when reserves were almost stable; from then to early 1965, it was inoperative while reserves were mostly declining; and it was reestablished during 1965 and 1966, again during a period of mostly downward imbalances. This inconclusive evidence suggests no firm relationship between this variable and the balance of payments.

CHART 11-6 (*Concluded*)

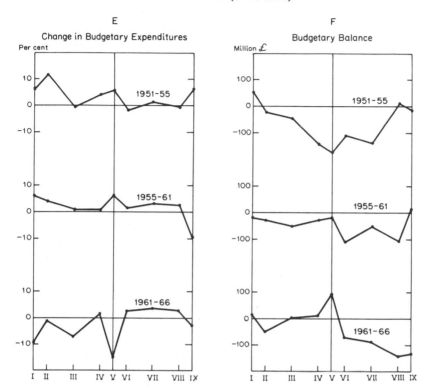

E

Change in Budgetary Expenditures

F

Budgetary Balance

A similar conclusion appears to hold for the variable of the Bank-of-England lending to the government. In Chart 11-1 two alternative series represent this variable—both recording the net flow rather than out-standing amounts. One shows the data of the government's net borrowing as the Bank's publications usually define it, covering only the government's transactions with the Banking Department. The other adds to this the change in government securities held by the Issue Department, which is the more substantial magnitude. The two series give very similar indications. They suggest that this variable cannot be associated in any consistent way with balance-of-payments fluctuations. The flow of lending was roughly constant most of the time. It was particularly high from about the end of 1959 to the end of 1960, when external reserves were mostly rising, and again from mid-1963 to the end of the period, when reserves were mostly falling. The lending was particularly low—in fact, mostly negative—from early 1962 to early

1963, when reserves were mostly rising. Major upward or downward movements of reserves do not seem to lead to any noticeable change in the level of this variable. It may thus be safely concluded that lending by the Bank of England to the Treasury did not respond consistently to balance-of-payments fluctuations. As will be seen later, a similar conclusion will be drawn for the government's budgetary deficit; and these two variables—the budgetary deficit and the Treasury's borrowing from the Bank—do appear to follow similar time patterns.

Commercial-bank credit is subject, it will be recalled, to a large amount of intervention by the Bank of England. The performance of this variable is described in column 3 of Table 11-1. The evidence does not suggest a regular association of this variable with the balance-of-payments position. The only period of any length in which the rate of expansion of bank advances varied in accordance with balance-of-payments requirements is that of the early 1950's, from 1951 to 1954. From then on, exceptions to this pattern of behavior were about as numerous as adherence to it.

Quite another conclusion is suggested, however, by other methods of observation. Chart 11-4 offers a reference-cycle analysis in which reference dates are determined by balance-of-payments developments. In Part B of this chart, the behavior of the rate of change of bank advances is described. If the rate of expansion of credit is governed by the need for balance-of-payments adjustment, the lines of this chart should have the inverted V-shape: the rate should be low at the trough, when reserves are low; rise towards the peak, when reserves rise; and fall back toward the trough. Indeed, the chart shows this shape almost consistently. It thus appears that if briefer fluctuations of the balance of payments are overlooked and longer-term movements analyzed, the rate of expansion of credit does behave in a manner consistent with the hypothesis that this rate is governed by the requirements of balance-of-payments adjustment.

In Chart 11-7 this hypothesis is examined by determining the cycles and their reference dates according to the rate of expansion of credit. In the trough-to-peak phase this rate is high; during the peak-to-trough phase it is low. The cycles are as follows:

Cycle	Trough	Peak	Trough
1951–53		IV 1951	III 1953
1953–58	III 1953	II 1955	I 1958
1958–62	I 1958	II 1961	I 1962
1962–64	I 1962	IV 1964	

CHART 11-7

UNITED KINGDOM: PATTERNS OF TARGET VARIABLES
DURING CREDIT CYCLES

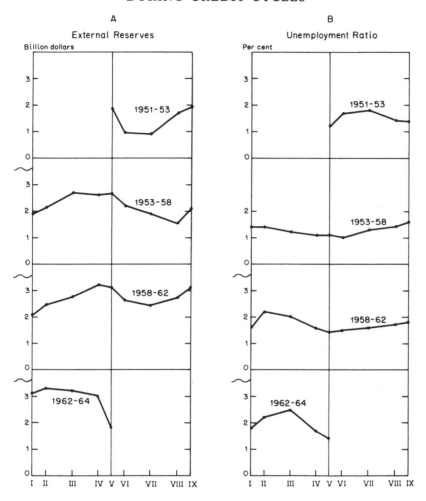

A
External Reserves

B
Unemployment Ratio

In Part A of this chart, the external reserve position is plotted along these cycles. Again, the hypothesis under consideration would require inverted V-shaped lines. In fact, a pattern close to it may be discerned, but it is far from being consistent. On the other hand, Parts B, C, and D of this chart do not reveal any other rule by which the rate of expansion of credit is governed. The variables of industrial production and of the

CHART 11-7 (*Concluded*)

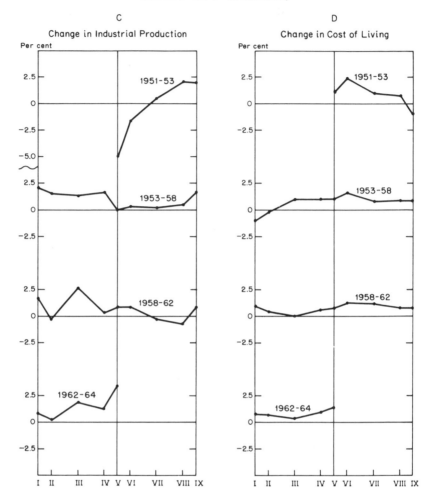

C

Change in Industrial Production

D

Change in Cost of Living

price level, represented in Parts C and D respectively, do not show any regularity of movement or position along the reference cycle under consideration. Movements of unemployment ratio, presented in Part B, would support an assumption that the policy variable in question was regulated by the need to maintain high employment if they had the inverted V-shape; in fact, the pattern revealed is partly the opposite. Likewise, in Part B of Chart 11-6, movements of the credit variable are presented along the unemployment reference cycle, and do not reveal any coherent pattern. This evidence does not support the assumption that movements of credit were determined by any of the possible targets of high employment, high rate of expansion of production, or price stability. This lends more support to the hypothesis that it was, in fact, the balance-of-payments position which directed the policy variable under consideration.

The combined outcome of these different analyses thus suggests that credit policy was intended to serve the needs of balance-of-payments adjustment. But this conclusion is not entirely firm, and applies to major, longer-term imbalances of payments rather than to shorter-term fluctuations.

A form of credit which may merit particular observation is that of advances by the clearing banks to hire-purchase finance companies. It is often asserted that hire-purchase restrictions have fulfilled an important role in balance-of-payments adjustment. These restrictions took the direct form of variations of the minimum amount of down-payments and the maximum duration of payments; but these variations must find some expression in the volume of hire-purchase credit. No direct measurement of the amount of this credit to consumers is readily available; but variations in it should presumably be reflected in the size of bank advances to hire-purchase companies. The latter (for which data are available since 1954) are given in Chart 11-1, and movements in the amount outstanding are analyzed in column 4 of Table 11-1. It appears, from this evidence, that no consistent association of this variable with the position of the balance of payments may be established; this would be true also if longer-term movements are analyzed. Roughly speaking, the volume of hire-purchase advances rises from early 1954 to the latter part of 1955, declines from then to the latter part of 1958, rises again until mid-1960, remains on a high level until late 1961, declines from then to the end of 1963, rises once more towards mid-1965, and falls back since then. By and large, these movements do not correspond to any uniform trends in the country's external position. It may be, of course, that the observed magnitude does not reflect accurately the variable of hire-purchase regulations. But as far as this evidence goes, it indicates that this variable was not in fact governed by the need for balance-of-payments adjustment.

The variable of money supply is represented in Chart 11-1 and is analyzed first by means of column 5 in Table 11-1. The analysis establishes no general association between this variable and movements of the balance of payments, with the possible exception of the first half of the 1950's—until about the end of 1955, changes in the rate of change of money supply do support the assumption that they were intended to serve the needs of balance-of-payments adjustment; from then on, however, movements of the variable were much more often in a disadjusting than in an adjusting direction. In particular, money supply seems to expand at a relatively high rate during recent years, from 1963 onward—a period distinguished by persistent balance-of-payments deficits.

The variable is further analyzed by means of Part C of Chart 11-4, where its movements along the balance-of-payments cycles are presented. The use of the variable for balance-of-payments adjustment would require the money supply curves to have an inverted V-shape— a pattern which is not found as a rule.

Still another form of analysis is the observation of the balance of payments along the money supply cycles—that is, cycles in which turning points are determined by the rate of change of money supply. This is done in Chart 11-8, in which the trough-to-peak phases represent periods of high level of the policy variable, while peak-to-trough phases represent a low level. The turning points of the cycles are as follows:[21]

Cycle	Trough	Peak	Trough
1950–52		III 1950	II 1952
1952–56	II 1952	II 1954	III 1956
1956–58	III 1956	II 1957	I 1958
1958–60	I 1958	I 1960	IV 1960

Part A presents movements of external reserves. If these movements were the reason for change in money supply, the curves would have to possess the inverted V-shape. In fact, something quite similar to this is found in the first 1½ cycles (until 1956), but no intelligible pattern appears later.

The results of all these methods of analysis suggest that money supply may have been controlled in a way which responds to the requirements for balance-of-payments adjustment until about the middle of the 1950's, although not after that. From Parts B, C, and D of Chart 11-7 it appears that the lack of such responsiveness was not due to the assignment of the instrument of money supply to the service of some other policy target, since no meaningful patterns are revealed in the level of employment, the level of industrial production, or the price

[21] No meaningful cycles can be distinguished after 1960.

CHART 11-8

UNITED KINGDOM: PATTERNS OF TARGET VARIABLES
DURING MONEY–SUPPLY CYCLES

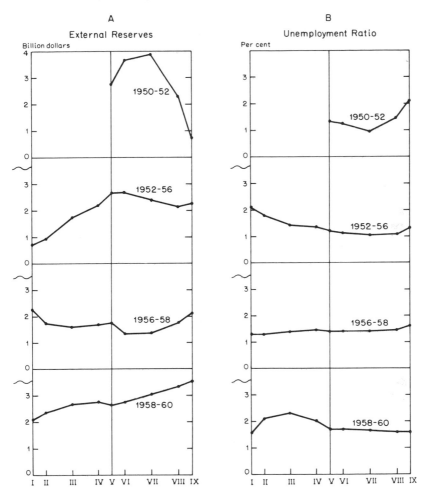

level. For the target of high employment, this impression is confirmed
also by Part C of Chart 11-6, where movements of the money-supply
variable along the unemployment cycles do not indicate any regular
pattern of behavior.

The analysis may turn now to the budgetary variables. Column 6
of Table 11-1 observes the rate of change of budgetary revenues. It

CHART 11-8 (*Concluded*)

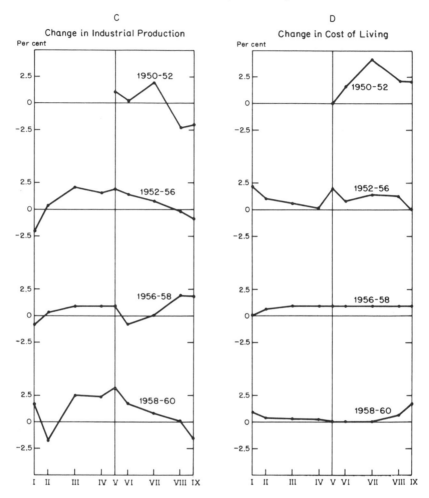

C

Change in Industrial Production

D

Change in Cost of Living

appears that this variable moved in the majority of subperiods as the needs of balance-of-payments adjustment would require; but the number of opposite movements is probably too large to warrant an assertion that this was a rule of behavior. In Part D of Chart 11-4, movements of the variable are represented along the cycle of the balance of payments. A movement in the adjusting direction would require the lines of this variable to have a V-shape; in fact, such a pattern cannot be found. When the rate of change of government expenditures is examined, the result is even clearer. From column 7 of Table 11-1, it may be seen that in the large majority of subperiods of imbalances, this variable moved in a disadjusting direction; whereas in Part E of Chart 11-4, no regular pattern of movements of the variable is apparent. It thus seems that government expenditures were not normally among the instruments used for balance-of-payments adjustment. This seems to be true also for the net result of the two magnitudes—the budgetary balance. From column 8 of Table 11-1 it appears that movements of this variable were about as often in an adjusting direction as in a disadjusting one. The impression of a lack of any consistent pattern of response of the budgetary balance to imbalances of payments is supported by observation of Part F of Chart 11-4. An adjusting response would require a V-shaped pattern, or at least a higher budgetary surplus (or, most often, a lower budgetary deficit) during the peak-to-trough phase (downward imbalances) than during the opposite phase; in fact, nothing similar to such a pattern can be distinguished.

In Parts D, E, and F of Chart 11-6 these three budgetary variables are examined along the unemployment cycle to see whether the lack of response to balance-of-payments requirements might be explained by responsiveness to the need to maintain high employment. In general, no consistent patterns of response are revealed. Only during the unemployment cycle of 1951–55 does the budgetary balance line have a clear V-shape, as the goal of high employment would require. Apart from this instance, it cannot be assumed that the lack of use of the major budgetary variables for balance-of-payments adjustment was due to their assignment to the task of maintaining full employment.

4. Summary and Interpretation

The clearest and most important conclusion which emerges from the preceding analysis is that the bank rate, the major instrument used by the Bank of England, was employed consistently in the service of balance-of-payments adjustment. The rate was almost always raised when the balance of payments deteriorated and lowered when the balance of payments improved.

Open-market operations, for which no data are readily available, were supposedly intended to reinforce movements of the bank rate. As such, they were thus also used for balance-of-payments adjustment.

But this cannot be asserted about other direct policy instruments at the disposal of the Bank of England. Minimum reserve ratios ("cash" and "liquidity") were, in the main, constant throughout. Even the measure of flexibility introduced into the system of minimum-reserve ratios by the method of "special deposits" at the Bank of England was not used, in any consistent way, to support balance-of-payments adjustment. Nor does Bank-of-England lending to the Treasury seem to be regulated by the needs for balance-of-payments adjustments.

Credit supply does seem to respond, by and large, to the needs of the balance of payments. This response appears to be much less consistent than that of the discount rate, but is nevertheless apparent, especially if shorter-term fluctuations are disregarded and major movements are concentrated upon. On the other hand, money supply, except perhaps for the few years before the mid-1950's, does not seem to respond in any consistent way to the fluctuations of the balance of payments.

British monetary policy certainly did not conform to the "rules of the game," as set by the Nurkse definition, according to which parallel movements of domestic and foreign assets of the central bank are required for the exercise of monetary policy. The greatest part of the Bank of England's domestic assets consists of loans to the Treasury, the movement of which was not in unison with movements of external reserves. Moreover, as has been discussed in the first section of this chapter, the rules of operation of the Exchange Equalization Account specify, in effect, a mechanism by which opposite movements of the Bank's foreign and domestic assets are automatically indicated.

Neither do the data indicate adherence to the alternative definition of the "rules of the game," which focus on money supply and interest rates, and which seem to have indeed served as rules of behavior for other countries which have been found in the present study to conduct monetary policy in a manner which responds to the external position. In this case, though, the disobedience is only partial, since the discount rate does respond to balance-of-payments requirements while money supply does not.

The pattern of behavior of British monetary instruments could conceivably be explained by more than one model. One probable explanation, which conforms with much of the reasoning found in the literature, runs along the following lines.

First, the role of the United Kingdom as a reserve country must be emphasized. The existence of very large sterling liabilities to the outside world, much of it of a short-term nature, makes it likely that fluctuations in the size of the country's external reserves, and, in particular, violent, short-term fluctuations, would be due to movements on capital account rather than on current account. This may make it easier to adjust imbalances by attempting to affect the capital account, avoiding measures which are intended to offset the current account and which must, by their nature, be more pervasive. Under such circumstances, movements of the bank rate may often be sufficient. By changing almost automatically the whole structure of short-term rates, they affect the relative cost of borrowing and holding funds in the United Kingdom and abroad. Also, when short-term capital moves out of the United Kingdom due to speculation against the pound, drastic increases of the bank rate are taken as a sign that devaluation is not imminent. In these ways, changes in the bank rate may be expected to have an immediate impact on the capital account of the United Kingdom's balance of payments.

Money supply is apparently not considered by policy makers in the United Kingdom to be a variable capable of exercising a major impact on aggregate demand. The availability of credit, on the other hand, is probably regarded as a more effective instrument. Aggregate demand is affected, of course, by changes in the cost of borrowing funds which are induced by changes in the bank rate. If additional changes are sought, however, the Bank of England tends to create them by influencing the amount of advances made by clearing banks. Such changes may be expected not only to affect the current account, through their impact on aggregate demand, but also to reinforce the effect of changes in the bank rate on short-term capital movements. The Bank of England seems to prefer, at least when substantial changes are called for, to effect the changes in the amount of advances by controlling this amount directly, rather than by changing the lending capacity of banks. Thus changes in advances have not necessarily been accompanied by operations which are intended to change bank reserves, such as Bank-of-England lending to the Treasury or (presumably) open-market operations.

The preceding analysis does not support the assumption that failure to use money supply as an instrument for balance-of-payments adjustment is due to the assignment of this instrument to other global economic targets. A more likely explanation is that money supply was thought to be of only secondary importance. The crucial variables in the monetary system were apparently considered to be the bank rate and, to a lesser extent, clearing bank advances. These—the latter less consistently than the former—were used for balance-of-payments adjustment, rather than for other economic targets. It may thus be concluded that the over-all pattern of use of monetary instruments in the United Kingdom was indeed geared to the requirements of balance-of-payments adjustment.[22]

This is not true, on the other hand, for the aggregate fiscal variables of the government's revenues, expenditures, and the budgetary balance. None of these appears to be related with any consistency to the requirements of balance-of-payments adjustment. Changes in various tax rates have often been submitted as part of "packages" of policies intended to adjust balance-of-payments deficits; but these changes could not have been of major significance so far as their quantitative effect on total government revenues is concerned.[23] As in the case of the monetary instruments, the failure to use these budgetary variables in the service of the balance of payments was not due to their assignment to other targets. Only during the earlier years of the 1950's can it be assumed that changes in the budgetary balances were intended to serve another major target—that of high employment. Just during this short period could it be assumed, therefore, that economic policy in the United Kingdom was pursued in a manner which allocated the use of fiscal policy to the domestic target of high employment, while monetary policy was assigned to the pursuit of balance-of-payments adjustment.

[22] It should be mentioned again that the present study seeks to find the mode of behavior, but not to appraise it. Whether the disregard of the variable of money supply is justified is a matter which could be debated, particularly in view of the persistence of deficits in the U.K. despite the response by means of the variables of bank rate and of credit supply. It may also be mentioned that in very recent years—1968 and 1969—some shift appears to have taken place among policy makers in the U.K. toward the use of money supply.

[23] It is conceivable, though, that such tax rate (and other) changes interfered with a movement in a disadjusting direction in which the relevant budgetary magnitudes would have been headed without these changes, so that the *ex post* aggregate results do not show adequately the net impact of the changes. This may explain the difference between the present findings and statements of policy makers and other analysts of the United Kingdom experience, which tend to attribute considerable importance to budgetary policy as an instrument used for balance-of-payments adjustment.

References

Bank of England, *Report,* annual, London, 1946/47–66.

Brandon, Henry, *In the Red, the Struggle for Sterling 1964–1966,* London, 1966.

Committee on the Working of the Monetary System, *Report, Principal Memoranda of Evidence,* and *Minutes of Evidence,* London, 1959, 1960.

Conan, Arthur Robert, *The Problem of Sterling,* London, 1966.

Dow, J. C. R., *The Management of the British Economy, 1945–60,* Cambridge, 1964.

Grant, A. T. K., *The Machinery of Finance and the Management of Sterling,* London, 1967.

Great Britain, Central Statistical Office, *Annual Abstract of Statistics,* London, 1875–1966.

Great Britain, Central Statistical Office, *Monthly Digest of Statistics,* London, January, 1946–66.

Great Britain, Central Statistical Office, *Financial Statistics,* monthly, London, 1962–66.

Great Britain, Treasury, *United Kingdom Balance of Payments,* semi-annual, London, 1945–66.

Hanson, John Lloyd, *Monetary Theory and Practice,* 2nd ed., London, 1962.

Harrod, Roy F., *The Pound Sterling 1951–1958,* Princeton, 1958.

Hawtrey, Sir Ralph, *Incomes and Money,* London, 1967.

Kirsch, Fred, *The Pound Sterling: A Polemic,* London, 1965.

Institute of Bankers, *The Bank of England Today,* London, 1964.

Johnson, H. G., "Recent Developments in British Monetary Policy," *American Economic Review,* Vol. 43 (May, 1953), pp. 19–26.

———, "The Revival of Monetary Policy in Britain," *Three Banks Review,* Vol. 30 (June, 1956), pp. 3–20.

Kenen, Peter B., *British Monetary Policy and the Balance of Payments 1951–1957,* Cambridge, Mass., 1960.

McMahon, Christopher, *Sterling in the Sixties,* London, 1964.

Organization for Economic Cooperation and Development, *Economic Surveys: United Kingdom,* annual, Paris. Reports for 1953–61 issued by the Organization for European Economic Cooperation.

Prest, A. R., *Public Finance in Theory and Practice,* Chicago, 1960.

Robertson, D. J., and Hunter, L. C. (eds.), *The British Balance of Payments,* Edinburgh, 1966.

Sayers, R. S., "English Policy on Interest Rates, 1958–62," *Banca Nazionale del Lavoro Quarterly Review,* Vol. 15 (June, 1962), pp. 111–26.

————, "The Development of British Monetary Policy, 1951," *Banca Nazionale del Lavoro Quarterly Review,* Vol. 5 (January–March, 1952), pp. 3–9.

Williams, D., "Some Aspects of Monetary Policy in England, 1952–8," *Yorkshire Bulletin of Economic and Social Research,* Vol. 12 (November, 1960), pp. 96–110.

CHAPTER
12

UNITED
STATES

1. Comprehensive Policy Instruments

The Federal Reserve System employs all three classical monetary instruments: the discount rate; minimum-reserve ratios; and open-market operations. In addition, subsidiary measures are often used, mostly to affect particular segments of the market. While emphasis is most often put on open-market operations, there seems to be no agreement among policy makers or analysts of monetary affairs in the United States that these operations alone signify the direction (easiness or tightness) of monetary policy. Likewise, there seems to be no general agreement about the use of some other variable, or combination of variables, as the proper indicator. Accordingly, a number of variables which are often mentioned as relevant (sometimes, by their respective proponents, as the "only" relevant variables) will be presented. These include the following:

The Discount Rate. Actual lending by the Federal Reserve System to commercial banks is normally very small, resorted to (in effect by Federal Reserve regulation) infrequently, and of the shortest possible duration (not over fifteen days). Not only the average, but also the peak amounts of this lending and fluctuations in it, are small in comparison with such other relevant magnitudes as total assets of the Federal Reserve System, or total reserves of commercial banks. Changes in the discount rate do not therefore greatly affect the cost of borrowed funds; they serve more as indicators of the direction of monetary policy. Yet, even this statement is probably less applicable to the United States than it would be to many other countries; according to the Federal Reserve System, changes in the discount rate are usually meant to follow the market (adjust to changes in the market rates which are caused by other developments), rather than to lead the market in new directions.

Treasury-Bill Rate. If monetary policy is designed to maintain some desired level of short-term rates, the yield of Treasury bills would probably be a good indicator of this variable. The Treasury-bill rate and the discount rate are normally quite close to each other; but the latter may sometimes remain unchanged for long periods, whereas the bill rate fluctuates continuously.

Reserve Ratios. Minimum-reserve ratios vary according to the type of bank and the type of deposit against which reserves are held. Most often, reserve ratios move together; but exceptions occur, so that the use of a single rate to represent the entire schedule may conceivably yield misleading impressions. This variable is therefore represented here by a weighted average calculated for purposes of the National Bureau's monetary studies.

Free Reserves. These are excess reserves held by member banks over and above the legally-required reserves (but not including "borrowed reserves," that is, advances from the Federal Reserve System). This magnitude is sometimes regarded as an indication of monetary policy: the larger the free reserves, the "easier" the policy.

Federal Reserve Credit and Open-Market Operations. A minor fraction of total Federal Reserve credit to banks is the Federal Reserve lending to commercial banks, mentioned earlier; but by far the greater part is created by open-market purchases. This is probably the most important *direct* instrument which the Federal Reserve System uses. By open-market operations the System determines the size of commercial-bank reserves and, combined with the use of minimum-reserve ratios, the lending capacity of banks. In terms of day-to-day conduct of monetary policy, open-market operations constitute by far the chief instrument through which the Federal Reserve System regulates the market. The Open-Market Committee of the Federal Reserve System, which directs open-market operations, is thus the crucial organ in the conduct of monetary policy in the United States.

The Federal Reserve System does not lend directly to the U.S. government, and Treasury deposits at the Federal Reserve Banks are normally minor. Net lending to the government is thus insignificant, so that the amount defined as "Federal Reserve credit" (which is, in turn, almost equivalent to the size of the open-market portfolio) is practically identical with the central bank's total domestic assets.

"High-Powered Money." Also often referred to as the "monetary base," this consists (except for a small amount of Treasury currency)

of the central bank's total domestic liabilities (commercial bank deposits at the Federal Reserve System and the amount of currency issued by it). Since the Federal Reserve's total liabilities must be equal to its total assets, the differences between this and the abovementioned Federal Reserve credit is roughly equal to the System's (net) foreign assets. Thus, this variable is affected both by changes in the central bank's credit (in the United States, this is by far the more important factor), and by changes in the external assets—gold (for the most part) and foreign-exchange reserves—which are held by the Federal Reserve System.[1] It is often argued that while movements of its foreign assets are not directly controlled by the Federal Reserve System, the System takes these movements into account in its decisions on the size of its credit (which has the same effect on the monetary base as movements of foreign assets); that is, the variable which the System intends to regulate is not just the amount of its credit, but the total of high-powered money.

Other Monetary Instruments. Two other variables will be observed which are further removed from the direct action of the monetary authorities but may be the magnitudes which they endeavor to manipulate. These are *commercial bank credit* and *money supply*. In both cases, as in the studies of other countries, rates of change rather than absolute amounts will be observed. Money supply will be represented by alternative definitions: the conventional one, which covers cash and demand deposits; and another which includes time deposits also. During a number of years, these alternatives exhibited somewhat different movements, and both may have had the attention of the monetary authorities.

Budgetary Variables. In the fiscal sphere, the three budgetary variables which are used in the studies of other countries, *budgetary revenues, budgetary expenditures* (both represented by their respective rates of change), and the *budgetary balance* will be observed here. All of these refer, as usual, to the cash budget.

---

[1] Strictly speaking, the gold is held by the Treasury, whereas the Federal Reserve System holds gold certificates. But this technical complication is not relevant for the present discussion. Gold certificates are regarded here as gold, and therefore as a "foreign" asset of the central bank although they are a claim of the Federal Reserve System on the U.S. Treasury.

2. Comprehensive Policy Patterns

The top five series in Chart 12-1 represent possible indicators of the balance-of-payments position:[2] gold and foreign-exchange reserves (including net IMF position), the balance on the "liquidity" basis, the balance on the "official-settlements" basis, the ratio of the country's external reserves to its liquid obligations to foreign official monetary institutions, and the ratio of these reserves to the country's total short-term obligations (that is, in practice, adding mostly liabilities to foreign commercial banks in the denominator of the ratio). The balance on the "official-settlements" basis is shown only during the years 1960–66, for which the estimate was readily available. But since changes in liabilities to foreign banks, which are the main source of differences between this concept and the "liquidity" concept of the balance of payments, were of relatively little importance in the 1950's, it may be assumed that not much information is lost by this partial omission.

All the series presented indicate a downward imbalance of payments existing almost continuously throughout the period. Since changes from deficit to surplus, or vice versa, in the balance-of-payments position were infrequent, an analysis of responses to imbalances of payments is very difficult indeed. Nevertheless, a few observations can be made.

First, it may be worthwhile to look for possible policy reactions to the few upward movements that did interrupt the long decline. If the slight, temporary surpluses during single quarters are overlooked—as they should be—only two periods of upward movement may be distinguished, one during 1951–52, and the other during 1956–57. Table 12-1 delineates these periods more precisely.

As may be seen from Table 12-1, the indications of the various series are not identical. A simultaneous upward movement in all series occurs, in fact, only during a single quarter in each of the two episodes. In general, the series of external assets presents a favorable movement for the longest duration, while the two series of ratios of external reserves to foreign liabilities indicate much shorter periods (and smaller extent) of improvement. The series of the balance of payments on the liquidity basis falls in between, and may also be assumed to have attracted a large amount of attention. It was thus decided to rely pri-

[2] See the discussion of the United Kingdom, the other "reserve country."

CHART 12-1

UNITED STATES: TIME SERIES OF SELECTED VARIABLES

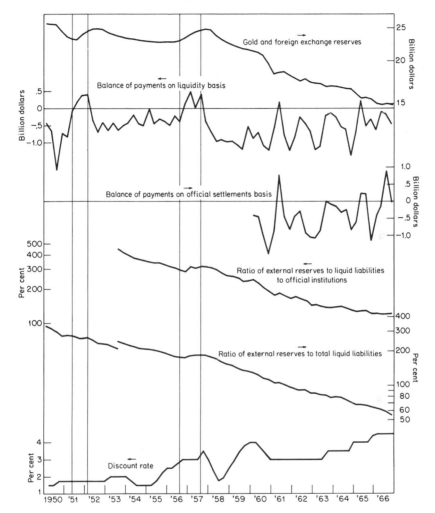

marily on this measure in the present analysis. Yet, for purposes of comparison with other periods, quarters in which external assets moved upward while the balance of payments series showed a deficit will be disregarded rather than considered as parts of periods of downward imbalance.

The two episodes of upward movement are thus judged to have

CHART 12-1 (*Continued*)

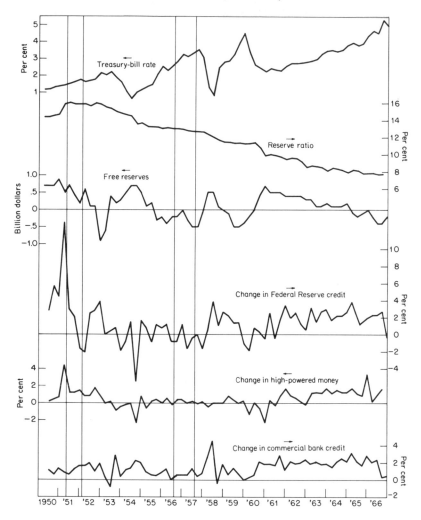

taken place during, first, the third quarter of 1951 through the first quarter of 1952; and, second, the fourth quarter of 1956 through the third quarter of 1957. The first of these will be compared with the six preceding quarters, from the beginning of 1950 to mid-1951, which was clearly a period of deficits; and with the following two years, 1953–54, again a period of clear deficits (the second half of 1952 being ignored altogether, for the reason mentioned above). The second

CHART 12-1 (*Concluded*)

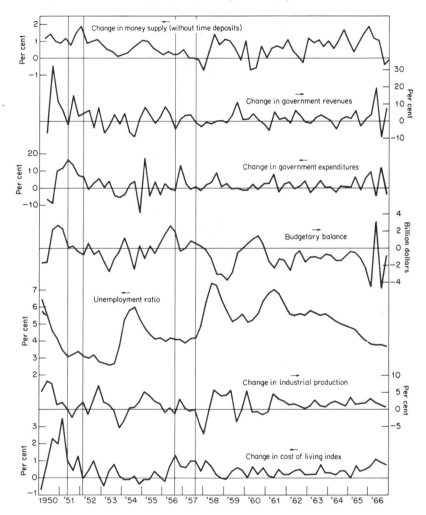

episode, that of 1956–57, will be compared with the two following
deficit years, 1958–59 (the last quarter of 1957 being ignored for the
same reason); and also with the preceding years, 1953–54 (1955
being a year of a rough equilibrium according to indications of external
reserves and the balance of payments on liquidity basis). The comparison, for each of the policy variables mentioned earlier, is carried out
in Table 12-2.

TABLE 12-1

UNITED STATES: INDICATORS OF BALANCE-OF-
PAYMENTS POSITION, 1951–52 AND 1956–57

Period	External Reserves (1)	Balance on Liquidity Basis (2)	Ratio of Reserves to Official Liquid Liabilities (3)	Ratio of Reserves to Total Liquid Liabilities (4)
1951 I	—	—		=
II	—	=		—
III	—	+		—
IV	+	+	n.a.	—
1952 I	+	+		+
II	+	—		—
III	=	—		—
IV	=	—		—
1956 I	=	—	—	—
II	=	—	—	—
III	+	—	—	—
IV	+	+	—	=
1957 I	+	+	+	+
II	+	=	=	+
III	+	+	+	=
IV	+	—	—	—

+ indicates an upward movement.
− indicates a downward movement.
= indicates stability.
n.a. indicates not available.

To show responsiveness to the position of the balance of payments, a policy variable would have indicated a more expansionary policy during each surplus episode than during the preceding and following deficit periods. Table 12-2 reveals such patterns only for the rates of change of commercial-bank credit, money supply, and government expenditures in the surplus episode of 1951–52, and only for government expenditures in the episode of 1956–57. In all other instances the evidence is either mixed, or suggests the opposite pattern of a more expansive policy during the deficit than during the surplus periods. Thus, only the single variable of the rate of change of government

TABLE 12-2

UNITED STATES: MOVEMENTS OF POLICY VARIABLES
DURING PERIODS OF SURPLUSES AND DEFICITS

		Deficit: I 1950 – II 1951	*Surplus:* III 1951 – I 1952	*Deficit:* I 1953 – IV 1954	*Surplus:* IV 1956 – III 1957	*Deficit:* I 1958 – IV 1959
Discount rate		stable	stable	fluctuates	raised	fluctuates
Treasury-bill rate		rises	stable	falls	rises	fluctuates
Reserve ratio		raised	stable	lowered	stable	lowered
Free reserves		stable	fluctuate	rise	fall	fluctuate
Federal Reserve credit	Average	+1.3	–.3	0	–.2	+.4
High-powered money	quarterly	+1.4	+1.2	–.3	+.2	0
Commercial-bank credit	rate of	+.9	+1.7	+1.2	+.7	+1.4
Money supply (without time deposits)	change,	+1.1	+1.4	+.5	+.1	+.8
Government revenue	per cent	+8.5	+7.6	–2.0	+2.0	+1.7
Government expenditure		+4.5	+9.2	–2.4	+4.0	+1.9
Budgetary balance (quarterly average, in billions of dollars)		+.7	–.3	–.9	+.3	–1.9

expenditures moves consistently according to the required pattern. But the effect of the Korean War on this variable (as, indeed, on most others) during the first episode must have been so strong that even here an inference of a causal connection from the positive association with the balance-of-payments position would most probably be unwarranted. Hence the evidence of Table 12-2 does not support the assumption that monetary and budgetary policy tended to be more expansive during periods of balance-of-payments surpluses than during periods of deficits. As will be shown shortly, it is easy to explain the differences among periods in the behavior of policy variables by domestic economic conditions, rather than by the balance-of-payments position.

In the period from 1958 onward, only a few sporadic quarters show balance-of-payments surpluses. No clear balance-of-payments fluctuations between positive and negative balances exist, therefore, in this period. It is possible, however, that the balance-of-payments performance might have been judged, during these years, by the *direction* of change rather than by the balance-of-payments position, and that, although the balance was negative throughout, only *larger* deficits were a source of concern such as to induce policy reactions. If this is true, the policy pattern should be found to be comparatively restrictive during periods of large deficits, and more expansive during periods of small deficits.

Table 12-3 tests this possibility by dividing the period 1958–66 into six subperiods of alternate large and small deficits, within which are measured the policy variables of discount rate, money supply, credit supply, and budgetary balance. Three indicators, presented in columns 1, 2, and 3, are used to estimate the size of the deficit: the decline of external reserves, the deficit on liquidity basis, and the deficit on official-settlements basis. As may be seen, these indicators agree with each other almost consistently, with two exceptions: for the subperiod of II 1962–II 1963, the liquidity and official-settlements measures show a substantial increase in the deficit from the preceding subperiod, while the decline of external reserves is moderate. Similarly, in the following subperiod, II 1963–III 1964, the rate of decline of reserves remains unchanged, while the two other indicators point out a very significant decline in the deficit. In both of these instances, liquidity and official-settlements definitions of the imbalance were used to determine the subperiods. It seems clear that the behavior of the four policy variables, presented in columns 4 to 7, does not support the assumption that

TABLE 12-3

UNITED STATES: MOVEMENTS OF SELECTED POLICY VARIABLES, 1958–66

Period	Loss of External Reserves (1)	Balance-of-Payments Deficit on "Liquidity" Basis (2)	Balance-of-Payments Deficit on "Official Settlements" Basis (3)	Discount Rate (change over the period) (4)	Money Supply (average quarterly rate of change, per cent) (5)	Commercial Bank Credit (average quarterly rate of change, per cent) (6)	Budgetary Deficit (quarterly average in millions of dollars) (7)
I 1958 – I 1961	505	896	—	—	.5	1.4	1.0
I 1961 – II 1962	158	577	239	—	.6	1.9	1.7
II 1962 – II 1963	90	863	986	—	.7	2.1	1.0
II 1963 – III 1964	96	351	159	+.50	1.2	2.0	1.2
III 1964 – I 1966	258	560	430	+1.00	1.2	2.3	2.0
I 1966 – IV 1966	80	242	surplus 225	—	.2	1.1	.8

NOTE: Columns (1), (2), and (3) are quarterly averages, expressed in millions of dollars.

policy tended to be more expansionary in periods of small balance-of-payments deficits. The hypothesis that comprehensive monetary or budgetary variables responded, from 1958 onwards, to balance-of-payments improvements or deteriorations, cannot be sustained.

An examination of longer periods may be more rewarding. As just mentioned, the period from 1958 onward is one of persistent, large balance-of-payments deficits, in which the external position of the country deteriorated with almost no interruption. For the period 1950–57, on the other hand, the net fall of the country's external reserves was slight; so also was the cumulative balance-of-payments deficit on the liquidity basis. Moreover, the level of reserves, judged by comparisons with past periods or with other countries, must have been regarded as particularly high; and increasing liabilities to foreign countries—signifying rising external reserves of those countries—may have been regarded favorably not only by the countries concerned but also by the United States. The ratio of the country's reserves to its foreign liabilities was falling throughout these years; but it was so high at the outset that, even by 1957, the decline may not have been a source of concern. From 1958 onward, however, the deterioration was much more persistent and large-scale, and the cumulative effect on the level of reserves and on the ratio of reserves to liabilities was very considerable. It is thus likely—as, indeed, statements of policy makers would suggest—that only from 1958 on has the balance-of-payments deterioration attracted serious concern. If aggregate policy reflected this concern, policy variables during 1958–66 would show a relatively contractionary tendency in comparison with the preceding years.

A comparison of changes in policy variables during the two periods is presented in Table 12-4. All of the variables, with the possible exception of interest rates, clearly indicate that an assumption of such greater responsiveness in the later period must be rejected. Two variables, the reserve ratio and free reserves, appear to move in about the same manner during the two periods. Other monetary variables—Federal Reserve credit, high-powered money, commercial-bank credit, and money supply—all move during 1958 and onward in a distinctly more expansive way than during the earlier years. This is true also for the budgetary variables. Although government expenditures rise at a slightly slower pace during the second period (a fact undoubtedly due to the huge impact of the Korean War during the earlier years of the first period), they rise at the same rate as (or even slightly more than) government revenues; whereas during the earlier period revenues

TABLE 12-4
UNITED STATES: MOVEMENTS OF POLICY VARIABLES
IN 1950–57 AND 1958–66

		1950–57	1958–66
Discount rate		raised	raised at about the same pace
Treasury-bill rate		rises	rises at about the same pace
Reserve ratio		lowered	lowered at about the same pace
Free reserves		no trend	no trend
Federal Reserve credit		+.2	+.6
High-powered money	Average	+.4	+.6
Commercial-bank credit	quarterly	+1.0	+1.7
Money supply: excluding time deposits	rate of	+.6	+.7
including time deposits	change,	+.8	+1.5
Government revenue	per cent	+2.8	+1.7
Government expenditure		+2.1	+1.8
Budgetary balance (quarterly average, in billions of dollars)		+.1	−1.2

increased much more than expenditures. An approximately balanced budget during the earlier period as a whole turned into a budget with persistent deficits during the later period. By most of the evidence, therefore, monetary and budgetary policies were distinctly more expansive during the period from 1958 onward rather than more restrictive, as responsiveness to balance-of-payments position would have required.

Interest rates, as the discount rate and the Treasury-bill rate indicate, did rise during 1958–66—as a restrictive policy would require. But no clear-cut conclusion about responsiveness to the balance-of-payments position can be drawn from this trend. For one thing, a rising trend of interest rates is evident during these years in other major countries as well, although rates in the U.S. do show some rise even in comparison with these other countries. It should also be noted that the trend toward increasing the interest rates, as shown both by Chart 12-1 and Table 12-3, started rather late—the discount rate started its steady climb only in mid-1963—and was not evident when balance-of-payments deficits were most severe. It seems reasonable to assume that the rise of interest rates was a cyclical phenomenon, due to the economic expansion of these years, and probably reinforced by large-scale governmental borrowing. From the evidence of the increased rate of expansion of money supply, it may be inferred that the monetary authorities did not contribute to the rise of interest rates but, on the contrary, mitigated it. The active monetary policy was, thus, most probably expansionary.

Yet, it may be argued that even though the monetary authorities did not initiate the rise of interest rates, they could have done more to prevent this rise; and that they did not is an indication of an intention to maintain a high level of interest rates, possibly to affect favorably the balance of payments. Some support for such assumption may also be derived from the fact that interest rates during the 1960–61 recession were not allowed to fall as much as they were in the two earlier recession periods, 1953–54 and 1957–58. That is, despite the undoubtedly major impact which domestic cyclical developments and requirements have continued to exert on interest rate policy, the balance-of-payments position may also be assumed to have been taken into consideration during the 1960's.

Finally, a cyclical analysis which uses cycles of policy variables may be attempted in a search for an association between policy instruments and targets. As may be seen from Chart 12-1, movements of many of the monetary variables could be divided into a number of cycles, at least until about 1960; but in some cases the turning points of these cycles would differ greatly among the various monetary indicators. A cyclical analysis based on the reference dates of a single variable could be repeated for each of these variables; but this could hardly be expected to be rewarding. Instead, reference dates for monetary policy were derived from a study by Brunner and Meltzer, in which the authors estimated "easiness" or "tightness" of monetary policy by a number of indicators—chiefly by what the Open-Market Committee itself specified as its guideline.[3] This study ends with the year 1962; and, in any case, it would be difficult to find significant cyclical policy movements from 1960 onward. The monetary policy "cycles" thus refer only to prior years, as follows:[4]

[3] Karl Brunner and Allan H. Meltzer, *An Analysis of Federal Reserve Monetary Policy Making,* Washington: Subcommittee on Domestic Finance, Committee on Banking and Currency, 1964 (in three parts). The "scaling" of policy decisions is provided in Appendix II, which appears in the third part ("An Alternative Approach to the Monetary Mechanism"), pp. 119–25.

[4] As may be seen from Chart 12-1 almost identical turning points are indicated by the discount rate.

Cycle	Trough	Peak	Trough
–1953		IV 1949	I 1953
1953–1957	I 1953	IV 1954	III 1957
1957–1959	III 1957	II 1958	IV 1959

The reference-cycle patterns of a few target variables are presented in Chart 12-2. Part A shows the pattern given by the rate of change of external reserves. Responsiveness to this indicator would be reflected in an inverted V-shape (that is, the "easing" of monetary policy would take place when reserves were rising, or falling only slowly, while "tightening" would be undertaken when reserves were falling rapidly). No resemblance to such a pattern seems to appear. Part B presents the balance of payments on the liquidity basis. Responsiveness to this indi-

CHART 12-2

UNITED STATES: PATTERNS OF TARGET VARIABLES
DURING MONETARY POLICY CYCLES

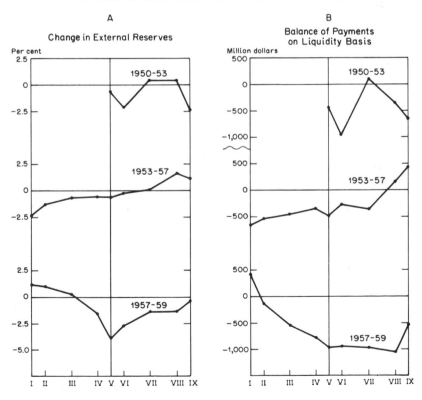

CHART 12-2 *(Continued)*

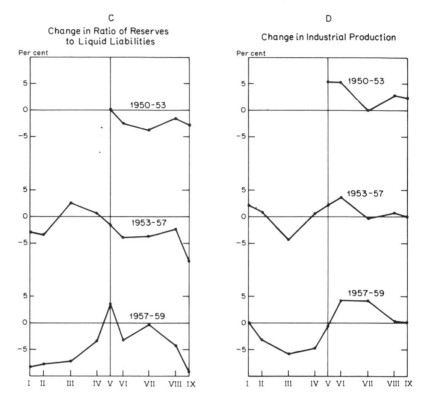

cator would be expressed, again, in an inverted V-shape; or at least in the balance of payments being higher (a higher surplus, or a lower deficit) during the easy-money phase than during the tight-money periods. Again, no such general pattern may be observed. Another alternative, the indication of the balance-of-payments position by the rate of change of the ratio of external reserves to the country's total short-term liabilities to foreigners, is tested in **Part C**. Again, responsiveness of monetary policy would be indicated by inverted V-shaped patterns. Such a pattern is found in the monetary-policy cycle of 1957–59; but this is probably too meager an evidence to suggest the existence of an association.

On the other hand, it may well be that the monetary-policy cycle could be explained by alternative economic targets. Part D presents the rate of change of industrial production. It appears clearly that this rate was negative during the easy-money, and positive during tight-

CHART 12-2 (*Concluded*)

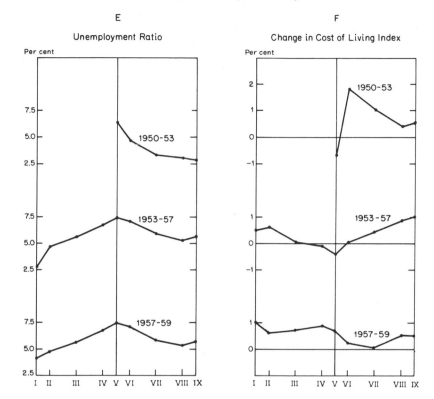

E

Unemployment Ratio

F

Change in Cost of Living Index

money, phases; monetary policy could thus be assumed to have responded to the need to maintain a high rate of expansion of production. Responsiveness of monetary policy seems to be even more convincingly shown for the target of high employment. In Part E, which presents the pattern of the unemployment ratio, an inverted V-shaped pattern would be consistent with the assumption that monetary policy reacted to the level of unemployment; this, indeed, is found consistently. No such consistency, on the other hand, is revealed for the target of price stability, which is analyzed in Part F. The V-shaped pattern which responsiveness to this target would require clearly emerges once, in the monetary-policy cycle of 1953–57, but not on other occasions.

From about the end of 1953 to the end of 1961, budgetary policy, too, could be explained by the targets of high employment and high production. It may be seen, from Chart 12-1, that if the series depicting the unemployment ratio and the rate of change of industrial production are shifted to the right by about two quarters, their dips and bulges match fairly consistently those of the series of the budgetary balance (in the case of the unemployment series, this would of course be an inverse relationship). Fluctuations of the budgetary balance may thus be explained as a response, lagging by about half a year, to fluctuations of the level of employment and of the rate of expansion of production.[5]

3. Specific Policy Reactions

The analysis thus far indicates that, through 1966, demand policy was still not primarily responsive to balance-of-payments requirements, although the country's external position may have had an impact on the level of interest rates. It would not be correct, however, to infer that the balance-of-payments problem was regarded lightly during this period. Unlike their reaction in earlier years, much greater concern was shown by U.S. policy makers in the 1960's with the need for balance-of-payments equilibrium. But this concern produced, for the most part, a large number of specific policy actions, rather than a responsive aggregate demand policy. Due to the particular importance of these measures in the United States, and the major significance of the United States for the international system, it may be worthwhile to mention briefly the most salient of these specific policies. For convenience, the measures will be divided into several categories, according to the type of balance-of-payments account on which each device was intended to have its primary effect.

The Current Account. Measures to affect the current account were not many and were largely related to U.S. economic and military foreign aid. One of these steps was an increased tying of economic aid to developing countries to the purchase of American goods. Another was concerned with military expenditures in Europe—primarily in Germany and Italy. Agreements were concluded by which these two countries undertook to buy military wares from the United States, to offset partially the impact of American military expenditures in these countries on the U.S. balance of payments.

Aside from these actions, a few minor steps to encourage exports

[5] Whether this responsiveness is discretionary, decided on ad hoc, or whether it is brought upon by automatic mechanisms, may be a very important issue for other purposes; but it is not a consideration in the present inquiry.

were undertaken. On the imports side, the main impact was sought in tourist trade: the amount of duty-free goods allowed to U.S. residents returning from trips abroad was reduced drastically—a step taken both for its direct impact on imports and, presumably, for its indirect effect on the inclination to go abroad.

Long-Term Capital Movements. This is probably the area in which the largest effort has been made—an effort which includes measures of taxation, quantitative restrictions, and agreements with foreign governments.

One step was the imposition, in 1963, of the interest equalization tax on lending to foreign countries (many of these countries, however, being exempted from the tax). The tax, equivalent to a one per cent rate of interest, is imposed on foreign bonds sold in the United States, or on bank loans with a maturity of over a year.

Another major effort to limit capital outflows has been through the "voluntary" agreements with U.S. companies along the line called for in the President's Balance-of-Payments Program of early 1965. These agreements have been concluded with some six-hundred corporations which, in the aggregate, form the major nonbank investors in foreign countries. Formally, each corporation was asked to draw a complete balance-of-payments account of its operations with the outside world and to suggest means of improving this balance in any of the account's components. In fact, the corporations were expected to make the improvement primarily by reducing their long-term capital outflow—either by investing less abroad or by financing more of their investments by borrowing in foreign markets.

Foreign central banks undertook to help limit the net flow of long-term capital from the United States by agreeing, since 1962, to purchase U.S. Treasury bonds denominated in foreign currency (the so-called "Roosa bonds"). The outstanding amount of these bonds reached the equivalent of $1.5 billion by early 1968. Another step in the same direction was the prepayment, primarily by Germany, of long-term debts owed by foreign governments to the U.S. Government.

Short-Term Capital Movements. In this area, two main policy forms may be distinguished. One is the attempt to affect the structure of interest rates in order to raise rates more significant for international capital flows relative to those important for domestic activity. Specifically, it has often been suggested that the Federal Reserve System attempted in the early 1960's to change the maturity structure of government securities by increasing the supply of short-term paper at the expense of long-term paper, so that short-term interest rates would rise relative to long-term rates. It is argued that the rise of the former is of relatively little significance to domestic economic activity, but of much importance to international short-term capital flows; whereas a relatively low long-term rate would encourage domestic activity without, it is presumed, having a considerable impact on international capital flows (especially when combined with the interest-equalization tax). While the argument seems convincing, it is doubtful whether the divergent movements of the two rates—which have indeed been substantial during the 1960's, particularly from the fall of 1961 to the fall of 1966—should be attributed to a specific policy rather than to the normal path expected when short-term rates rise.[6]

Another change in the structure of interest rates has been brought about by a gradual increase, during the 1960's, of Regulation Q ceilings on interest rates paid by commercial banks on savings and time deposits, particularly for longer-term time deposits. It is argued that the foreign depositors are primarily interested in this type of deposit, and that this is the reason for the relative increase of ceiling rates for these deposits.

The other main measure in this area was the introduction, in early 1965, of quantitative restrictions on foreign lending by commercial banks. Each bank was asked not to let its outstanding lending exceed by the end of 1965, 105 per cent of the outstanding amount at the end of 1964. For the end of 1966, the ceiling was determined at 109 per cent of the 1964 base.

Stabilizing Activities. In addition to the measures listed above, the Federal Reserve System (and, to a smaller extent, the Treasury) began to intervene in the early 1960's in the foreign-exchange markets. This intervention was always carried out for very short durations, being intended to counter disruptive speculative outflows of funds. The means of intervention in the market were provided primarily by a system of bilateral "swap" arrangements, which the Federal Reserve System has concluded with all the major foreign central banks and with the Bank for International Settlements. Started in the spring and summer of 1962, with an initial amount of some $700 million, these agreements have gradually widened in scope through the addition of more central banks and, to a much greater extent, through raising the agreed amount in each bilateral arrangement, until the total amount of the "swap" ar-

---

[6] See Franco Modigliani and Richard Sutch, "Innovations in Interest Rate Policy," *American Economic Review*, LVI (May 1966), pp. 178–97.

rangements exceeded $7 billion by early 1968. Although drawings under these arrangements were in principle bilateral, most of the drawing has in fact been done by the United States. The other major drawing country was the United Kingdom; when the United Kingdom drew dollars by this arrangement, the United States sometimes offset part of this by drawing other currencies. In this way, the system of bilateral arrangements became in fact multilateral, with the United States serving as a clearing center.

Drawings under the "swap" arrangements were always for a very short time: about half of all commitments was repaid within three months, and the greater part of the rest within six months. Intervention by the Federal Reserve System (and, in the early 1960's, the Treasury) was carried out in both the spot and forward markets for foreign exchange. Forward purchases of dollars by the authorities may be viewed as a means of raising the interest rate on dollar holdings and of inducing in this way a short-term capital inflow. But, in practice, these interventions were sporadic and always for short durations; they seem to have been intended to combat speculation rather than to serve as a permanent way of attracting short-term capital.

4. Summary and Conclusions

The evidence examined here indicates that the United States did not direct its aggregate monetary and budgetary policy primarily to meet the needs of balance-of-payments equilibrium during the period under consideration. This is true both for the earlier years—in which the level of the country's reserves must have been considered high enough for the country to afford balance-of-payments deficits, or even welcome them as being required for the international monetary system as a whole— and for the later years, in which this could no longer have been the prevailing view among policy makers. During the entire period the major monetary and fiscal instruments of aggregate-demand policy were, it appears, responsive to the needs of the targets of high employment and high production, rather than to those of the balance of payments.[7] It seems possible, though, that while no responsiveness to

---

[7] This, of course, is neither a novel nor a surprising finding. After all, the Council of Economic Advisers was specifically established within the framework of the Full Employment Act. Likewise, the Federal Open-Market program of the

changes in the balance-of-payments position is revealed, the high level of interest rates during the 1960's may have been maintained partly due to the chronic downward imbalance of that period.

An awareness of the balance-of-payments problem since the late 1950's has resulted primarily in a few specific measures taken in an attempt at adjustment. These measures seem to follow a definite pattern, with certain common attributes. First, it appears that the major thrust of these policies was directed at the capital account of the balance of payments, rather than at the current account. Second, most of these measures appear to be of a temporary nature—even though their life span was not necessarily determined in advance. This pattern of policy responses could be given a few explanations, each probably having some validity, which could be regarded as complementary rather than as mutually exclusive.

First, it should be noticed that the deficit in the U.S. balance of payments was derived totally from the capital account; the current account was always in surplus over the period studied, offsetting part of the deficit on capital account.[8] It is conceivable—as would follow from a few policy statements—that policy makers drew from this phenomenon the inference—which most economists would reject—that the adjustment of the balance of payments had to be carried out by improving performance in those items in which the deficit was shown; that is, that corrections should be sought in the capital account, whereas the current account, which was in surplus anyway, did not require any adjustment. This interpretation of policy motivations may find some support from the fact that, within the current account, the major item attracting attention from policy makers was the tourist trade—an item in which the United States has continuously had a substantial deficit.

Another possible explanation is that policy makers wished to prevent a conflict between the U.S. measures and accepted conventions or tendencies in world transactions. A variety of institutions or agreements

Federal Reserve System usually bases its deliberations explicitly on the situation of domestic economic activity. For studies reaching similar conclusions, see William G. Dewald and Harry G. Johnson, "An Objective Analysis of the Objectives of American Monetary Policy, 1952–61," in Dean Carson (ed.), *Banking and Monetary Studies,* Homewood, Ill., 1963, pp. 171–89; and Thomas Havrilesky, "A Test of Monetary Policy Action," *Journal of Political Economy,* June 1967, pp. 299–304.

[8] This statement refers to the period ended with 1966. Subsequently, the surplus on current account began to shrink, and in 1968 it turned into a deficit. Even while the surplus on current account was large, moreover, the question remains how much of it was attributable to capital outflows.

would call for serious reactions from U.S. trade partners to interference with trade in goods; the capital account—and, to some degree, tourist services—are considered less objectionable areas for specific state intervention.

Still another explanation may be found in the assumption that the U.S. deficit was temporary and likely to reverse itself. If this is so, measures having a small impact on the economy as a whole would find favor. Temporary restrictions of capital movements, whose effect on the domestic economy is, in the short run, marginal, would thus tend to be preferred to measures whose impact would be felt through aggregate demand in the economy. Likewise, measures to increase the country's reserves, and thus the country's "breathing space," would be particularly attractive in this situation. Indeed, U.S. policy makers invested considerable effort in this direction during the 1960's.

Finally, as suggested earlier in this study, it may also be possible that U.S. policy makers have felt that the small size of the country's trade, in relation to its total economic activity, did not justify an adaptation of aggregate-demand policy to balance-of-payments requirements, and that the situation called for the adjustment of the balance-of-payments deficit in ways which would not have a direct adverse impact on the domestic economy.

It may be remarked, parenthetically, that during most recent years—which partly transcend the period covered by the statistical investigation—some new elements have been introduced into the system. On the one hand, a new dimension has been added by the war in Vietnam, which contributed significantly to the deterioration of the U.S. balance of payments, both through the direct military expenditures and through the impact of the ensuing domestic inflation. On the other hand, the establishment in 1968 of the so-called "two-tier" gold market has in effect transformed the international system largely into one based on the dollar standard, in which dollar assets accumulated by foreign governments are not converted into gold. This process (which, without any specific agreement, was largely in effect also during much of the 1950's), enables the U.S. to have, at least temporarily, sustained deficits in its balance of payments without feeling the direct pressure imposed by loss of international reserves. Thus, despite further balance-of-payments deficits, and a deterioration of the current account, the immediate need for an adjusting policy has not presented itself with the same urgency as in earlier years.

References

Ahearn, Daniel S., *Federal Reserve Policy, Reappraised 1951–1959,* New York, 1963.

Barger, Harold, *The Management of Money,* Chicago, 1964.

Bernstein, E. M., "The Adequacy of United States Gold Reserves," *American Economic Association, Papers and Proceedings,* Vol. 51 (May, 1961), pp. 439–46.

———, "Domestic and International Objectives of United States Monetary Policy," *Journal of Finance,* Vol. 18 (May, 1963), pp. 161–73.

———, "The Role of Monetary Policy," *American Economic Review,* Vol. 48 (May, 1958), pp. 88–98.

Board of Governors of the Federal Reserve System, *Annual Report,* Washington, D.C., 1914.

Board of Governors of the Federal Reserve System, *Federal Reserve Bulletin,* Washington, D.C., 1914–66.

———, *The Federal Reserve System—Purposes and Functions,* Washington, D.C., 1954.

Brunner, Karl, and Meltzer, Allan H., *An Analysis of Federal Reserve Monetary Policy Making,* Subcommittee on Domestic Finance, Committee on Banking and Currency, Washington, D.C., 1964 (in three parts).

Burtle, J., *et al.,* "The Balance of Payments of the United States: Discussion," *American Economic Review,* Vol. 51 (May, 1961), pp. 447–54.

Chamber of Commerce of the United States, *The United States Balance of Payments Position.* (Report of the Committee on Economic Policy, 1961; revised 1963) Washington, D.C., 1963.

Committee for Economic Development, *National Objectives and the Balance of Payments Problem: A Statement on National Policy by the Research and Policy Committee,* New York, 1960.

Dale, William B., *The Foreign Deficit of the United States: Causes and Issues,* International Industrial Development Center, Stanford Research Institute, Menlo Park, Calif., 1960.

Dewald, William G., and Johnson, Harry G., "An Objective Analysis of the Objectives of American Monetary Policy, 1952–61," in Dean Carson (ed.), *Banking and Monetary Studies,* Homewood, Ill., 1963, pp. 171–89.

Economic Report of the President, annual, Washington, D.C., 1947–66.

Egle, W. P., "American Reaction to the United States Balance of Payments Deficit," *Weltwirtschaftliches Archiv,* Vol. 93, Part 2 (1964), pp. 273–83.

Fatemi, Nasrolah S., *et al.*, *The Dollar Crisis, The United States Balance of Payments and Dollar Stability,* Fairleigh Dickinson University Press, 1963.

Federal Reserve Bank of New York, *Annual Report,* New York, 1915–66.

Federal Reserve Bank of Philadelphia, *Monetary Policy: Decision Making, Tools and Objectives,* Philadelphia, 1961.

Frank, H. J., "The United States Balance of Payments Problem, Causes and Cures," *Economia Internazionale,* Vol. 13 (May, 1960), pp. 306–25.

Friedman, Milton, and Schwartz, Anna Jacobson, *A Monetary History of the United States 1867–1960,* Princeton, 1963.

Furth, J. H., "Unbalanced International Accounts: Diagnosis and Therapy," *American Economic Review,* Vol. 51 (May, 1961), pp. 430–38.

Hansen, A. H., "Monetary Policy," *Review of Economics and Statistics,* Vol. 37 (May, 1955), pp. 110–19.

Harris, Seymour E. (ed.), *The Dollar in Crisis,* New York, 1961.

Hayes, Alfred, "Monetary Policy and the Balance of Payments," remarks of the President of the Federal Reserve Bank of New York before the National Foreign Trade Convention, November 16, 1959.

International Economic Policy Association, *The U.S. Balance of Payments, An Appraisal of the U.S. Economic Strategy,* Washington, D.C., 1966.

Jacoby, N. H., "Fiscal Policy of the Kennedy-Johnson Administration," *Journal of Finance,* Vol. 19 (May, 1964), pp. 353–69.

Kareken, J. H., "Federal Reserve System Discount Policy: An Appraisal," *Banca Nazionale del Lavoro Quarterly Review,* Vol. 12 (March, 1959), pp. 103–25.

———, "Post-accord Monetary Developments in the United States," *Banca Nazionale del Lavoro Quarterly Review,* Vol. 10 (September, 1957), pp. 322–51.

Kenen, Peter B., *The U.S. Balance of Payments and American Economic Policy,* New York, mimeographed, 1961.

Knipe, James L., *The Federal Reserve and the American Dollar: Problems and Policies 1946–64,* Chapel Hill, 1965.

Lary, H. B., "Disturbances and Adjustments in Recent U.S. Balance of Payments Experience," *American Economic Review,* Vol. 51 (May, 1961), pp. 417–29.

MacDougall, Sir Donald, *The Dollar Problem: A Reappraisal,* Princeton, 1960.

Mao, C. T. (ed.), *Readings in International Finance,* Ann Arbor, 1962.

Martin, W. M., Jr., "Monetary Policy and International Payments," *Journal of Finance,* Vol. 18 (March, 1963), pp. 1–10.

Modigliani, Franco, and Sutch, Richard, "Innovations in Interest Rate Policy," *American Economic Review*, Vol. LVI (May, 1966), pp. 178–97.

Morton, W. A., "Development and Implication of Federal Reserve Policy," *American Economic Review*, Vol. 47 (May, 1957), pp. 229–43.

Neisser, H., "The Aims of Federal Reserve Policy, 1951–1960," *Review of Economics and Statistics*, Vol. 42 (August, 1960), pp. 258–61.

Organization for Economic Cooperation and Development, *Economic Surveys: United States*, annual, Paris. Reports for 1953–61 issued by the Organization for European Economic Cooperation.

Ott, David J., and Ott, Attiat F., *Federal Budget Policy*, Washington, D.C., 1965.

President's Advisory Committee on Labor-Management Policy, *Conference on Fiscal and Monetary Policy, Washington, D.C. 1962*, Washington, D.C., 1963.

Prochnow, Herbert V. (ed.), *The Federal Reserve System*. New York, 1960.

Ritter, L. S., "Official Central Banking Theory in the United States 1939–61: Four Editions of the Federal Reserve System: Purposes and Functions," *Journal of Political Economy*, Vol. 70 (February, 1962), pp. 14–29.

Roosa, R. V., "Reconciling Internal and External Financial Policies," *Journal of Finance*, Vol. 17 (March, 1962), pp. 1–16.

Salant, Walter S., *et al.*, *The United States Balance of Payments in 1968*, Washington, D.C., 1963.

Schmidt, Wilson E., *The Rescue of the Dollar*, Washington, D.C., 1963.

Smith, W. L., "Monetary Policy, 1957–60: An Appraisal," *Review of Economics and Statistics*, Vol. 42 (August, 1960), pp. 269–72.

Stabilization Policies, A Series of Research Studies Prepared for the Commission on Money and Credit, Englewood Cliffs, N.J., 1963.

Triffin, Robert, *The Balance of Payments and the Foreign Investment Position of the United States*, Princeton, 1966.

U.S. Board of Governors of the Federal Reserve System, *The Federal Reserve and the Treasury: Answers to Questions from the Commission on Money and Credit*, Englewood Cliffs, N.J., 1963.

U.S. Congress, Committee on Banking and Currency, *Background Information on U.S. Balance of Payments*, 89th Congress, 1st Session, Washington, D.C., 1965.

U.S. Congress, House Committee on Banking and Currency, *Recent Changes in Monetary Policy and Balance of Payments Problems*, 88th Congress, 1st Session, Washington, D.C., 1963.

U.S. Congress, Joint Economic Committee, *The United States Balance of Payments—Perspectives and Policies*, 88th Congress, 1st Session, Washington, D.C., 1963.

U.S. Congress, Subcommittee of the Committee on Banking and Currency, *Federal Reserve Monetary Policies: Hearings,* 85th Congress, 2nd Session, Washington, D.C., 1958.

U.S. Congress, Subcommittee on Economic Statistics of the Joint Economic Committee, *The Balance of Payments Statistics: Hearings,* 89th Congress, 1st Session, Washington, D.C., 1965.

U.S. Congress, Subcommittee on International Exchange and Payments of the Joint Economic Committee, *Factors Affecting the United States Balance of Payments,* 87th Congress, 2nd Session, Washington, D.C., 1962.

U.S. Congress, Subcommittee on International Exchange and Payments of the Joint Economic Committee, *Outlook for United States Balance of Payments: Hearings,* 87th Congress, 2nd Session, Washington, D.C., 1963.

U.S. Department of Commerce, Bureau of the Census, *Statistical Abstract of the United States,* annual, Washington, D.C.

U.S. Department of Commerce, Office of Business Economics, *Survey of Current Business,* monthly, Washington, D.C.

U.S. Review Committee for Balance of Payments Statistics, *The Balance of Payments Statistics of the United States: A Review and Appraisal,* Washington, D.C., 1965.

Walker, Pinkney C., *Essays in Monetary Policy in Honor of Elmer Wood,* Columbia, Mo., 1965.

Wallich, H. C., "Recent Monetary Policies in the United States," *American Economic Review,* Vol. 43 (May, 1953), pp. 27–41.

Whittlesey, C. R., "Central Bank Policy in the Light of Recent American Experience," *Weltwirtschaftliches Archiv,* Vol. T8 (1957), pp. 17–44.

Wood, Elmer, *Monetary Control,* Columbia, Mo., 1963.

———, "Recent Monetary Policies," *Journal of Finance,* Vol. 10 (September, 1955), pp. 315–25.

Young, R. A., "Federal Reserve Flow of Funds Accounts," *International Monetary Fund Staff Papers,* Vol. 5 (February, 1957), pp. 323–42.

Youngdahl, R., "Monetary Policy in Recent Years," *American Economic Association Papers and Proceedings,* Vol. 45 (May, 1955), pp. 402–8.

Zassenhaus, M. K., and Dirks, F. C., "Recent Developments in the U.S. Balance of Payments," *International Monetary Fund Staff Papers,* Vol. 2 (April, 1952), pp. 213–62.

APPENDIX:
A FEW EXPERIMENTS WITH
FORMAL CORRELATION ANALYSIS

As I have pointed out in the discussion of the study's approach, much of the method amounts, in essence, to a correlation analysis; but due to the small number of observations (the "subperiods"), it is a mostly intuitive inference, rather than formal. I have also argued, in that discussion, that a formal analysis based on a large number of observations, in which each quarter is taken as a unit of measurement of the variables concerned, is not likely to be very helpful. Nevertheless, I have carried out a number of experimental correlation analyses, which are described here.

First, Table A-1 presents the outcome of the simplest experiment, in which the size of each dependent variable in a given quarter is assumed to be a function of the sizes of the independent variables in the same quarter. The dependent variables are, in turn, three monetary variables: the discount rate; the rate of change of money supply; and the rate of change of credit supply. The independent variables are the four targets assumed in this study as conceivably guiding monetary policy: the balance-of-payments position, measured by the change in external reserves and designated by B; the price level, measured by the change in the cost-of-living index and designated by P; the employment position, measured by the unemployment ratio and designated by U; and, finally, the growth target, measured by the change in the industrial-production index and designated by G. The table records only correlation coefficients which are significant at the .95 level. When a coefficient appears with the right sign (that is, the sign expected from the assumption that the instrument in question responds to the need of the target in question), the coefficient is *italicized*.

The results of Table A-1 are quite meager. Little dependence of the monetary instruments on the major economic targets is revealed. The highest R^2 recorded (.538) is in Germany, with credit supply as the dependent variable. But in this case, as also with the variable of money supply in Germany, the result may be discounted altogether. Credit

TABLE A-1
COEFFICIENTS OF CORRELATION OF MONETARY
INSTRUMENTS WITH TARGET VARIABLES

Country and Dependent Variables	Multiple Correlation		Partial Correlations with Independent Variables			
	r	*Adjusted R²*	*B*	*P*	*U*	*G*
Belgium:						
Discount rate	.601	.320	—	—	−.573	—
Money supply	.440	.142	.302	—	—	−.252
Credit supply	.440	.106	.310	—	—	—
France:						
Discount rate	.581	.286	—	.407	—	—
Money supply	—	—	.351	—	—	—
Credit supply	—	—	—	−.344	—	—
Germany:						
Discount rate	.583	.297	.351	.250	.486	—
Money supply	.428	.131	—	—	.394	—
Credit supply	.750	.538	—	—	526	.504
Italy:						
Money supply	.559	.257	.323	—	−.410	.378
Credit supply	—	—	—	—	—	.400
Japan:						
Discount rate	—	—	—	−.284	—	—
Money supply	—	—	—	—	—	—
Credit supply	—	—	—	—	—	—
Netherlands:						
Discount rate	.446	.147	—	—	−.408	—
Money supply	.517	.220	.496	—	—	—
Credit supply	.396	.102	−.336	—	—	—
Sweden:						
Discount rate	—	—	—	—	—	—
Money supply	.442	.140	.317	—	—	.382
Credit supply	—	—	—	—	—	—
U.K.:						
Discount rate	—	—	−.279	—	—	—
Money supply	—	—	—	—	—	.330
Credit supply	—	—	—	—	—	—
U.S.:						
Discount rate	—	—	—	—	—	—
Money supply	—	—	—	—	—	.310
Credit supply	—	—	—	—	—	—

supply and money supply appear, in Germany, to be dependent on the employment situation; but this is patently due to general trends of falling unemployment and falling rates of expansion of money and credit in this country. Outside Germany, the highest correlations (R^2) are within the range of about .3, which is very low indeed.

It should be pointed out that despite the meagerness of the results, they largely conform with those arrived at in the main body of analysis of this study. Thus, with the exception of one instance (Sweden), all the cases of dependence of one monetary instrument or another on the balance-of-payments position (Belgium, France, Italy, Netherlands, and the U.K.) have been demonstrated before. But the opposite is not true: many instances of such demonstrated dependence are *not* revealed by the correlation analysis. A glaring example of this is the case of Japan.

Table A-2 presents the results of a similar analysis, except that it introduces a time lag: the size of the dependent variable (monetary instrument) in each quarter is assumed to be a function of the size of the independent variables (the targets) during the preceding two quarters. The outcome as a whole is again quite disappointing. Table A-2 shows a clear improvement over the performance of Table A-1 in two countries: France, and the U.K. In both instances, the outcome agrees with the findings arrived at by the main body of analysis of this study. In other cases, however, there are mostly fewer and less meaningful findings when the time lag is introduced than without it.

Particularly baffling is the outcome concerning the discount rate. Table A-1 shows a significant (but quite small) correlation of this instrument in the right direction in only one instance: in the U.K., it appears to depend on the target of the balance of payments. In Table A-2, some improvement is apparent: a dependence of the discount rate on the balance-of-payments position is seen also in France, where the discount rate appears to depend also on the unemployment situation. Dependence of the discount rate on the price level appears in Germany and the Netherlands, and in the latter also on the unemployment position. All these positive findings still amount to quite little. Table A-3 presents the result of an attempt to improve this performance by observation of selected points only. There is a general tendency, in almost all countries, not to vary the discount rate very often but, at most, about once or twice a year on the average. Thus, long periods may be found in which the target variables move, but the discount rate remains stable. It might be expected that if these periods are abstracted from,

TABLE A-2
COEFFICIENTS OF CORRELATION OF INSTRUMENTS WITH VARIABLES, WITH TIME LAG

Country and Dependent Variables	Multiple Correlation		Partial Correlations with Independent Variables			
	r	Adjusted R^2	B	P	U	G
Belgium:						
Discount rate	.583	.292	—	—	−.549	—
Money supply	.413	.115	—	—	−.276	—
Credit supply	—	—	—	—	—	—
France:						
Discount rate	.758	.542	−.422	.483	−.377	—
Money supply	.460	.151	.317	—	—	—
Credit supply	—	—	—	—	—	—
Germany:						
Discount rate	.552	.259	—	.409	.399	—
Money supply	.487	.186	—	.374	.326	—
Credit supply	.652	.386	—	—	.546	—
Italy:						
Money supply	—	—	—	—	−.302	—
Credit supply	.543	.235	—	—	—	.536
Japan:						
Discount rate	.513	.210	—	−.363	—	—
Money supply	—	—	—	—	—	—
Credit supply	—	—	—	—	—	—
Netherlands:						
Discount rate	.678	.424	—	.315	−.552	−.270
Money supply	.353	.066	—	—	—	—
Credit supply	.451	.150	—	—	—	.408
Sweden:						
Discount rate	—	—	—	—	—	.271
Money supply	—	—	—	—	—	—
Credit supply	—	—	—	—	—	—
U.K.:						
Discount rate	.480	.179	−.412	−.379	—	—
Money supply	—	—	—	—	—	.319
Credit supply	.577	.289	−.407	—	.327	—
U.S.:						
Discount rate	—	—	—	—	—	—
Money supply	—	—	—	—	—	—
Credit supply	—	—	—	—	—	—

TABLE A-3

COEFFICIENTS OF CORRELATION OF DISCOUNT–RATE
CHANGES WITH TARGET VARIABLES

Country	Multiple Correlation		Partial Correlations with Independent Variables			
	r	Adjusted R^2	B	P	U	G
Belgium	—	—	—	—	−.503	—
France	.858	.605	—	—	−.642	—
Germany	—	—	—	—	—	—
Japan	—	—	—	—	—	—
Netherlands	.797	.531	—	.688	—	—
Sweden	.860	.624	.843	—	—	.710
U.K.	—	—	—	—	—	—
U.S.	—	—	—	—	—	—

and only periods of changes in the discount rate are left, the real motivations of these changes stand a better chance of being revealed. Thus, Table A-3 presents coefficients of correlation of the discount rate with the target variables when only quarters in which discount-rate changes took place are considered, and each such change is assumed to be a function of the target variables during the preceding two quarters. The results of this procedure are again disappointing: if anything, the performance is even worse than in Tables A-1 and A-2. The discount rate appears to depend on any of the target variables in only four instances. In Belgium, a dependence of the rate on the unemployment position is shown; but the multiple-correlation coefficient, which would show the dependence of the rate on all targets combined, is insignificant. In France, a dependence of the rate on the unemployment position appears, as it has also appeared in Table A-2; but the level of unemployment in France has been so low, throughout the period, that such a dependence would be hardly credible. In the Netherlands the rate seems to be correlated with the price-level target—a finding which would agree with that of the study's text. Finally, in Sweden the rate appears to be correlated, even strongly so, with the rate of change of industrial production—a somewhat surprising finding not only in view of the main body of the study's analysis, but also when compared with Tables A-1 and A-2.

Lastly, Table A-4 presents the outcome of an attempt to tackle the problem on hand in a somewhat different manner. The balance-of-payments target is taken here as the *dependent* variable, and the three monetary instruments as the independent variables. The multiple correlation coefficient would then show the association of the target with all the three instruments combined; whereas the partial correlations would show the association with each separate monetary instrument. The results, again, are not encouraging. Once more, Japan is the most obvious case: no significant correlation of the balance of payments with monetary policy appears at all in this country. But other associations as well, though significant, seem to be quite weak. Among the separate instruments, associations of the balance-of-payments target appear for money supply in Belgium, France, Italy, and the Netherlands; and for credit supply in Belgium. These findings agree with those of the study's text; but they represent only a small fraction of the latter. Again, particularly disappointing is the performance of the discount rate, as it is represented here.

All the experiments demonstrated in this appendix appear, thus, to have been unsuccessful. If conclusions had to be drawn from their findings, they would have been grossly misleading in many instances. It is, of course, conceivable that an improved performance of this method

TABLE A-4

COEFFICIENTS OF CORRELATION OF MONETARY
POLICY WITH BALANCE-OF-PAYMENTS POSITION

Country	Multiple Correlation		Partial Correlations with Independent Variables		
	r	Adjusted R^2	Discount Rate	Money Supply	Credit Supply
Belgium	.430	.146	—	.297	.264
France	.374	.091	—	.287	—
Germany	—	—	.303	—	—
Italy	.442	.164	—	.393	−.341
Japan	—	—	—	—	—
Netherlands	.588	.315	—	.483	−.390
Sweden	—	—	—	—	—
U.K.	.273	.046	—	—	—
U.S.	—	—	—	—	—

could be achieved in a variety of other ways, such as by the elimination of extreme observations; the introduction of a variety of time lags, not necessarily uniform for all targets, and possibly of some model of distributed lags; the removal of trend factors; and the like. The amount of experimentation required for these improvements would undoubtedly have been very large—and its outcome of doubtful validity.

INDEX OF NAMES

SUBJECT INDEX